been a child survivor of the Theresienstadt concentration camp. With irreverent humor and deep insight, The True Adventures of Gidon Lev presents an improbable love story—of a man who had every reason to be bitter but instead fell in love with life.

Yossi Klein Halevi, senior fellow, Shalom Hartman Institute, author of "Like Dreamers" and "Letters to my Palestinian Neighbor"

"How do we remember in order to learn, and learn in order to build a better world—while not letting the Holocaust eclipse our life-affirming purpose and values? In The True Adventures, truth—that is to say searching, love, humor, anger, despair, hope—is not shrouded in dark clouds, but aglow amidst them. Wonder of wonders, it is exactly through this tale, a tale with the Holocaust at its essence, that a new light is shed on Jewish possibility and purpose."

Rabbi Susan Silverman, author of "Casting Lots: Creating a Family in a Beautiful, Broken World"

THE TRUE ADVENTURES OF GIDON LEV

JULIE GRAY

with
GIDON LEV

Publisher's Cataloging-In-Publication Data

(Prepared by The Donohue Group, Inc.)

Names: Gray, Julie, 1964- author. | Lev, Gidon, 1935- author.

Title: The true adventures of Gidon Lev : rascal. Holocaust survivor. optimist / by Julie Gray, with Gidon Lev.

Description: [Ramat Gan, Israel] : [Julie Gray], [2020]

Identifiers: ISBN 9781735249704 | ISBN 9781735249711 (ebook)

Subjects: LCSH: Lev, Gidon, 1935- | Lev, Gidon, 1935---Political and social views. | Holocaust survivors--Israel--Biography. | Jewish children in the Holocaust--Czech Republic--Karlovy Vary--Biography. | Theresienstadt (Concentration camp) | Holocaust, Jewish (1939-1945)--Personal narratives. | LCGFT: Biography.

Classification: LCC DS135.C97 L48 2020 (print) | LCC DS135.C97 (ebook) | DDC 940.531809224371--dc23

CONTENTS

For the children who were in or transported through Theresienstadt and never came back.

For the children everywhere who suffer the terrible consequences of the intolerance, hate, and war that grown-ups create.

For the children.

INTRODUCTION

On the face of it, *The True Adventures of Gidon Lev* is the story of an elderly Holocaust survivor—a man who made it through horrifying events and lived to tell the tale. But Gidon (pronounced "Gid-awn") did more than survive—he thrived. Gidon's is the story of a little boy who never truly grew up, with a desperate need to belong and to build a family for himself. His story spans the beginnings of a fledgling country, a first marriage gone seriously wrong, a second marriage that lasted for over forty years and a late-in-life relationship with a writer and editor, thirty years his junior with whom his adventures continued, apace.

～

I moved from Los Angeles to Israel in 2012 on the heels of great grief and loss. Everybody thought I was crazy. But the heartfelt memoir I would write about my experiences would prove everybody wrong and heal all of my wounds. This was going to be my *A Year in Provence*, my *Under the Tuscan Sun*, my *Eat, Pray, Love*. I just had to wait for it all to make sense. But it didn't exactly happen that way.

It turns out that you can't really outrun grief and that regaining a sense of purpose can take time. In my case, a lot of time and a very special person named Gidon Lev.

When I was a kid, I saw a miniseries about the Holocaust on television. Starring Meryl Streep and James Woods, among others, the series aired in four parts. I was shaken to my core. Ovens? Gas chambers? Later in life, I learned much more about the Holocaust through films, books, and museum exhibits. By then, I had converted to Judaism. But the Holocaust—the lowest moment in human history, the absolute nadir of humankind— wasn't part of my family history, nor of anyone's that I knew, even tangentially.

When I came to Israel, I was aware that many Holocaust survivors lived here. Israelis are accustomed to their presence in the social fabric. Every year, on Yom HaShoah (Holocaust Remembrance Day), sirens blare out over the whole country in every city, village, and town. Cars pull over to the side of the road, and freeways come to a standstill. The whole country simply stops and stands, heads bowed for what seems like forever but is really only two minutes. My first encounter with this annual ritual of mourning left me with a deep sense of sadness and respect for the millions of victims of the Holocaust and the way that Israel, as a nation, chooses to mark the day each year.

I didn't know it at the time, but only two months after I arrived in Israel in 2012, Gidon Lev lost his wife of over forty-one years. Susan's death was a terrible blow for Gidon and the whole family. It was that great sorrow and a need to keep busy that allowed him the time and space to reflect for the first time in a long time through writing down the story of his life. It was through his writing that my life and Gidon's overlapped.

Gidon's life can be, in some ways, expressed through numbers, symbols, and dates. He was born in 1935, an only child. He was put on Transport M as number 885 and imprisoned in the Térézin (or Theresienstadt) Nazi concentration camp from the ages of 6 to 10. He is one of 92 children estimated to have survived the camp. His father was sent to Auschwitz, where he was tattooed as prisoner B12156.

Gidon lost 26 family members in the Holocaust. He was liberated in 1945 and came to Israel in 1959. He was a soldier in the Six-Day War, responsible for an FN 5.56 caliber Belgian automatic rifle. He was a husband to two wives, father to six children, and grandfather to fourteen. Gidon was also a two-time survivor of cancer. As of 2020, he had lived for 85 years.

There are an estimated two hundred thousand Holocaust survivors left in the world today. Gidon is one of a rapidly disappearing generation. There may be fewer living eyewitnesses to the Nazi atrocities of World War II when you finish reading this book than when you began it. We must share their stories and we must make these stories matter.

The research, writing, and reading that I did while working with Gidon on this book were, naturally, distressing for me on many levels. We like to believe that the human race has progressed and improved—on the continuum of human history, seventy-five years ago is but a negligible blip. On the contrary, it saddens me that, for many, the Holocaust seems like it happened eons ago on a scratchy black-and-white newsreel. We have become alarmingly removed. "History," as Mark Twain may or may not have actually said, "doesn't repeat itself, but it often rhymes."

The Holocaust has not defined Gidon's life—he has not allowed it to—yet he found himself feeling responsible for conveying his experiences at the hands of the Nazis. Even so, he didn't want that terrible experience to be the focal point of his life story. For me, this was sometimes tricky to navigate. I felt responsible as a curator of Gidon's Holocaust testimony, as well as of his many other sometimes painful life experiences. I did not want to cause him or his family any more pain or grief than they had already endured.

As we worked on this book together, it became clear to me

that Gidon's deepest feelings of anger and hurt were reserved for his mother. It took me some time to understand why. He didn't always express his emotions directly or dramatically on any topic, but I decided to err on the side of simply observing Gidon being Gidon in whatever way was natural to him. That seemed and seems the right decision to me. He didn't owe me or anyone else any kind of performance. I have seen people almost genuflect before Gidon when they find out he is a Holocaust survivor. He is suddenly a saint, a relic, or both. I think I did that at first, too, before I came to know him in all of his complex, flawed, sometimes hilarious, opinionated humanity.

Things began to get pretty dire in the world as Gidon and I worked on *The True Adventures* together. There were fires and hurricanes and political upheavals and migrants drowning in the sea. Then there was a global pandemic. The book became more than the story of one man; it became the tale of two people telling an important story in times that desperately needed perspective and hope.

There is history in *The True Adventures*—I think it's important to put things into context—and there is also poetry and laughter and singing. *The True Adventures of Gidon Lev* is about living through dark times and uncertainty and taking chances. It's about reinvention, resiliency, and joy. It's also about one of the most colorful characters you'll ever come across; there is absolutely nobody like Gidon Lev.

Gidon Lev did something extraordinarily courageous; he allowed his most deeply held narratives and beliefs to be challenged by viewing his life events with the benefit of time and a different perspective. All of us should be so brave.

I hope that Gidon's story allows you the grace and the courage to carry on—even when it's hard. "You don't get the life you want," Gidon once said. "You get the life that you get." A very simple principle is embedded in those words—gratitude.

CHAPTER 1
GIDON LEV

Gidon Lev needed an editor. He'd written a book, and he was, among other things, a Holocaust survivor—would I mind meeting him for a cup of coffee? He sounded very sweet on the phone with his slight, unidentifiable accent and impeccable English. I didn't have any experience editing life stories, but it was no skin off my teeth to keep an old man company for half an hour. It would be the nice thing to do. Plus, didn't I owe a Holocaust survivor at least a little of my time?

Gidon made a spectacular arrival with his phone dangling from a cord around his neck and a red clipboard stuffed with papers, notes, and receipts tucked neatly under one arm. I later learned he never goes anywhere without that clipboard. With his merry blue eyes, shock of white hair, and mischievous grin, Gidon Lev did not fit my image of a Holocaust survivor. But then, he was the only one I had ever met in person. He was energetic and cheerful—a force of nature. This was no lonely old man; this was a gregarious talker and inveterate charmer. Gidon ordered a cup of tea and launched into his story with gusto. I must admit I was a bit taken aback by how much he shared with me and how quickly.

Gidon told me about his experience in the Térézin

concentration camp then he kept right on talking. He told me that after he was liberated in 1945, he had been in a socialist Zionist youth group in Canada. (I had no idea what he was talking about.) Then, in 1959, he had come to Israel, where he became a devoted kibbutznik and taught folk dancing. He worked in a dairy. He had fought in the Israeli Army and had taken fire from Syrians; he lost his pants crossing the Jordan River, holding his rifle over his head. He had been stationed at an Israeli enclave on Mount Scopus in Jordanian-controlled East Jerusalem.

Then, mostly for the shock factor—I think—he added that two of his children had been kidnapped. *Okay*, I thought, *time's up. This guy is crazy.*

"Uh, how many children do you have?"

"Six."

Gidon wasn't done yet. He told me how he searched for his two children in California where their mother had taken them. Along the way, he said he had gone to a nude beach, gotten poison oak, and worked on a farm. Then, he made a split-second decision in a California parking lot that changed the direction of many lives forever. He also had lived in Wales for a time with his second wife.

"But, how many wives did you have?"

"Just two." Gidon grinned. "That was enough."

This man was something else. I had heard stories about Holocaust survivors who were lonely, isolated, depressed, or sometimes heroic activists. Gidon was none of those things; he was more like a mischievous Peter Pan.

Gidon needed someone well-versed in Israeli history, not to mention Holocaust studies, and he needed someone with a whole lot more patience and time than I had. I wasn't qualified to take on such a project, I explained as nicely as I could, and reassured him that, with no doubt, there were any number of editors who would be a perfect fit. Just not me.

But I was troubled. Gidon's story was important; I knew

that. How could I walk away from a Holocaust survivor, an eyewitness to atrocity? Surely he would find a qualified editor out there somewhere, I told myself.

But Gidon was so friendly and outgoing, I thought it might be nice to be—and to have—a new friend. After all, if I was honest with myself, *I* was lonely. So I called Gidon up a couple of days later and asked if he wanted to meet for coffee again. Just to visit with each other, not to discuss his book, which I clearly could not, I emphasized, help him with.

"Sure. I just need to shave and put some shoes on!" he said. *Oh—now?* I hadn't planned on that. Half an hour later, we sat across from each other at another café in the suburb of Tel Aviv where we both happened to live.

During our second visit, Gidon told me about his adventures working on dairies on various farms in Israel, and how he tested the milk for quality, and what type of cow was the best for milk, and how often the cows need to be milked. He told me about his six children, where they lived, and what they did. He wanted to know about me, too. Why was I living in Israel? How long had I lived here? How was my Hebrew? Did I want to go to his nearby home and see some of his artwork, family pictures, and books?

Gidon Lev, this father, son, grandfather, dairyman, husband, builder, dancer, doer, and—evidently—mischief-maker, was something else. I was quite taken by my new friend. He was a character, to say the least, and a welcome new presence in my life. We began to meet regularly for coffee and the strudel that he so loved. Soon, our coffee dates began to include going to the movies and shopping for groceries together. Cheerfully, Gidon started to show up and make repairs and improvements in my apartment. We went camping and traveling. We swam in the Mediterranean and subsequently nursed our jellyfish stings. We shopped, cooked, and ran errands together. Before long, we spent almost every day together.

In Israel, there is a saying: "For every lid there is a pot." There is somebody for everybody, in other words. Though it was a book project that I was not—and I repeat *not*—going to work on that initially brought Gidon and me together, it didn't take long for us to realize that we made great life partners, or Loving Life Buddies, as I came to call us.

If there's one trait that stood out the most about Gidon, it was his persistence. He was dead set on his book. It was a subject that he brought up at every opportunity.

In Gidon's office, there was an avalanche of mysteriously labeled, jumbled computer files of his writing, which he had paid a young man to upload to his computer for him. He'd printed it out in batches held together by paper clips. A blizzard of Post-its covered the mass. There was the yellow star he'd had to pin on his jacket that read, in large, ugly letters, *JUDE*. I had a physical reaction to it; I had never seen such a thing if it wasn't in a film or behind a glass case. Gidon showed me his transport papers and those of his mother. Gidon was on Transport M and he was number 885. I had never seen such a thing, either. It was sinister, written so neatly with such detail.

Along with his recollections of his time in Térézin, Gidon had written thousands of words and hundreds of painstakingly detailed pages about the regular stuff we all do in our lives: camping trips, birthday parties, changing jobs, and moving house. I tried to tell Gidon that these kinds of details wouldn't interest people outside of his family. He did not agree, and I could not persuade him.

Maybe, I thought, in my spare time, I could simply help Gidon get organized, proofread what he had written, and get the whole thing printed at a local copy shop. We'd put his photo on the cover, and Gidon would be happy. But Gidon wasn't crazy about that idea. Somehow, instinctively, he knew that there was much more to his story than his personal experiences. He realized that his memories were not, in themselves, a narrative. The historical and cultural background of his life had been complicated. He needed someone to join him in his project. That person, he insisted, should be me. I didn't choose this project. It—and Gidon—chose me. That seemed to me a kind of cosmic beckoning, an invitation that I would have been foolish to ignore. I was in. If there were aspects of history or Israeli culture that I didn't know or understand, I would learn.

I made an appeal on a Facebook group for writers and journalists. I thought that perhaps by crowdsourcing the early organizational stages of this project, I could give this sprawling project some kind of shape. I was amazed by the number of responses I received. Dozens of people volunteered their help, advice, and encouragement. Some offered to go over the original writing and organize it by subject. Others offered to type handwritten pages. With the help of dozens of generous volunteers, a mountain of files and piles of paper had been corralled. A significant step forward had been taken.

I found a helpful tool—a roll of whiteboard paper that was sticky on one side. I unspooled it in the hallway, so Gidon could match dates up with events. Gradually, I noticed something beginning to emerge on that whiteboard, something in between the lines: Gidon hadn't ever *really* looked back at his most traumatic experiences on an *emotional* level. He was in a Nazi concentration camp at an age when he wasn't able to contextualize it in any way, then he immigrated to America where he didn't have the language to speak about it. Afterward, and for decades, nobody really talked about their Holocaust experiences at all; the postwar world was busy rebuilding and leaving the past behind. There were many other hurts, experiences, and traumas that Gidon had gone through as well. He'd had a painful relationship with his mother—who was by all accounts a very difficult person—a dramatic, tragic breakup with his first wife; two painful, life-threatening bouts of cancer; and then, to top it all off, the love of his life—the weave and the weft of his emotional well-being—Susan, passed away long before her time.

Finally, the penny dropped for me. Gidon had reached the stage in his life when he *needed* to look back and he *wanted* to be heard. And, importantly, he'd found a safe, supportive, and loving companion to do that alongside him.

Finally, after months of transcribing, typing, retyping and organizing, we simply started at the beginning:

 GIDON "I was born in Karlsbad, or Karlovy Vary, in Czechoslovakia, in 1935. Originally, my name was not Gidon. I was born Peter Wolfgang Löw. Peter —not a Jewish name. Wolfgang—because my grandfather played the viola. I guess he liked Mozart. So he gave me the middle name. Löw was my family name.

The truth is, my grandfather owned a Stradivarius viola. When the war came, he gave it to someone for safekeeping. I still have the receipt. But my grandfather died in the Warsaw ghetto and the viola was never to be seen again."

Taking a bird's eye historical view, I decided, was not just important but critical in understanding the times during which Gidon lived. Adolf Hitler was elected the führer of Germany in August 1934, about six months before he was born. When Gidon was just six months old, the Nuremberg Race Laws stripped German Jews of their rights, and an inexorable horror ground into motion.

In 1938, when Peterl, as his mother called him, was just three, Germany annexed the Sudetenland in the Munich Agreement. That was where Gidon's family lived: a part of Czechoslovakia that is just east of Germany. After Hitler's annexation, the Jewish population in the Sudeten fled eastward to Prague. Gidon's family packed up, too. Gidon's stern, diminutive mother, Doris, had been trained as a milliner, and his father, Ernst, owned a scrap-iron lot. Everything was left behind.

GIDON "I remember happy times and being with my mother, father, and grandparents celebrating my third birthday. The highlight was a beautiful red tricycle with black rubber handlebars. I was so overjoyed that I rode it until I collapsed in bed each night. However, slowly, things began to change, and I couldn't make sense of it. After all, I was only three years old; I didn't know about Hitler, Germany, or even what or who Jews were. When we fled to Prague, I had to leave my tricycle behind and it broke my heart."

The family crowded into a small flat in Prague: Gidon, his mother and father, and his paternal grandparents, frightened and unsure about what would happen next. For three years, they lived in fear and dread along with thousands of others who had fled Hitler's murderous regime hoping they would stay safe.

 GIDON "Arriving in Prague in 1938 was a tremendous relief for my parents, at least at first. We rented an apartment not far from the center of the city. There, we waited for our household furniture and belongings to arrive, but they never did. I learned later that the mover we hired took everything."

Three years later, in 1941, Gidon was transported with his mother and grandfather to the Térézin (Theresienstadt) concentration camp, just over 30 miles north of Prague. His father had been sent on a transport to the same camp two weeks earlier. Peter—Gidon—spent four years in the camp. In fact, of the estimated fifteen thousand children who were imprisoned in or transported through Térézin, only ninety-two are known to have survived. Gidon is one of those children.

Although Gidon and his mother survived, his father, great-grandmother, three grandparents, aunts, great-aunts, uncles, great-uncles, and cousins all perished in Auschwitz, Buchenwald, Treblinka, and Majdanek and in the Izbica and Warsaw ghettos. What had been a large family spread across Czechoslovakia and Austria was reduced to two family members: Gidon and his mother, Doris.

"But we had to go to Prague, before you could really understand the rest," Gidon added.

"Yes, yes, next chapter. Hold your horses," I said. "That hasn't happened yet."

The book was in its early stages, and Gidon wanted to hear and comment on every word and page. That seemed fair enough to me. It was his life story, after all. But we would have to try to come up with a routine.

"Let's make a deal," I said. "Once a week, I'll either read the new pages to you or print them out and you can read them. If there's something you want to change or add, just tell me."

"Every day."

"Every week."

I had by then learned that Gidon tended to be stubborn—but he was also right an annoying majority of the time, which meant I took him seriously. But I had to have some latitude, or the book Gidon wanted so badly would never get written. Finally, we agreed that we would go over every chapter together, weekly, and that Gidon's notes and comments would focus on those matters of great importance—not just facts, dates, and the like, but his feelings. This would come to be a routine that we both enjoyed, but I was surprised, over and over, by the things that caught Gidon's attention for comment or correction and those that did not. His comments (or lack of them) offered a valuable insight not just into Gidon but into the nature of memory itself.

CHAPTER 2
PRAHA

There are a lot of things I didn't think about before I met Gidon. For instance, in my mind's eye, there was Europe before World War II: tumultuous but sophisticated, cultured, and European—that ineffable, superior quality we Americans adore. Then there was Europe during World War II: a kind of hell with billowing black smoke and lines of tanks and concentration camps. Then there was Europe after World War II: cafés, fountains, and cathedrals of historic grandeur.

Why did I have such images of postwar Europe as a glamorous place to go when, in fact, Europe was devastated, in every respect, for years?

With the postwar rebuilding and innovation in Europe, optimism in America, and worldwide hope, a new era of consumerism and tourism was born. Hollywood films showed American audiences romantic images of Europeans sitting in cafés, riding Vespas, and smoking insouciantly. It was an image cultivated to encourage tourism and economic growth. An American could be forgiven for buying into this hopeful, glamorous vision.

The truth was that Europe had to be rebuilt, and several international organizations we take for granted now were formed posthaste. The UN (United Nations), UNICEF (UN International Children's Emergency Fund), WHO (World Health Organization), and the World Bank were just a few. Indeed, under the U.S. Marshall Plan, the United States sent more than twelve billion dollars in foreign aid to Europe.

Another thing I hadn't noticed before was that World War II and the Holocaust were often understood differently in popular culture. For some, World War II occupied the foreground, with places and names such as Dunkirk and Normandy and Winston Churchill, Adolf Hitler, and General Patton. The war brought up visions of muddy battles, tanks, bombers, ruins, and rations.

The Holocaust was the horror happening in the background. It was different. It brought up images of corpses, ovens, barbed-wire fences, and ominous, chugging trains full of terrified, doomed Jews. Names such as Adolf Hitler, Heinrich Himmler, Adolf Eichmann, and Hermann Göring and places like Auschwitz and Treblinka came to mind.

How did it come to pass that one conflict, which exploded into thousands of conflicts and acts of brutality and war across Europe, Africa, and the Pacific, could be seen as separate narratives? Wasn't the Holocaust synonymous with World War II? And what was the Shoah, anyway?

I was not familiar with the word *Shoah* until I saw French director Claude Lanzmann's epic 1985 film by the same name. *Shoah*, a documentary of 556 minutes (nine hours and twenty-six minutes) is considered a masterpiece and was hailed widely by critics. Roger Ebert wrote of the film: "It is not a documentary, not journalism, not propaganda, not political. It is an act of witness".[1] I saw the film at UC Santa Barbara. It was shown in three-hour increments over a period of three days. I remember emerging from the dark theater into the bright California sunshine and feeling a sense of deep disconnect and sorrow. The sunshine and palm trees outside could not wash away the first-person testimonies and long shots of railroad tracks that had been projected on a screen inside.

Shoah is a Hebrew word that means *catastrophe*. Over time, many Jews have come to prefer this term to the word *holocaust*, which comes from the first Greek translation of the Hebrew Bible, called the Septuagint, and dates back to the third century BCE. Scholars agree that *holocaust* means "wholly burnt" and refers to a burnt sacrificial offering.

The word *holocaust* was first used to describe the Hamidian (or, in modern terms, Armenian) Massacres perpetrated by the Ottoman Turks from 1894 to 1896. Although many believe that a word that implies an offering is unsuitable to describe the Jewish genocide, "the Holocaust" has become synonymous with the murder of six million Jews (and millions of others) at the hands of the Nazis.

Gidon felt it was important to show me the place of his birth, his flight, and his imprisonment. Of course, he was right. We made plans to go to the Czech Republic. We were to fly to Prague, stay for a few days, then travel to Karlovy Vary and, finally, Térézin.

Though Gidon had twice been back before, in 1989 and in 2008 with his family, this time his feelings were complicated. Maybe he intuited that he might never see these places again. Or perhaps he was nervous about whether the places he had described to me in such detail would be as he said they were.

The plane we boarded at Ben-Gurion International Airport held all the usual suspects: crying children, harried parents, and young travelers. There was also a group of about twenty yeshiva (orthodox religious) students from Brooklyn who had been studying in Israel.

"Oh, great," Gidon muttered darkly as we took in the black-clad group of youths. Moments later, we discovered that our seatmate was one of the yeshiva boys. He and Gidon had a pleasant conversation about Prague and Gidon's history. I was relieved that the topic of Jewish religious observance did not come up.

～

There is a curious and often painful divide between secular and religious Jews in Israel. This is sometimes expressed with secular Jews feeling that the very religious (i.e., the ultra-orthodox) are backward, superstitious, and intolerant and with the ultra-orthodox viewing secular Jews as having abandoned what they see as the basic obligations of being a Jew.

Gidon's family was, like many Jews living in central and western Europe before the war, entirely secular and very much a part of the local culture. Gidon did not have a ritual circumcision, bar mitzvah, or any of the typical rites of passage for male Jews. In fact, he didn't realize he was Jewish until he was in a concentration camp. After the war, Gidon never considered a Jewish religious identity for a moment. For him, being a Jew meant building a country. Religion had nothing to do with it.

That said, and although the ultra-orthodox make up only about 12 percent of the population in Israel, many argue their political influence is outsized. A familiar source of friction within Israel, the argument for many comes down to who is a Jew or who is Jewish enough.

～

Prague (*Praha* in Czech) is one of the top tourist destinations in Europe—and for good reason. Gidon proudly showed me the towering spires and fairytale buildings which, he observed with some wonder, had been significantly renovated and beautified since the fall of the Soviet Union. This was the Prague that Gidon remembered and loved.

Like other European capitals, Prague has a long, windy history of kings, invasions, destruction, and rebuilding. It struck me as a city where the cool kids live: artists, writers, and intellectuals. Prague is a city in which one could linger for weeks, going to museums, reading novels, and sitting in cafés, soaking up the atmosphere as the sun slips over the pointy buildings and creates deep shadows. There are plenty of shadows in Prague.

66 **GIDON** "A few months after we came to Prague in 1938, restrictions on the Jews were announced. Jews, young and old, had to wear the yellow Star of David with *JUDE* written in black on it on the left side of their chest. Later I learned that these stars were available for a sum of money in every postal and government office and, adding insult to injury, we were required to buy them for ourselves; not wearing it was punishable by death. Soon after, Jews were forced to follow a curfew and to be home at 8 p.m. All bank accounts belonging to Jews were confiscated and became the property of the Third Reich. The same went for safety deposit boxes, no matter what they held. Jewelry, cameras, typewriters, and especially radios of any size were to be handed in to the authorities. Even public transportation was restricted for us, including where we were allowed to sit if we were lucky enough to get on a tramway at all. Every day it seemed there was a new ordinance."

On our second day in Prague, Gidon and I made our way over the cobblestones and through the crowds to the Pinkas Synagogue in the old Jewish quarter. A synagogue dating back to the sixteenth century, today it is run by the Jewish Museum. Inside the synagogue/museum is a permanent exhibit of the names of the estimated seventy-eight thousand Czech Jews murdered during the Holocaust. The names are written according to village or region—regions with Hapsburg-y names such as Moravia and Bohemia in the country then called Czechoslovakia. It took Gidon and me only a few minutes to find the names of his father and grandparents. Nearby, the yeshiva boys we'd seen on the plane were gathered in a circle and singing a traditional song of grief and mourning in Hebrew. Their voices rose above us and echoed.

I tried to photograph the family names inscribed on the wall, but I couldn't zoom in enough on the names that were relevant only to Gidon. There were just too many. Round and round the walls the names went.

Outside the Pinkas Synagogue is the old Jewish cemetery, which is one of the oldest Jewish cemeteries in Europe. Enclosed by walls and crammed into a relatively small, stony, mossy place, it radiates with a jagged and solemn atmosphere, packed with gravestones peppered with stones, which are the traditional Jewish expression of the permanence of memory at a gravesite, rather than flowers that wilt and fade.

There in the cemetery, Gidon and I came upon the yeshiva boys yet again. Our airplane seatmate recognized us, greeted Gidon warmly, then looked immediately over Gidon's head.

"You guys!" he called. "Come here, quick!" Gidon had told the young man a bit about his history on the plane. Only a moment later, Gidon was surrounded by the eager and awestruck faces of the boys.

"So where's your number?" one asked, gesturing to Gidon's arm. Gidon explained that it was only at Auschwitz where Nazis tattooed numbers on the arms of prisoners and that, furthermore, children sent to Auschwitz generally did not survive to show their numbers anyway.

A few other tourists, overhearing the conversation, listened in. Gidon loved the attention, but I saw his energy flagging. We bid our goodbyes, and Gidon stooped to pick up a branch that had fallen on the ground and used it as he walked away regally. The yeshiva boys and tourists stared after him.

As we made our way back to our hotel, we passed by the Old

New Synagogue, Europe's oldest operating synagogue, completed in 1270. Legend has it that, in the attic of the synagogue, there is a box containing the body of the Golem. The Golem is a figure from a centuries-old Jewish myth; it is a powerful, avenging creature made of mud, with superhuman strength and an inability to speak. If this sounds at all familiar, it is because the myth of the Golem was famously borrowed by Mary Wollstonecraft Shelley as the tragic character of her novel *Frankenstein*, as well as dozens of other literary works, including *The Amazing Adventures of Kavalier & Clay* by Michael Chabon. The Golem has even been associated with the Gingerbread Man and a Slavic myth called "The Clay Boy."

The Golem in the attic has a purpose. It lies dormant until it is brought to life to protect the Jews from pogroms. A pogrom is a massacre that takes place when a violent mob enters a Jewish neighborhood or village and sets fire to and destroys everything and everyone in sight with guns, knives, and even bare hands. There is rape. There is murder. Pogroms were an unspeakably horrible and regular fact of life for Jews living in Europe for centuries. The Golem is a legend that arose from sheer desperation.

Legend says that if one wrote the Hebrew letters *aleph, mem,* and *tav* ("truth") on its forehead, the Golem would come to life and obey whoever commands it. Erase the *aleph* on the Golem's forehead and what remains is *mem* and *tav* ("death") and the Golem stops—until further notice.

It was interesting, I thought, that "truth" brings life and that "death" is only temporary.

Outside the Old New Synagogue, shops did a brisk business selling Golem cookies, keychains, magnets, and other Golem-shaped tchotchkes. Naturally, I wanted to buy something Golem-related, but Gidon was ready to go.

We dined at a café along the Vltava River overlooking the Charles Bridge, surrounded by tourists and souvenir shops. There, we had a view of the huge, many-spired Prague Castle, which overlooks the Vltava River and all of Prague. The castle, the seat of power for the kings of Bohemia since the ninth century, once had an unwelcome guest. On March 15, 1939, Hitler spent the night there and, reportedly, looked out over Prague—his latest conquest—with pride. The previous day, Czech president Emil Hácha had suffered a heart attack when he was informed that if he did not agree to allow a complete Nazi takeover, Prague would be bombed.

Perusing the café menu, distracted by the horrible idea that Adolf Hitler himself had also been in Prague, I thought about a terrible fact: Before the war, approximately ninety-two thousand Jews lived in Prague. Today, there were about five thousand.[2]

I ordered a glass of absinthe even though I had heard that it's doubtful any absinthe ordered at a café in Prague—particularly a tourist café—was authentic. I was too tired and sad to care. It was jewel green and pretty. Gidon tasted it and made a face. He was right. It was awful.

The following day, Gidon was to show me the building that he and his family took shelter in for three years, from 1938 until 1941.

CHAPTER 3

ITALSKA

GIDON "There were five of us who lived in the small flat on Italska 7 Street. I shared a bedroom with my grandfather because my grandmother was very ill and needed her own room. I remember going to kindergarten, and I remember being sick quite often, with colds and sometimes a fever, too. When I stayed home from school, I would sit at a small table, sewing little garments for my doll while my mother worked on hats for her clients. My mother had gone to a millinery school when she was growing up, and this was her profession, and it helped us to survive since neither my father nor, even less so, my grandfather could find work because nobody would hire Jews. We lived close to a lovely playground, where my grandpa Alfred would take me from time to time. I remember the swings there, one in the shape of a canoe, which I particularly loved. One day, I came home from kindergarten to find my father terribly aggravated and angry with my mother. It was my mother's regular practice to air out our bedding on the windowsill every day, and, that day, one of the pillows had fallen down to the street. My father had run down the four floors of steps only to find an elderly lady who had picked up the fallen pillow. After my father thanked her profusely, he had come back upstairs with the pillow, and only then did it become clear to my mother why he was so upset. My family had hidden all of my parents' money inside that pillow."

Italska Street is in what is now an up-and-coming neighborhood in Prague, with cafés, a yoga studio, and frozen yogurt shops. But the building at Italska 7, although not lacking in character, was not as well-kept as the neighboring buildings.

I took a picture of Gidon on the steps of the building, wearing his backpack, looking curiously like a child as he peered into the glass front doors. Inside, a Czech janitor was mopping the floor disinterestedly. He caught sight of us and opened the door, a cigarette dangling from his lip. I tried to explain that Gidon used to live in the building long ago, but the janitor only shrugged and continued working.

I wasn't sure how Gidon was feeling or how he was taking all of this. He seemed cheerful enough and was energized to be in Prague. But I didn't want to pry or to project my own feelings onto him. I just wanted to let him be and allow him to show me his past without expectation. Was there a way that Gidon was *supposed* to be feeling? It wasn't for me to judge. It seemed to me that Gidon had told his story so many times throughout his life that he had become accustomed to it.

I have seen him weep, overcome with joy or with sadness in unexpected moments—maybe because of a sad television commercial or an old song. I get it. Some things are too much to think about directly even when they are right in front of you.

GIDON "Public parks were only for 'Aryans,' and so were public playgrounds. My grandfather could no longer take me to the park, where my favorite canoe swing had once lifted me away from our dark reality. The German Gestapo entered the homes of Jews without the slightest warning or provocation. I was fearful of any knock on our door and would hide in the darkest corner of our apartment lest it be the feared intrusion of the Gestapo. If they did find something, they not only confiscated it, but the entire family also was taken away, never to be heard from again."

Ignoring the sulky janitor, I took a picture of the stairs coming down to the lobby. Long ago, a six-year-old Gidon and his mother clunked down these very stairs with their suitcases and rucksacks on a cold autumn morning in 1941, obeying orders to report to the train station.

GIDON "A new announcement came that said all Jews would be resettled in Térézin, a village and army camp from the Great War, just 55 kilometers north of Prague. The first two transports would be men between the ages of eighteen and fifty, who, if they volunteered, would be joined by their immediate family within a few weeks. Hearing this, my father and grandfather signed up and, just before they boarded the train, came to visit me in the hospital. I had just had my tonsils removed. So here I was in the hospital and could not even say goodbye to my beloved grandfather and my dad. They gave me a big hug, and brought me *zmrzlina* (ice cream), the only thing I could eat, because I couldn't speak at all, it hurt so much. They said they would be okay, assuring me that we would see each other soon. I didn't quite understand and was very sad, but later my mom explained to me and, thinking that we would soon be together again, I calmed down, somehow."

Suffocating dread must have crept up slowly on Gidon's parents and so many others. The small humiliations. The arrests. The yellow stars. The posters pasted on the city walls and lampposts ordering the Jews to do this and that, no longer allowing them in this park or that café or this bus. The appearance of German soldiers sporting their gray uniforms, marching down streets and over bridges. The wondering where the neighbor went or if the neighbor talked. The pulling down of the blinds at night. The radio announcements. Going out to shop with clipped ration cards. Trying to live when your bank account has been confiscated by the Reich. The knock on the door. The order to report to the train station. The dread. The disbelief. What do you pack? Bring your valuables, they said. And something warm.

 GIDON "Within ten days of my father and grandfather's transport, my mother and I received a notice from the Germans that we, too, were to be shipped out to Térézin. I remember being quite happy—aha! The Germans are keeping their promise, and we are going to be reunited! I helped my mother pack our suitcases and roll up our blankets. We arrived at the central *Bahnhof* [train station] with all our personal belongings by 12 p.m. the next day, December 12, 1941. It was sheer madness. What to take, what to leave behind? How much can we carry? What about blankets, sheets, pillows? Warm clothing, winter things, which shoes, how much and what food for how many days? We took as much as my mother and I could carry and hoped for the best. We were motivated by our fear of the Germans, and the hope that we would be reunited with my dad and granddad. It is hard to imagine something like five hundred women and their children all camping out in the train station hall on the bare floor. We were one on top of the other, every centimeter accounted for. It was my first encounter with hell on earth. I tried not to cry, and even to be helpful to my mother, who was, most of the time, aggravated and tense. For two days, we slept there, ate whatever we had brought with us, stood in hour-long lines to relieve ourselves, and somehow also kept warm. It was, after all, December, the middle of the winter and bitterly cold."

How frightened Gidon and his mother must have been. What did Doris tell Gidon, and what did he really understand? I wondered if I could have kept my cool with my kids. Doris had no real idea of what her future held.

Peeking out from behind the last building on the block only half a block away were a steeple and lush green treetops. Was that the same park Gidon remembered? We walked over, and, sure enough, there was the small park his grandfather Alfred used to take him to. The square, called náměstí Míru, is presided over by the towering Church of St. Ludmilla and lined with neatly clipped grass and flowers. The playground is gone. We sat on a bench, and I made small talk with a grandmother with her grandchild in a stroller. The baby had so many teeth.

"Yes!" the grandmother exclaimed proudly. "Even the dentist says so!"

There was something else Gidon wanted to do while we were in Prague. We took a taxi to the New Jewish Cemetery, which was only a few minutes away. This lush, sprawling, stately cemetery is where Franz Kafka is buried, and we beelined to see his grave, which was festooned with stones, poems, and other remembrances from literary tourists. But that's not why we were there. We were there to find the grave of Gidon's grandmother.

Theresa, or "Theresie," as she was affectionately called, was Gidon's paternal grandmother. She had passed away a few months before the first transports started and was buried in Prague. In some ways, I thought, she was spared: she never made it on the transport to Térézin with the rest of the family. Had she done so at her age, she likely wouldn't have lasted very long. Her husband, Alfred, was dead within a year after his arrival there.

Theresie's resting place is toward the back of the cemetery, along with other people who didn't have elaborate grave markers or family plots. On a past visit, Gidon couldn't find his grandmother's grave; there was too much snow on the ground. But not on this warm summer day; the ground was musty and loamy, covered with ivy and leaves. The cemetery was quiet, as they are wont to be. The dense foliage of trees created scattered patterns of moving sunlight over the graves. Gidon and I had the crinkled paperwork showing us which part of the cemetery Theresie was buried in, and which plot. But even with the help of a tall, silent cemetery worker in dirty overalls, look as we might, we could not find her grave. We searched for over an hour, scraping dirt and ivy back from marker after marker. The cemetery worker apologized and ruefully disappeared back over the vines and into the trees. Gidon sat down on a bench, full of emotion but silent.

"It's a pity," he said finally.

On our way out of the cemetery, Gidon and I noticed memorial plaques along the cemetery walls. On them are the names of family members killed in the Holocaust. No exact dates of death, but the years of transports and the camps they were sent to. Treblinka, Auschwitz, Dachau, Belzec, Majdanek, and others. What a miserable constellation of places to die a horrible death. As we passed by the office of the cemetery, I was inspired to push for more information. Maybe we could show the man in charge our paperwork and ask again. There had to be a way to find Theresie. Gidon might never have this chance again.

The nice man in the office spoke to Gidon in Czech and in German. A few words in English were thrown in, too. How could this be, we asked? We knew Gidon's family had salvaged at least some resources when they fled to Prague. We knew that they buried Gidon's grandmother here. The man explained that, at the time Gidon's grandmother died, Jewish burials were done quickly and secretly. Jews didn't want to draw attention to themselves. Later, he went on, during the forty-year Soviet rule over Czechoslovakia, religious institutions and especially Judaism were under an "officially sanctioned hostile policy," so synagogues and cemeteries were neglected and fell into a state of disrepair. Only in recent years were the more remote sections of the cemetery being cleared and help offered to locate graves for those looking.

What the man didn't mention to Gidon and me, and perhaps he didn't know, was that in the early 1980s, over one hundred thousand Jewish headstones were looted by the Soviet regime to "revamp" Wenceslas Square in the center of Prague's historic district. In May 2020, as Prague set to again revamp and restore this large public square, Jewish headstones were discovered. They had been taken from Jewish cemeteries in Prague and broken into pieces and used as paving stones.[1] Gidon and I had spent so much time on our hands and knees looking for Theresie's headstone, thinking we would find it under the ivy. In reality, she might have been right under our feet, and under those of thousands of tourists, the whole time.

Gidon and I hopped on a vintage-seeming trolley car back toward the part of Prague where we were staying. Very quickly, we realized that we were on the wrong trolley and wound up on the other side of the Vltava, the side that had not been spruced up or "revamped" for tourists. Here the buildings and streets were slightly dilapidated and bore the Brutalist stamp of the former Soviet occupiers. We sat at a café, ordered ice cream, and watched a miniature street-sweeper clean up the detritus of the recent past.

CHAPTER 4
KARLOVY VARY

Karlovy Vary is a name that rolls around on my tongue like something sweet, like the holiday season. It is more widely known as Karlsbad, its German name. The Czech Republic is cupped on its north, southeastern and southwestern sides by Germany and bordered by Poland on its northeast side; it sits north of Austria. Slovakia is directly to the southeast.

It is interesting how the tumbler of time has arranged and rearranged European empires, dynasties, and nations over and over again. In my lifetime, many countries have disappeared into new ones. Former Czechoslovakia is one of those, splitting, in 1993, in the "velvet divorce" into Czechia and Slovakia. Yugoslavia is now Bosnia and Herzegovina, Croatia, Serbia, Slovenia, Montenegro, and North Macedonia. The former Yugoslavia and Czechoslovakia were both parts of the Austro-Hungarian Empire, as were Hungary and Austria. And others. It gets confusing.

Gidon's family were from all over the Austro-Hungarian Empire. They came from Vienna and various small villages that dotted the landscape all the way to Karlovy Vary, which is in the C-shaped region that borders Germany. During the twentieth century, this area came to be known as the Sudetenland, so named after a mountain range. In 1921, it was estimated that more than three million ethnic Germans lived there. This population saw itself as different, as German rather than Czech. The fact that they lived side by side with Czechs was not a big issue. Until it was.

With the rise of Hitler, who sought to rebuild a German empire (i.e., a Reich), German inhabitants of the Sudetenland saw a chance to be reunified with Germany. Many of those German Czechs were enthusiastically on board with Hitler's hateful anti-Semitic rhetoric. Things heated up with the rise of Hitler, and in the 1930s, there were pogroms across the Sudeten. Jews living in this area were not large in number, comparatively speaking. Still, as their German-Jewish counterparts lost their rights in the Nuremberg Laws, they must have been terrified.

Anti-Semitism wasn't new to European Jews, though. It was forbidden for Jews to live in Karlovy Vary for almost three hundred years, from 1499 to 1793, after which Jewish peddlers were allowed to do business and be on their way. A permanent Jewish presence in Karlovy Vary didn't gather any kind of momentum until after 1848. It must have been sometime around then that Gidon's ancestors arrived.

In Europe at that time and for centuries before, Jews were considered Jews first *then* conditional sub-citizens depending on social whims and political expediency. This conditionality was shared by Jews throughout Europe. Whether religious and living in small villages (*shtetls*) in eastern Europe, or secular (typically in the more urban areas of western Europe), Jews were at times merely tolerated and at other times savagely attacked in pogroms. Surely, in the modern age of the 1920s and '30s, anti-Semitism would fade away, wouldn't it?

"Hope," as Thucydides said, "is an expensive commodity. It is better to be prepared."

~

Karlovy Vary is not far from Prague, as the crow flies: about 70 miles. But the day Gidon and I traveled there in our rental car, over miles and miles of countryside, there was roadwork. A lot of roadwork. But it didn't seem to bother Gidon. The closer we got to this western part of the Czech Republic, the more animated he became. He had already told me again and again how beautiful it was, the place of his birth—how wooded, how spectacularly beautiful, how historic. From what I could see out the window, I was beginning to have serious doubts. I saw nothing but miles of flatland and fields and road construction.

The villages were few and far between and looked stuck in time (and not in a quaint way) with the indeterminate architecture of a vaguely post-Soviet kind. The farther we got from Prague, the more uneasy I felt. I had read about the current rise of anti-Semitism in Europe and in the Czech Republic as well. We looked for a place to eat lunch in yet another village that had seen better days. We sat down in a dark, mostly empty pub-like restaurant with some locals who were drinking beer at a table in the corner. They glanced up at us inquisitively. Whether they were unaccustomed to tourists or were merely curious, I did not know. I found myself hauling out all the stereotypes of Eastern Europeans: big-boned and muscular, pale, a bit flabby, hard-edged, and vaguely thuggish.

Where had I gotten such ideas? Too many movies, I supposed. I wondered what would happen if I said that Gidon was from there, that he was a Jew, that he had been in a concentration camp, that his family had been murdered. Would these locals be interested or defensive? Why did I even have that train of thought? Should they feel guilty or responsible for something they likely had nothing to do with?

Gidon was a bit quieter than usual, I noticed. I figured he was simply hungry, tired, and anxious to get to Karlovy Vary.

· · ·

Gidon was right. Karlovy Vary is incredibly beautiful. It is located at what amounts to the bottom of a densely forested ravine with a river winding through it. A mile or two away is the larger, more modern city that the tourists skip. Nestled as Karlovy Vary is, in such alpine geography, it reminded me of the part of northern California where I had grown up. Scents of pine needles, tree sap, moss, rustling rivers, and dying leaves wafted over everything. As did the smell of sulfur. The big draw in Karlovy Vary is and has been, for hundreds of years, the mineral water hot springs and geysers. Famous figures from history who came to Karlovy Vary for the health benefits of the water include people like Johann Wolfgang von Goethe, Frédéric Chopin, Ludwig van Beethoven, and a long list of now-obscure European royalty. Taking the cure in the form of balneology was all the rage.

Karlovy Vary is a spa town all right, but not the kind that I am accustomed to, with mauve carpeting and piped-in music and hot stone massages. No, this is old-school. The main street is lined with spas touting not just the health benefits of the water but numerous other health treatments as well. Things like the cleansings of toxins and minor medical procedures that are, I am quite sure, probably illegal in most places.

The stately Imperial Hotel, built in 1912, overlooks the town. White and very Stephen King-esque, it was designed to help some of the seventy thousand-plus annual tourists who came to visit Karlovy Vary (previous to the First World War) find more luxurious digs. I was particularly keen to see the famed Grandhotel Pupp. I know it's not pronounced *poop*, but far be it from me to skip an opportunity for humor on this emotionally arduous trip. In any event, the Grandhotel Pupp is purportedly the visual inspiration for the Wes Anderson film *The Grand Budapest Hotel*, and the resemblance is clear. To be fair, though, the Imperial Hotel looks quite similar, so this Hollywood myth might have some holes in it. Inside the lobby of the Grandhotel, there was an enormous, stylized photograph of Morgan Freeman, who apparently is a fan of the Grandhotel Pupp, as were many other celebrities whose names are engraved on little gold stars that litter the hotel driveway and sidewalk like a walk of fame.

I wondered what this now-thriving spa town had been like just after the war, whether the spas were still open and, if they were, who went. They weren't, I later learned, and people didn't. The occupying Soviet Army made good use of the Imperial Hotel, though, sending officers there for recuperation. Both the Imperial Hotel and the Grandhotel Pupp had been nationalized during the Soviet era. In the 1990s, as the Soviet Union began its fall apart, the hotels were privatized for pennies on the dollar. The getting must have been good. The end of the main drag that the Grandhotel Pupp occupies is populated by a decidedly wealthier class of tourists enjoying gelato and luxury shopping experiences. The other end is comprised mainly of budget tourists, like Gidon and me. We strolled through the streets, took pictures, bought Gidon a funny hat, and ate spicy sausages with horseradish, mustard, and pickles.

I was struck by the incongruous fact that Gidon hailed from a resort town, a vacation spot. Well, when in Rome, as they say. I booked an appointment at the illustriously named Spa Number Five. We were in a spa town, and I wanted a spa experience. Gidon and I sank into deep, stainless-steel tubs of a decidedly medical nature. I snapped a photo of Gidon in his tub. In the picture, he is giving a big thumbs-up and grinning. Later, we sat in the salt cave in awkward chaise lounges of the rickety variety. Valiantly, patiently, we tried to enjoy the benefits of sitting awkwardly in rickety chairs in a salt cave. It was clammy.

At its height, in 1930, the Jewish community in Karlovy Vary numbered about 2,200 Jews. In 1945, after the war ended, only twenty-six individuals returned. Of those, Gidon and his mother were two. The synagogue had been destroyed, and homes and property were in the hands of other, new owners (or, perhaps,

between the front desk and the parking garage; she was the only employee at the front desk of this Russian-owned hotel with more than 150 rooms. Many of the big hotels in Karlovy Vary were owned by Russians. The concierge said she was from Bulgaria, and that, yes, she missed her family very much but was happy to have a job. She apologized for the inconvenience, but the management kept reducing the staff. She gave us a business card and scrawled her mobile phone number on the back. That seemed normal. I tried not to let my imagination wander too far into the mists of the predatory, post-Soviet privatization, and probable conditions for the thousands of spa town workers in Karlovy Vary. Today was a new day, and we were headed east.

"Northeast," Gidon added.

Today was a new day, and we were headed northeast.

CHAPTER 5
THE FORTRESS

When the U.S. Holocaust Memorial Museum first began to document the concentration camps, it was thought that the list would total about seven thousand. Researchers discovered that, in fact, there were around 42,500 camps. Of those, 30,000 were slave labor camps; 1,150 were Jewish ghettos; 980 were concentration camps; 1,000 were prisoner of war (POW) camps; and 500 were brothels filled with sex slaves.[1] Thousands of other camps were used for euthanizing the elderly and infirm, Germanizing prisoners, or transporting victims to killing centers. For example, there were more than three thousand camps in and around Berlin. Auschwitz alone had fifteen subcamps.

Térézin also had a subcamp, and this one was in Litomêrice, where Gidon and I stayed at the improbably named Hotel Roosevelt, only a few kilometers away from Térézin. Judging from their helmets and assorted gear, the other guests were cyclists, mostly older, slim, and lithe with the kind of sun damage that made them look leathery. The cyclists were touring southeastern Germany and the northern part of the Czech Republic. Quietly, studiously, they dined on the copious amount of cold meats, cheese, and black coffee provided at the hotel. Yet again I was struck by the normalcy of life so near to what had been a kind of hell only decades ago. Gidon and I swiped a couple of rolls for later, and I shoved them into my backpack, which also contained a roll of toilet paper for the tears I knew were inevitable. Today, Gidon would visit the place of so much pain and fear from his childhood, and I would experience my first visit to a Nazi concentration camp. I wasn't sure if I could be strong enough to give Gidon the loving support he would need.

Our first stop would be the "small fortress," which is 2 kilometers outside of the village of Térézin.

The fortress of Theresienstadt was built about 240 years ago by the Hapsburg Emperor Joseph II and named in honor of his mother. It's near the Elbe River and was built to protect the empire from Prussian invaders. When the Nazis annexed Czechoslovakia in 1938, the fortress and adjacent garrison village were efficiently put to use.

The non-Jewish Czech residents of Térézin, who lived in the village near the fortress, were evacuated in stages by the Germans. The entire village needed to be repurposed to serve as a concentration camp. Because it had served as a military garrison in the past, the village was like a "company town" if you will, with streets, shops, and apartment buildings but also barracks for soldiers. On November 24, 1941, the first prisoner transport of 342 men arrived. The men were told that if they "volunteered" to "upgrade" the village and barracks before it was repopulated with more prisoners, their families would come to join them. They were not told that families would not be allowed to live together, that children over the age of fourteen would live separately without their mothers or fathers, or that they would be slave laborers until they became too weak to be useful. Prisoners were denied the possession of money, medications, cigarettes, lighting, and any correspondence outside of the camp. The prisoners of Terezin were regularly subjected to being lined up outside in the freezing cold to be counted, beaten and given orders. Gidon's father Ernst arrived on Transport J, as prisoner 895, on December 4th, 1941.

Between January and February 1942, nine young men were hung in the main square. Their crime? Trying to send letters to friends or family in the outside world. The population was forced to gather and watch.

As we were working on the book, Gidon told someone that he indeed remembered the 1942 hangings in vivid detail. But on another occasion, he said he had no memory of these events at all. Gingerly, I asked Gidon which it was, a memory or a blank. He was just a little kid – not quite 7 years old – I reminded the both of us. A bit chagrined, Gidon admitted that all he *really* remembered was that on one particular occasion, as the prisoners were lined up in the courtyard and he strained to see what was going on, his mother suddenly yanked his head to her breast and the crowd gasped. That's it, he said, a little apologetically. That yank – that gasp – that sense memory is something he carries with him to this day.

Térézin was meant to appear to function as a ghetto—a Jewish village surrounded by walls, with limited freedom of movement for the residents to enter or leave the village. But Térézin had no such freedoms. Prisoners were not allowed to leave—ever. The Germans went to great lengths to hide from the prisoners the fact that the main function of Térézin was as a transportation hub to the death camps. In fact, Térézin served many purposes for the Nazis. More than a transport hub, it was also a pseudo-ghetto and, as such, a valuable propaganda tool for the Nazi regime. In fact, in both form and function, Térézin was an awful kind of "waiting room." Between October 1941 and May 8, 1945, more than 155,000 Jews passed through Térézin. Roughly 80 percent of those prisoners died. Fewer than 3,100 are thought to have survived.[2]

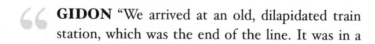 **GIDON** "We arrived at an old, dilapidated train station, which was the end of the line. It was in a

village called Bohušovice, about two and a half
kilometers from Térézin. We disembarked with
the German guards shouting at us, and we started
walking, carrying whatever we could. My mother
had two large suitcases and a blanket roll on her
back, and I had a rucksack and a bag that was quite
heavy for me. So we trudged along, my mother
shouting at me to keep up, and I tried. But it was
so heavy, I dropped the suitcase halfway along the
way. I just couldn't go on; I needed a rest. Of
course, I started to cry. Then, finally, a kind man
walking next to me offered to help me out with the
suitcase, and I was so relieved, even though my
mother was fearful that he would not give it back
to me. But, of course, he did return it, just as we
arrived at the gate to the camp, that as far as I
could see was enclosed by a high, barbed-wire
fence. The Germans started shouting at us once
again, dividing us into groups of a hundred or so,
and took each group to one of the two-story
barracks, which had a single entrance and iron bars
on the windows. How depressing and horrible it all
looked, and it was so cold. We children kept
looking for our fathers, but they were nowhere in
sight.

My mother and I were assigned to Room No.
212, together with five other mothers and their
children, and as soon as we got in, we collapsed on
one of the double bunk beds from sheer
exhaustion and hunger. I climbed up to the upper
bunk with the last ounce of my strength and fell
asleep. A while later, we were ordered to the
central parade ground—just a large yard in the
center of the barracks—and told to bring a pot or
cup or whatever for our first meal: a thin, watery

turnip soup. The only good thing about it, as I recall, was it was wet and warm.

When we asked about our fathers and when we would see them—after all, they had promised us a reunion, didn't they?—we were told we would see them only in the morning, and we should look out the windows around 6 a.m. So, the next morning, a lot of us kids clambered around two half-meter windows to get a glimpse of the men as German guards shouted at them to march swiftly. I looked for my father and my grandpa, but, sadly, I did not see either one of them that morning. The barracks that we were in were specifically for mothers and small children younger than ten years old. Fathers and grandfathers, older brothers, or sisters were in a totally different barracks, and we didn't see them except when we looked out the windows and watched them march by going to work."

Térézin is not that far from Prague—about 43 miles. Another 60 miles north is Dresden, Germany. The distance between Térézin and Auschwitz, in Poland, is 312 miles, or about five hours and forty minutes by car. Auschwitz was one of the main destinations for transports out of Térézin.

The "small fortress" of Térézin was used to torture political prisoners, escapees, and other troublemakers, and where numerous executions took place. Now it has an adjacent parking lot, which, on the day we visited, was populated by two or three tour buses. Nearby was a brisk micro-economy of small kiosks selling water, snacks, and maps. The presence of tourists made me glad, though. This was an odd corner of Europe to tour. You'd have to be visiting Prague for it to be convenient to go to

Térézin. These people had opted to spend a day here, I thought, when they could be at the Mucha Museum or having coffee on the banks of the Vltava or buying Czech glass.

Tour guides speaking Spanish, Italian, English, or Russian expertly guided groups through the place at a rigorous clip. It's all pretty overgrown, but one relic looked to be refreshed regularly.

Arbeit Macht Frei is painted in large letters over the entrance to the central courtyard of the fortress. Translation: Work makes you free. The letters are black, the background white. It stopped me in my tracks. I had never actually seen these words in real life. I felt a surge of white-hot rage. *Work makes you free?!* I looked around for Gidon, ready to swoop him up in my arms because, surely, he was overwhelmed, too. But he was some distance away; he had stopped to chat with a group of student tourists who were gathered around him with interest and admiration. Gidon was doing all right emotionally, or so it seemed. I wasn't sure how to behave or what to feel, but I wanted to respect Gidon's boundaries and his unique way of being. Gidon likes talking to people. So he talked.

GIDON "Hunger! It never left us, not by day and not by night. My mother worked in a factory, splitting into thin slices mica that the men had mined nearby for twelve hours a day, starting at 6 a.m. They marched to work, and they marched back every day. I hardly saw my mother. My father, I only saw two times in the almost four years that he and I were in the camp.

In the camp, even us kids worked. In some ways, this actually helped us to survive, giving us something to do. Since the kids in my barracks were younger than the rest, we were not allowed to go to any kind of school to learn to read or write. From time to time, we managed to find, steal, or beg for a piece of bread or scrape the jam barrel for a bit of jam.

One of our greatest fears was to be sent off to the east—to one of the camps. We didn't really know that whoever was shipped to a place like Auschwitz, Dachau, Birkenau, Treblinka, or some other horrific camp, that their chances of them surviving were very small. We didn't really know that there were gas chambers. But there were rumors of things like that. And some people said, 'What do you think? The Germans are killing everybody by gas?' It was known, and yet, it was so horrific that it was almost unfathomable. And the Germans were fairly successful in keeping it a secret. Maybe they were afraid that if the people in the concentration camps such as Térézin found out what was really going on, they would rise up and fight! But as long as the Germans left open a glimmer of hope for us, somehow we carried on."

The various rooms in the small fortress are heavy, dark, and claustrophobic. The torture room has large cruel-looking hooks in the walls at various heights. One has a pulley. As my eyes wandered unwillingly over these tools of torture, I imagined the screams, the iron smell of blood, and the muffled cries.

Suddenly, I saw something from the corner of my eye. Up in the eaves of the torture room, starlings were swooping in and out of nests. There were half a dozen of them. How had I not noticed the fluttering of their wings? Outside, there were more. Diving up, under the eaves on the outside of the buildings, they pulled bits of string and straw in after them.

"Did you see the execution ground?" Gidon had rejoined me. I had. Somewhere between 250 and 300 people were executed at Térézin, mostly by a firing squad. There were also hangings. The gallows are still there, as is the pockmarked wall against which prisoners were shot.

~

The Nazis forced Jewish community leaders to form a committee of elders, which they called a *Judenrat*, to administrate their own imprisonment. The Nazis then created a flowchart visualizing the various functions within the camp. The committee had to elect representatives to oversee the running of the camp. There were administrators, a health branch, workers, and technicians. While families had been separated by design, to destroy the basic social unit and further dehumanize the prisoners, a new social fabric emerged stubbornly and created a thin veneer of normalcy.

The Youth Welfare Office, headed by Egon Redich and Fredy Hirsch, two left-wing Zionists and experienced youth group leaders, did its utmost to make life for the children in the camp less harsh than it was. They sought to educate, amuse, and otherwise keep the children occupied in this horrible, inhumane, but—they hoped—surmountable situation. There were newsletters and activities. There were even sports leagues: this dorm against that dorm. The children played with balls made of rags. Some children were taught in secret about their Jewish heritage. The children were encouraged to create art and to write, and some even kept coded diaries. There were marionette shows and concerts.

One small group of prisoners was forced to do more than administrate; they were forced to verify and catalog stolen Jewish religious objects for later use in a Nazi-planned Museum of the Extinct People. In Bram Presser's *The Book of Dirt*, he reveals that his grandfather, a prisoner in Térézin, had been part of this secret group called the Talmudkommandos.

~

The Jewish Virtual Library explains a unique aspect of Térézin: "There were so many musicians in Térézin, there could have been two full symphony orchestras performing simultaneously daily. In addition, there were a number of chamber orchestras playing at various times."

But why did Térézin, among all of the concentration camps, have such a disproportionately high number of artists and musicians? From the Jewish Virtual Library: "Notable musicians, writers, artists, and leaders were sent there for 'safer' keeping than was to be afforded elsewhere in Hitler's quest to stave off any uprisings or objections around the so-called civilized world. This ruse worked well for a long time."

In June 1944, under pressure, the Nazis invited the International Red Cross to inspect the camp. Ahead of the visit, thousands of elderly, infirm, or sick prisoners were sent to the death camps, so that Térézin wouldn't look as horribly overcrowded as it was. Then the beautification began. The Nazis forced prisoners to plant flowers, paint buildings, and otherwise make the village look normal and presentable. They also printed fake money and gave prisoners new clothes (all of which had been taken from them in the first place) to wear. They forced the musicians in the camp to put on a performance. And they filmed it all. Those who volunteered to appear in the film were told that they would receive special consideration for their trouble. In the days after the Red Cross visit, those who appeared in the film were transported directly to death camps.

Apparently, the propaganda film was shown four times to audiences unknown but never released to the general public. Today, you can see the film when you visit Térézin. Watching it marked the first time during our visit that Gidon's determined façade began to falter. We sat there on uncomfortable wooden stools as the film flickered, our jaws slack. The soundtrack had rousing, happy music. The faces on the screen had strained smiles. Some faces looked outright bewildered, hungry, and scared. We were looking at the faces of the dead.

I wondered if Gidon recognized any of the faces in the film. I wondered if he or his mother, Doris, appeared unwittingly in a frame or two. I strained to look but didn't see them. I'm not sure I would have recognized them anyway. A part of the film shows a soccer game with a cheering crowd. I touched Gidon's elbow. Did he remember going to soccer games?

"Yes," he said without taking his eyes off the screen, "but not that one."

CHAPTER 6

TÉRÉZIN

Gidon and I decided that we needed to sit down before we moved on from the small fortress to look at the village of Térézin itself. There, we'd see the barracks, the crematoria, the remnants of the railroad tracks, and the museum. But before that, we needed some lunch. We were both already emotionally and physically exhausted. Our visit to the Czech Republic was proving to be intense.

I ordered a potent Czech beer, and Gidon and I dived into a lunch of mashed potatoes and sausage. Gidon was doing all right, or so it seemed to me. He was doing better than I was, anyway. How was he able to keep his cool? Where was he putting his horror, his grief, his anger? He'd had a long life to incorporate these feelings, I supposed. To me, none of this was grounded in anything outside of history books or movies. But today, at Térézin, on this unseasonably warm August day, my intellectual understanding of the Holocaust was made real by standing in a place where it had happened. There were worse Nazi concentration camps than Térézin; I know that. Camps that were more brutal, more humiliating, more efficient in their killing. But that fact only magnified the horror welling up inside of me.

The Térézin museum, like most museums, was crammed with facts, photos, and exhibits—and tourists. More people were here than at the small fortress. They shuffled along, listening to their tour guides. I shifted into Dutiful Museum Visitor mode and proceeded to examine every exhibit with great care and studiousness. Gidon was pleased by how the museum had grown and become more sophisticated since his last visit, almost twenty years prior, and besides, he liked facts. But as we wandered through the museum, both Gidon and I grew a bit detached. By the look of the other tourists, so did they. It was too much to take in and one became numb—even bored. Holocaust museums all over the world have tried many approaches to make the information presented more personal, bone-deep, and effective, yet it seemed to me that day, that we still have many miles to go. Times are changing, and people are changing along with them.

Gidon and I learned that between September 1943 and October 1944, eighteen transports were sent from Térézin to Auschwitz. There were 37,232 people on these transports, a thousand of whom were children. One of the people on one of the last of these transports was Ernst Löw, Gidon's father. He was forty-five years old.

Ernst was on the last train that left Térézin for Auschwitz-Birkenau on October 28, 1944. Of the 2,038 people on the train, 1,589 were gassed immediately upon arrival. But not Ernst. He didn't know it, but he still had about two miserable, nightmarish months to live.

In Térézin, as far as the prisoners knew, people were put on lists and simply "sent east." On one occasion, five thousand prisoners disappeared from Térézin on a single day. Imagine the impact that would have on a captive population forced to pretend that life was carrying on as usual while others were vanishing with regularity. A Jewish committee was forced to draw up the deportation lists. At first, it was the elderly, the sick, the people with mental disabilities. Then it was those who had recently fallen ill or been injured. All the youth leaders were sent to the death camps. The musicians who had performed concerts, too. The man who designed the layout of the camp. The elders on the committees. Then it was entire barracks.

 GIDON "I remember that my great-grandmother Rosa arrived in Térézin on one of the last transports from Prague, and we went down to the train station to see her. There was this old, sad, and forlorn lady standing in the corner of the transfer building, still full of poise, meticulously dressed, even with a little funny-looking hat. My great-grandmother Rosa considered herself more German than Jewish—she spoke only German, was assimilated, and loved the German culture. I wasn't aware of it at the time, but I learned later that she stayed in Térézin for about two months before she was sent to Treblinka and murdered."

In 1942, 30 percent of the population in Térézin suffered from highly contagious bacterial infections such as scarlet fever, typhoid, and diphtheria. Viral illnesses with potentially devastating outcomes, such as polio or encephalitis, were present in equal numbers. That didn't include other, more ordinary illnesses such as the flu or bronchial infections. Think, for a moment, how important nutrition, hygiene, and rest are in fighting disease. Take into consideration the impact that lice infestations, overcrowding, beatings, and despair had on physical and mental well-being. Imagine the elderly. And the children.

From my childhood, I remember waiting for the ice cream truck and being read aloud to on someone's lap. I remember singing, clapping, and kindergarten, pets, and cookies. What must it have been like to be without those things? With no hot baths, no favorite book, no soft kittens to pet? With hunger and fear so bone-deep and unrelenting? When the social fabric consisted of shouts and blows and missing people? How grim-faced those children must have become. How did those who survived manage to build or regain a sense of normalcy, of play? Of joy? I circled back to the thing about Gidon that astounded me. Not just that he saw these things and that he lived them, but that he wanted to keep being a part of this world afterward.

GIDON "I knew one woman and her daughter, who, for a while, was living in the same room as we were, and I remember being in 'love' with her. I mean, I was seven or eight years old, and she was very pretty, and she was also very agile; she did tumbling, standing on her hands, and stuff, and one day they received the notice that we all feared: They have to report to the train station for the next transport to the east. I was so heartbroken that, for days, I would not speak to anyone, not even my mother, who couldn't understand why I was acting so strange. Of course, they never came back, and I cried silently for days, and I didn't even know that they were sent to their deaths. I missed them, especially my 'girlfriend.' She was the first girlfriend I ever had."

I wondered if little Gidon had noticed the enormous numbers of other people who were suddenly not there anymore. How the cold wind of bottomless despair must have blown in Térézin. How intense the anxiety, the grief, the anger, and the fear. Day in and day out, trains came to Térézin and stood motionless in the cold as prisoners from the camp were lined up —after having been asked to turn in their ration cards and ID numbers—and shouted at, beaten, and forced into cattle cars. At least eighty people were in each cattle car, with no food, no water, nowhere to sit down, and a freezing-cold journey that lasted for hours and was headed straight toward the death camps. Then new trains came with new prisoners who spoke different languages and who were used to perform all manner of tasks needed to keep the camp running. Until they were of no use.

 GIDON "On one a rare occasion, my father got permission to visit us—my mother and me—for a short half hour, and he spent a few minutes with just me. I was conflicted, filled with both joy and sadness because it was so quick, and he also told us that Grandpa Alfred had died. He said, 'Peterl, I need to spend a little time with your mom. Maybe they will give me permission to see you again?' Like so many promises and hopes before, this one, too, was crushed. I never saw my father again. A year or so later, my father sent a note to us that he was being sent to the east, to Auschwitz, and that my mother should try to come down to the train station the next day. He had something for her. I don't know how, but my mother did manage to get to the train just as it was pulling out and saw my father, who threw a little package to her as the train picked up speed. She took the parcel and ran before a German officer could shoot her. It was a necklace with a charm. It was the emblem of the town of Térézin, carved with the date April 8, 1944. I don't have any idea how he got this made or how he paid for it. I have it with me to this very day. I wear it from time to time, on special occasions, to remind me that I once had a father."

Gidon was wearing that pendant that day at the Térézin museum; it was indeed a special occasion. Gidon had always believed that the date on the emblem was the date of his father's departure. But we found that this was not true: Ernst was sent to Auschwitz on October 28, 1944. So what did the date signify? As far as we could tell, it didn't correspond to any notable dates at Térézin, nor did it correspond to any birth or anniversary dates in Gidon's family. Maybe Ernst traded his bread for an emblem that already had the date on it, and it meant something to someone we will never know. Or perhaps that date says something that was only between Doris and Ernst.

Hoping that the pendant might hold some clue that might have meaning to the museum curator of Térézin, we had emailed in advance to make sure we could meet with him. The dates must have gotten mixed up because we were told by the kind security guard who sat on a folding chair at the museum's entrance that the curator was on holiday. The guard had worked there for many years, he told us, and no, he wasn't Jewish. But—he patted the place on his chest—as a Czech, he felt it was important to remember what happened to the Jews. With nothing to lose, Gidon showed him the pendant and asked if he'd seen others like it. The security guard peered at the pendant. No, but would we like to email the curator?

Disconcertingly enough, there was once again an actual village where people lived. There was a laundromat, a hardware store, an ice cream store, and a couple of cafés, although the streets were almost entirely empty of people other than tourists. What a strange place the village is today—both an open-air museum and an actual town. The barracks are set apart; some are crumbling, and others are now apartments that have been renovated, I presume, for today's Térézin village-dweller-by-choice. The Dresden, the now-dilapidated barracks where Gidon once lived, was cordoned off and marked as dangerous to enter. Peering inside the broken windows, we saw trash and graffiti, remnants of some other, more recent, life.

We came upon a trio of young backpackers with wiry beards and indistinct accents. They were not touring the camp; they were simply trekking across it to reach some other, more interesting destination. The hikers were friendly, though, and told us where to look for what remained of the railroad tracks upon which prisoners arrived and were "sent east."

It wasn't as dramatic as the emblematic shot from the nine-hour documentary *Shoah*. It was just some railroad tracks, overgrown with weeds. Still, Gidon and I plucked a few nearby wildflowers and laid them down there.

CHAPTER 7

HOWL

The next day, Gidon wanted to go to Lidice, a small village about 14 miles northwest of Prague. I didn't want to go. We were back in Prague for only one day, and I lobbied hard to go to the Mucha Museum. Gidon was having none of it.

Something had happened at Lidice, Gidon told me. Something terrible. A massacre, a reprisal. He had never, on previous visits to the Czech Republic, gone to see Lidice. Now, Gidon felt it was time. Out of respect, he said, and a loyalty to fellow Czechs who had suffered Nazi atrocities.

I had no idea that anything could be more excruciating and disturbing than what we'd already seen. But it was. To say that the massacre at Lidice, which took place on June 10, 1942, was savage would be to understate what happened by a magnitude of ten thousand.

~

Resistance to the Nazis in Czechoslovakia was an impassioned one. Still, when Hitler appointed Reinhard Heydrich the *Stellvertretender Reichsprotektor* (Deputy/Acting Reich Protector) of Bohemia and Moravia, the resistance went into overdrive. By way of placing Heydrich on the scale of malignant Nazi evil, a highlight of his career was chairing the Wannsee Conference, at which the "Final Solution" was devised. Heydrich was, in other words, one of the most sociopathic Nazi bastards imaginable.

A plan was set in motion by the Czech government-in-exile to assassinate him in what was called Operation Anthropoid. The assassins, part of the Czech Resistance Movement, were parachuted into Czechoslovakia five months before the planned date of their attack. On May 27, 1942, as Heydrich's car rounded a hairpin curve, one of the assassins stepped into the road and took aim with his gun. It jammed. The other commando in the operation acted swiftly and threw a bomb under the wheels of the car. The bomb went off. Heydrich sustained fatal injuries, succumbing in a hospital a few days later. There is an urban myth that Heydrich died because he refused the medical care of Czech doctors, preferring only German doctors.

Hitler was enraged. He ordered that ten thousand Czechs be killed outright. He wanted to show the Czechs that resistance would not be tolerated. Instead, thirty-six thousand homes in Prague were raided. By June 4, 157 Czechs had been executed. But Hitler wasn't done. He ordered that any village with ties to the assassination should be entered and that his soldiers were to:

1. execute all adult men
2. transport all women to a concentration camp
3. gather children suitable for Germanization, place them in SS families in the Reich, and bring the rest of the children up in other ways
4. burn down the village and level it entirely

Bring the rest of the children up in other ways? We would soon find out what that meant.

A visit to a museum perched on a hill overlooking what had

been the Village of Lidice took Gidon and me through the events of that day. On June 9, 1942, late at night, the villagers of Lidice were awoken by the sound of crunching gravel. The killing team had arrived. The villagers were told to pack warm clothes and gather in the town square. In the early morning hours of June 10, the killing began.

Sources vary, but between 173 and 192 men and boys over the age of fifteen were lined up and blindfolded. At first, the men were lined up five at a time and shot, but that was too slow, so they were lined up ten at a time. When they fell, the next ten men shuffled forward, were shot, and fell on top of the previous bodies. Mattresses were placed behind them so the bullets wouldn't ricochet. It took all day. The women were sent to concentration camps, primarily Ravensbrück, 56 miles north of Berlin. Some of the children were placed in the homes of SS officers to be "Germanized." More than eight children were deemed not passable as Aryan and sent to Chelmno, where they were gassed in the back of a truck.

The houses in the village were blown up—the church, too. The town was set on fire. All pets and beasts of burden were slaughtered. The trees were cut down, and the graveyard dug up, the bodies looted for any valuables. Within days, a German workforce was dispatched to Lidice to reroute the stream that ran through it and to reroute the road to Lidice as well. Topsoil was brought in, and crops planted. Lidice was wiped off the map as though it had never existed.

Of the 105 Lidice children swept up in the rampage, only a tiny handful returned home. They weren't the same, though. They had been separated from their mothers for years. Many of them now spoke only German; they had forgotten their native Czech language—and their prior lives.

The black-and-white footage in the museum's informational film showed the aftermath: stained, torn mattresses, heaps of rubble, household goods strewn about. A crater where the church once was. There were photos of the blindfolded men stumbling forward, pale, their faces stricken. The bodies of the men killed just before them were sprawled in front of them. The Nazis documented the destruction on film. The savage fate of Lidice, unlike other Nazi atrocities, was publicly revealed by Hitler with pride. Lidice was an example.

That was a mistake. Allied media found the footage, and the news of the fate of Lidice raced around the world. Funds to help remember the victims were raised from as far away as England. Towns in Mexico, Venezuela, and Brazil renamed themselves Lidice. In Illinois, a neighborhood of Crest Hill was renamed Lidice.

There is a grainy film clip of the 1947 Lidice war crimes trial held in the People's Court of Pankrác. It is titled "The Trial of the Butcher of Lidice." The soundless clip is only forty-eight seconds long. In it, dozens of defendants sit, stony-faced. Some wear translation headsets. I scanned their faces over and over to look for remorse or maybe fear. The film shows men who, mostly, look somewhere between bored, resigned, and defiant. The camera pans to show several women listening to the proceedings. They look pale and serious. It's hard to tell what they are thinking. An official shuffles papers and uncaps a pen. The film ends.

~

When Gidon and I stood outside, overlooking the green hills where Lidice had once been, I noticed a semitransparent photograph of the village as it used to be. It was positioned so that it was superimposed over the current-day emptiness. We took turns looking through it in silence. Village. Nothing. Village. Nothing.

At length, Gidon spoke. "They weren't Jews." His voice broke; he seemed to swallow some deep emotion that was threatening to make him cry. I understood what he meant.

Fascism had no loyalty, no mercy. It mowed down everyone and everything in its path, like a voracious machine.

Nearby the museum, there is an art gallery with more information about the massacre. We peeked inside and noticed that the exhibits were minimalist, modern abstract art. I wasn't usually drawn to art like that, but we went inside and found that, actually, these wordless exhibits of slashed color or empty space, broken records, or nails were exactly the right response in the speechless void that the Holocaust wrenched out of us like a gasp.

One video exhibit created by Bulgarian artist Pravdoliub Ivanov stayed with me, though I was not sure why. In the video, a line of black-clad police stands rigidly, ominously, on the perimeter of a government building, their hands folded behind their backs. A disquieting, distorted low whistling sound, like an unearthly howl, grows as black balloons drift and bump around the policemen's legs in increasing numbers.

Lidice is but one example of such Nazi reprisals. Here are some others:

- *Ardeatine Caves, Rome.* March 24, 1944: 335 Italian prisoners were forced into a cave and made to kneel. They were shot point-blank to save bullets.
- *Marzabotto, Italy.* September 29-October 5, 1944: More than 770 villagers—men, women, and children—were massacred when Nazis used flamethrowers and bombs to set the entire village on fire. Villagers who tried to escape were shot.
- *Borovë, Albania.* July 6, 1943: Nazis set the village on fire after 107 villagers, mostly children and elderly women, were forced inside the burning church.
- *Oradour-Sur-Glane, France.* June 10, 1944: 642 villagers

were killed. Men were forced into a barn and shot in the legs with machine guns before Nazis set the barn on fire. Nazis also forced women and children into a church, and a bomb was detonated on the side of it. Those who tried to escape were shot with machine guns.

I felt parts of my conscious thought struggling to connect, to process. I just couldn't make it work in my brain. It seemed to me that like time, or the universe, or death, the Holocaust was a kind of super object that defied our ability to make sense of it. This thing—this cataclysmic orgy of horror, cruelty, debasement, and violence—not only happened but also happened in a sustained way, in millions of connected moments, some of which occurred in Lidice, or in Térézin, or in front of freshly dug ditches and countless forests. Other connected moments happened in a town square in Poland or a barn set afire in France or in Italy while people burned alive inside. The Holocaust occurred in courtrooms and on the streets and on hooks in walls and classrooms and trucks and gas chambers and cities and villages.

In the late 1930s and through 1945, hatred and brutality spread across Europe like a forest fire. Soon, it was unstoppable. My mind reeled when I thought about other genocides and atrocities in history: Cambodia, Bosnia, Serbia, Rwanda, Darfur, and the Armenian genocide.

Gidon and I returned to Israel after our trip to the Czech Republic in two different moods. Gidon, it seemed, felt a sense of sadness, yes, but also of closure and reckoning. But I was going through an awful rite of initiation into the unspeakable. In addition to our visit, I had read dozens of books about the Holocaust and watched hours of documentaries about the Final

Solution; the Nuremberg trials; Himmler; Goering; Goebbels; Ilsa Koch, "the bitch of Buchenwald"; and the capture and trial of Eichmann and John Demjanjuk. I read Eli Wiesel. I read Primo Levi and Victor Frankl. I visited three Holocaust museums and read hundreds of articles and lists of atrocities. I had become a student not just of Gidon's life, not only of the Holocaust but also of man's inhumanity to man, full stop. Worse, the gap was closing; things that seemed like distant black-and-white newsreel footage were becoming real for me by my exposure to them, my relationship with Gidon, and the news of the day. Now it seemed that there was a bridge between Gidon's lifetime and my own.

In fall 2017, not long before I met Gidon, I traveled to Sarajevo, Bosnia. I spent a week there and went to Srebrenica, where, in July 1995, in the space of three days, eight thousand Bosnian-Muslim men and boys were massacred and buried in mass graves in the forest. The area was preternaturally quiet, lush, green, and still. It was gloomy that day, I remember, and there, too, birds swooped overhead. It seemed as though nature had drawn a curtain over the past and was letting it grow over with weeds. I felt in the stillness a tense feeling in the air, as if the spores of evil could reanimate if there were a big enough gust of wind or a sudden downpour.

Thinking back to that visit, an embarrassing memory made its way into my consciousness. After touring the large, silent cemetery in Srebrenica—marked with white markers for those bodies that could be identified after being exhumed from mass graves sometimes even years later—I came upon two young men who were visiting the grave of a relative. Both men had been there but had been toddlers and so were spared. Without warning, I burst into wracking tears and asked if I could hug them.

"I'm sorry. I'm sorry," I wept into their somewhat surprised arms. Here, before me, were people who had been directly touched by the massacre. They made it real to me.

Remembering this, I got it. I suddenly, completely understood why people sometimes do this to Gidon: cry, ask to hug him, take his photo. Survivors are the embodiment, the proof of such things that we cannot imagine.

What will happen when none are left?

CHAPTER 8

LIBERATION

GIDON "In the early spring of 1945, we saw and heard, up high in the sky, huge formations of American warplanes flying toward Germany to bomb the hell out of them for weeks. We would shout with joy and satisfaction until some German guard would yell and then shoot at us. We didn't really know, for sure, but we felt that this war and our suffering were coming to an end. We had little proof, without phones, radios, or newspapers, but our senses told us that the end was finally coming. Some of us noticed that there were fewer and fewer guards watching over us, and there seemed to be a constant exit of fully loaded German trucks leaving the camp, not only with household goods but with the German families themselves."

I'm not sure how far the sound of the Boeing B-17 Flying Fortress bombers carried as they flew in squadrons and dropped their bombs from the sky a little over 3 miles overhead. But Dresden was only 60 miles north of Térézin and Prague only forty-five minutes to the south, so Gidon must have heard and seen many low-flying bombers crisscrossing the sky regularly in the weeks before his liberation.

According to the U.S. Air Force, the Allies dropped more than 238,000 tons of bombs over Berlin, Hamburg, Munich, Cologne, Leipzig, Essen, and, famously, Dresden, which was wholly destroyed in February 1945. Dresden, in particular, became the subject of the inadequacy of the Hague Conventions, which had not been updated before the aerial bombardments of World War II. To Gidon and the survivors of other concentration camps, these bombers and others must have sounded like the roar of a vengeful and victorious God. They could not have known the toll on civilians but then, living in a flattened, Dali-esque nightmare netherworld themselves, this knowledge would come much later and become yet another fragment of the shattered pieces of the world as they knew it.

What Gidon did not realize was that both the Allies and the Russians were closing in on the Nazis in late 1944 and early '45. There was a flurry of activity: The Nazis rushed to destroy evidence of their atrocities and redeploy soldiers toward the threats from both directions. The wheels were flying off the Nazi machine. Maps were being redrawn in real time. The Russians were coming.

 GIDON "It was also at this time that almost daily transports arrived from the eastern camps—such as Dachau, Buchenwald and others—with totally emaciated, hungry, sick, half-dead people whom the Germans had evacuated as the Allies and the Red Army advanced. When we saw some of these poor souls (they were housed separately for fear of a typhoid epidemic), it was painful. I was afraid to get close enough to ask if any of them had seen my father.

One day in May, in the afternoon, as I was lying on my cot, suddenly I heard a very loud shouting coming from the outside. I jumped to the window to see what was happening. My mother shouted at me to get away from there. I saw other people from the buildings around us doing the same. Some were shouting, 'The Americans are here!' Others were shouting, 'No, it's the Russians! The Russians have come to free us!' And, yes, it was the Red Army.

We ran to the barbed-wire fence; several tried to bring it down. I saw the first Russian tank and another behind it, where two officers stood saluting us. I was overwhelmed with excitement. I didn't know what to do with myself. Finally, we were free.

The Russians showered us with candy and cigarettes before they continued to Prague, where the Germans were still holding out, damaging that beautiful city. At one point, the Russians caught up with one of the German trucks, took the occupants to a nearby forest, and, without any pity, shot them then and there. To me, a ten-year-old, it was all a bit shocking, but, by then, I had seen so much that I didn't think twice about it. I am numb today when I think about that and the other things that I saw as a child. I don't really know how to describe it.

Still, a feeling of elation had taken over my soul that was stronger than the fear of the unknown— even the fear of the likely loss of my dad and the rest of our family. Somehow I felt that since my mother and I had survived those years in the camp that we could survive whatever was in store for us.

Confronted with the possibility of freedom, my mind raced with questions. Could we leave the camp? Would we see our families? Would we get some food and walk around the camp without German soldiers shouting at us, beating us, even shooting at us? What was freedom like? Would we ever get our things or our homes back? There were very few answers from my mother or anyone else.

The Russian unit that was assigned to deal with Térézin, once they realized that this was a German concentration camp for Jews, gradually began to deal with us. The cavalry left their tired horses in the camp to roam in the central square, where there was a green lawn, and us kids would catch and take hold of them and ride them bareback. That sure was fun. For the first time in four years, we were not hungry—it was like a revelation! Soup was real soup, potatoes were real, and even very small amounts of meat were in our diet. This alone was a reason for rejoicing. We were not allowed to go out of the camp for the first few weeks and were told there were still a few German units out there —that would surely take revenge on us if they caught us!"

In my naïve, movie version of things, liberation was immediate and jubilant. But a humanitarian crisis of a magnitude never before seen was unfolding in Europe. Millions of victims of the Nazi war machine who had been deported, expelled, and displaced were now herded into displaced persons camps run by several refugee organizations, chief among them the United Nations Relief and Rehabilitation Administration (UNRRA), which was established in 1943 ahead of the coming tsunami. UNRRA provided billions of dollars in U.S. aid and helped something like eight million refugees. For Jewish displaced persons, recovery and rehabilitation were a bit more complicated. Even with the help of UNRRA and the American Jewish Joint Distribution Committee, Jewish refugees quickly found that returning to their former homes was not realistic. They simply weren't wanted.

Journalist Michele Chabin elaborated on what many Jewish survivors encountered after liberation:

> "Although many survivors returned to their home villages or cities after the war in hopes of finding relatives and recovering their property, they were often met with hostility. There were some Jews in Czechoslovakia, Poland, Hungary who did move back, but they weren't home, Dr. David Silberklang, Senior Historian at Yad Vashem's International Institute for Holocaust Research, told me.
>
> 'Their communities were destroyed,' he said, 'their families were destroyed, their way of life was destroyed.'
>
> In Poland and Ukraine, many of the survivors who returned home were threatened by their countrymen. Some were physically attacked for daring to return, and others were murdered. Even in places where killing wasn't widespread, the survivors felt endangered. Jews who returned home found that their possessions 'had disappeared,' Silberklang said.
>
> 'Someone had taken their home, or their silverware and their bedsheets. The Germans or the local people had taken over Jewish businesses. It might have been a shoemaker shop or something bigger.'
>
> When Jews tried to get their businesses and property returned, they were rebuffed and ridiculed. The communist regimes that had taken over had nationalized these properties. When communism fell, and a survivor's children or

grandchildren sought redress, Silberklang said, 'They were met with "Who are you?" and told that the Nazis, and not the communists, had seized the property, "so we're not responsible."'

Many of the people who tried to help Jews during the war and its aftermath were considered traitors by the local population and tried to hide their actions.

There was no meaningful, lasting return home."

It was, I discovered, rare that survivors returned to their homes and stayed for any length of time. But Gidon and his mother didn't go home to Karlovy Vary right away. There were some stops along the way.

 GIDON "When the Red Cross arrived, together with the Russians, they set up a number of recuperation centers in the surrounding countryside for us children—all of us being undernourished—all of these being set up in abandoned country mansions or castles that the Germans had used for their own officers and their families. So I found myself, together with another fifty or so kids, mostly ten years old or younger, in this beautiful country house, in an area that just looking out from one of the windows, all I could see was gently sloping green hills, trees, and, in the far distance, high mountains. Girls and boys were sleeping in separate rooms, on cots, about ten to a room, and we had good food, and I enjoyed the activities, like sports, playing football, or going on hikes in the surrounding forest.

This, it turned out, was somewhat of a dangerous activity because the retreating German army would often throw away their military gear (so they wouldn't be caught by the Russians and shot!), which also included hand grenades, which, on contact, would very often explode and kill or injure anyone within ten meters. We were warned not to stray from the trodden path. It was for the first time that we kids sat together and shared our sorrow with each other. It truly brought us closer together!

Altogether, I recall my experience at this mansion as being very nourishing, both physically and spiritually; however, there was one incident that left me with perturbed and strange feelings. In our room, one of the boys—I think his name was Jirži; he was bigger and older than all the rest of us —would, from time to time, climb out of his bed and go to one of the boys' beds, lay down with him, and do things to him, which most of us didn't know what it was. We only knew that the small boy would cry and moan and call out for help, and we all were petrified, scared to move, scared to do anything, scared to tell anyone. And each night, we wondered who would be the next victim and hoped that Jirži would fall asleep and leave us alone. I was only ten years old and never spoke about this to anyone."

Wait. What? Rewind the tape. Could the Holocaust possibly have been worse?

I spoke with Ronnie Sarnat, the writer and director of a documentary called *Screaming Silence*, which aired on Israeli television in 2015. The film brings to light the long taboo subject of the sexual abuse of children in concentration camps, recuperation centers, and elsewhere during and immediately after the war.

Sarnat explained that the war and its attendant chaos was a

prime feeding ground for sexual predators. Children who were abused, as Sarnat highlighted in her film, remained silent for decades. As is often the case with rape, sexual abuse, and assault under any circumstances and during any era, a toxic veil of secrecy and shame burrows into the victims like a biological weapon and can remain in hibernation for a lifetime. Such, too, was the case with children of the Holocaust.

After a few months in a shared flat in Prague, Gidon and his mother returned to Karlovy Vary and lived with some friends in the house with the stable and the "Ja, ja, after the war" woman, whose name I forget. It must have been so strange to be back. It must have been hard for Gidon's mother to comfort and reassure her son. What could she say? Where was her husband, her mother, her father, half-brother, and grandparents?

 GIDON "Shortly thereafter, my mother and I returned to Karlovy Vary and lived in a small apartment in a house owned by some old friends from before the war, but it was a totally changed place. I was skinny and underweight since, in Térézin, we survived mainly on a watery soup and an occasional slice of black bread. I could hardly read or write since we were not allowed to go to any sort of school while in the camp. Returning to school, though, I was older than the other kids, which was something I was happy about.

Every morning, I would get up early, kneel near a chair, and pray, '*Lieber Gott*, please bring my father back!' One day, my mother saw me praying, and she berated me and told me not to be so foolish."

When I thought about Doris and her harsh words, I thought about how in *The Drowned and the Saved*, Primo Levi wrote, "We who survived the Camps are not true witnesses. We are those who, through prevarication, skill, or luck, never touched bottom. Those who have, and who have seen the face of the Gorgon, did not return, or returned wordless." Doris simply didn't have any words with which to comfort her son.

Despite all his prayers, Gidon eventually learned the truth about his father.

 GIDON "After a few months of searching, hoping, and praying, we were told by several survivors of the war that my father had collapsed on one of the death marches that the Germans organized as they retreated before the Russian and American armies. He was just too weak from hunger and cold, so they shot him. After that news, I stopped praying to God and never believed in him again. If there is a god, I thought, he's awfully cruel, and I didn't want to believe in such a god."

CHAPTER 9

1947

In 1947, Pan American Airlines offered the first-ever round-the-world ticket, the Treaty of Paris was signed, and Christian Dior unveiled his New Look, upending the world of fashion. Chiang Kai-shek and his forces massacred eighteen thousand protesters in Taiwan, and Jackie Robinson became the first African American baseball player to sign a Major League Baseball contract. Billie Holiday was arrested for possession of narcotics, and something weird happened in Roswell, New Mexico. Al Capone and Henry Ford died. David Bowie, Mitt Romney, Farrah Fawcett, Elton John, and David Letterman were born. In Karlovy Vary, Peter Wolfgang Löw—Gidon—had been liberated from a Nazi concentration camp for a scant two years. He was twelve years old.

After four years of abuse and malnutrition, Gidon was starting to fill out again. In a photo taken at the time, he had jug ears and wore an ill-fitting suit. By then, he knew his father was not coming back, and his mother, Doris, had even begun dating again. In particular, she was dating a man named Julius Cohn, "Jus" for short (pronounced *Yoos*).

GIDON "Jus became my stepfather and was a part of my life for many years. He was an accountant by profession and lived in Karlovy Vary with his wife and son, who was two years older than I was. Our two families were friends, and before the war and the Nazi takeover, they used to get together from time to time and go out dancing or to the theater. Jus was also an avid stamp collector and had thousands of stamps, some very valuable ones. As all the Jews of Czechoslovakia were transported to concentration camps, some through Térézin and some directly to Auschwitz, Jus, together with his wife and beloved son, found himself in front of the selection table with an SS officer deciding who goes to the left (the gas chamber) and who goes to the right—meaning who stays alive as long as he can work and survive the inhumane conditions.

When it came to Jus's turn, he was sent to the right, but his wife and son to the left! Suddenly Jus broke out of the lineup and burst forth to try and retrieve his dear son. The Germans reacted immediately, by almost beating Jus to death with their rifle butts. And, then, bleeding and injured, threw him back into the group that would live, at least for a while, while his son remained with his mother to be sent to the gas chamber.

One would think that that incident would have broken this man, but it didn't. Somehow, he managed to survive not only this but also another two firing squad shootings, which we never found out how, where, or when, because he refused to talk about it to us. Others that had been with him in Buchenwald and Auschwitz-Birkenau told my mother how much he had suffered, and only his will to stay alive and hope perhaps to see his family again made the difference.

Jus, after the war, did return to Karlovy Vary, and, realizing that his family would not, he met my mother, whom he had known from before the war, and a warm relationship developed between them. I actually liked him: he treated me well, he taught me things about stamp collecting (he had somehow retrieved his very extensive collection), and taught me how to fix, repair, and renew used bicycles, which we then sold. This was a good little business after the war since there was a shortage of everything. He would also take me on biweekly trips to the country to fetch fresh butter and milk from the farmers.

Once, I remember, on a pretty steep hill, the chain came off my bicycle—it must have been too loose—and I almost broke my arm and legs but managed somehow to end up in a bush on the side of this country road, just with a couple of scratches. It was scary, and we agreed not to tell my mother, because she would have prohibited my going with Jus into the country, something I really enjoyed doing."

Though Gidon welcomed Jus in his life, he was lonely and aimless. He needed to make friends, to belong. He joined a Jewish youth group, and it changed the direction of the rest of his life.

In America and Europe, outdoorsy, lean-to-building, campfire-sing-along scouting groups were a way to instill values in kids and to teach them skills that they might not ever need but would earn them badges and create a strong sense of bondedness.

Jewish youth groups at the time had a greater goal in mind: Zionism.

~

Zionism is a word that even for Jews is a bit complex, but in general, it refers to the desire of the Jewish people to live in their ancestral homeland, from which they had been forcibly exiled, most notably by the Romans in 70 CE. Sold into slavery and otherwise forced out of what today we call Israel, the idea of returning to the land has been a central part of the Jewish experience for millennia (see Appendix A).

After the Holocaust, though, Zionism became utterly imperative to many. Europe had just demonstrated to the Jews that they were more than unwanted; they were the object of deep hatred and genocide. A slow trickle of early Zionists had immigrated to Israel for more than four decades before World War II. Afterward, thousands of Jews who survived the Holocaust sought to live in Israel. Jewish Zionist youth groups became an important mechanism not just to energize the Zionist dream but also to prepare youth for a very different life there.

 GIDON "In my youth group, Dror Hechalutz Ha'tzair (the young pioneers), we learned about Israel, and about how kibbutzim were established. We even learned in summer camp how to use a stick for self-defense because, at that time, Israel had very few guns, so they wanted to teach us how to use a stick as a weapon. We began to learn krav maga using broomsticks we cut in half. Our counselor told us that we must prepare ourselves for two tasks: one, to make our way to Israel, as soon as possible, the country really needed us and, second, that we must learn to fight to defend ourselves, even without real arms."

Jewish youth groups symbolized a cultural earthquake in Jewish life in the 1920s; heretofore activities for Jewish youths had been almost exclusively religious in nature. Now, there was a modern alternative to "yeshiva," or Jewish religious school training, akin to Sunday School for Christians.

Whether Doris allowed Gidon to become an active member of a Zionist youth group as a way to keep him occupied while she tried to put her life back together again or whether she championed Zionism as an idea, Gidon did not know, although the former seemed most likely.

For Gidon, this was, perhaps, one of the most pivotal experiences in his life. On outings and hikes and in camps on mountains, the Jewish Zionist youth movement spoke to the young campers about their heritage, their values, and their traditions and, crucially, about living an agricultural kibbutz life in Mandatory Palestine, which was, they understood, in the middle of a pitched civil war.

Mandatory Palestine (sometimes referred to as the British Mandate) had been established by the League of Nations at the end of the First World War as a result of the defeat of the Ottoman Empire, which conceded the territories of Palestine and Transjordan to the British administration. The British promised to provide the Jews with a national home while they administrated the land. This was called the Balfour Declaration.

But Jewish pioneers arriving and settling down had another agenda: to ultimately wrest Palestine from the British. They accomplished this by creating a sort of subgovernment and suborganizations to suit their own needs. A guerilla war broke out, with Jewish militia groups fighting the British. The British Mandate was not going so well, to put it lightly. When the partition of Israel/Palestine was announced by the United Nations in 1947, Britain was more than happy to wash its hands not only of the Jewish insurgency but also of the untenable situation between Jews and Arabs that already had been simmering and erupting for decades. The youth groups kept their members apprised.

 GIDON "In the youth group, we talked about the U.N. special committee that was deliberating about the proposed partition plan that was to divide the territory under the British Mandate into two states: a Jewish state—Israel—and an Arab state. A great deal of the proposed borders comprising the Jewish state was based on the centers of the Jewish populations and, especially, on the existing kibbutzim and moshavim (collective communities and farms). To me, it all sounded pretty precarious and frightening, even though I hardly knew or understood at the time what it really all meant. Were we ever going to have our own country, and how large or small would it be?

On Parents Day, we prepared a little presentation, and the *shali'ach* [emissary] who had been sent from Israel to lead us and to train us taught us a song about Emek Yizr'el (the Jezreel Valley). And to this day, I remember the song. When I sang it, of course, I had no idea what I was singing about or what the words meant. It is all about the Jezreel Valley and the wonderful country and being guardians of the country."

Gidon may not have understood the Hebrew words correctly at the time, but he got the gist: The Jezreel Valley was a place of spiritual and emotional importance in Israel, and he was inculcated with a longing for it.

Ba'ah m'nuchah layageya
umargo'a le'amel.
Layla chiver mistareya
al sdot emek Yizr'el.
Tal milematah ul'vanah me'al,
mibeit Alfa ad Nahalal.

Mah, mah layla mileil
Dmama be' Yizr'el
Numah emek, eretz tif'eret
anu lecha mishmeret.
Numah emek, eretz tif'eret
anu lecha mishmeret.

In quiet rest and protection
Rest has come to the weary
Tranquility to the toiling
A pale night covers
Over the fields of Jezreel Valley
Dew beneath, the moon above
From Beit Alfa to Nahalal.
What of the night?
Silence in Jezreel.
Sleep, o valley, land of splendor,
We are your guardians

[Shir Ha'Emek. Words by Nathan
Alterman][1]

GIDON "I went to the winter camp in Czechoslovakia in 1947. It was bitterly cold, with snow everywhere my eyes could see. It was so beautiful here, nothing but snow-covered hills and thick pine forests all around us. I was twelve years old, and we spent two weeks in the highest mountains in Bohemia, the Krkonose mountains on the Czech −Poland border. Camp was fun because we were divided into groups of girls and boys of different ages, and each group was located in a special building, very far apart from each other. There was a central lodge where every morning we would come for breakfast and where all the cultural and other activities took place.

In the morning we would get up, wash our faces, get on skis, and ski for ten or fifteen minutes to the lodge. We had a young woman who was our *madricha*, our counselor, and I remember falling in love with her. Of course, she didn't take it seriously, but I did. She was from Israel, from Kibbutz Ginegar, which still exists in the Jezreel Valley, very close to Afula and Nazareth. I swore to myself that I would find her one day in Israel.

I didn't want to go to America. I wanted to go to Israel. The country needed young people. But the *shaliach* of our group, who was from Kibbutz HaHotrim, south of Haifa, said, 'Peter, don't worry. If you want to go to Israel, you will get to Israel also from America. We have our organization there. There is a shaliach there. You will find them. They will find you. And if you want to really come to Israel, you will come to Israel.'"

Doris, however, had no intention of immigrating to Israel, a place that to her must have seemed like a wilderness in the middle of a war. She wanted to go to America.

CHAPTER 10
MY BONNIE LIES OVER THE OCEAN

GIDON "My mother's grandmother's sister lived in Brooklyn, NY. Her great-aunt, I suppose you would say. Flora was interested in finding any relatives who were still alive. Living with her and taking care of her was her niece Leonie, who was employed by an agency that was looking for professional people who had survived the war, like doctors, lawyers, and engineers, and through this organization, my great-aunt located my mother and me. I don't remember the name of the organization, and I am afraid there is nobody around who I can ask because they are not alive."

Doris and Gidon were located by a cousin named Leonie, and Flora, a great-aunt in Brooklyn. Leonie must have been extremely determined, not just to find any surviving family members but also to scale the mountain of paperwork, requirements, and deadlines required to bring Doris and Gidon to Brooklyn. Once they had been found, Gidon remembered receiving monthly care packages from Leonie and Flora, carefully wrapped, heavy with canned sardines and, Gidon recalled, M&M's. Finally, two and a half years after liberation, Gidon and Doris got the okay in 1948 to immigrate to the United States. Flora didn't know it yet, but her sister, Rosa, Doris's grandmother, had been transported to Térézin in July of 1942. Three months later, she was sent to Treblinka and the gas chambers.

> **GIDON** "In 1948, my mother and I got on a train to France and spent three days in Paris. I don't remember much of that time except eating bananas. I had not ever before seen or tasted one, and I ate them until I got sick! Then we got on the *S.S. America*, which was a beautiful boat. I never had been on such a ship, of course. It even had a swimming pool. I learned how to swim, even though my mother was totally against it. She was afraid of water and swimming because of an incident years before. I remember I had to sneak out of our cabin into the swimming pool, and I taught myself to swim without her finding out."

"When I got to America and passed the Statue of Liberty, I was so disappointed!" Gidon added. "It was much smaller than I thought it would be!"

While Gidon had one experience, his mother, naturally, had another. It wasn't hard for me to imagine how frightening it must have been for Doris to disembark in Brooklyn in 1948, a widow, suffering from the shock and grief of her experience, with the knowledge that her family was murdered, and toting a thirteen-year-old at her side, her son, looking to her for cues and guidance. It wasn't easy to emigrate from the only place she had ever called home.

In *After Such Knowledge: Memory, History, and the Legacy of the Holocaust*, Eva Hoffman writes:

> "Emigration is an enormous psychic upheaval under any circumstances. It involves great, wholesale losses: of one's familiar landscapes, friends, professional affiliations; but also of those less palpable but salient substances that constitute, to a large extent, one's psychic home—of language, a webswork of cultural habits, ties with the past. Perhaps even ties with the dead."

"Less palpable but salient substances"—like belonging, familiarity, cultural habits. Gidon was too young to take his mother's state of mind into account, but it strikes me as interesting that he didn't write anything, even in retrospect, about Doris's frame of mind during this time. Though he did concede at least one important point:

> **GIDON** "Of course, to her credit, my mother did look after my basic physical needs, especially in Térézin, the concentration camp, though even there, there were long periods when she was ill and in the sick room, and I cannot recall who looked after me. I think for the most part I must have looked after myself."

Neither Gidon nor his mother spoke English when they arrived in America. Well, that's not entirely true; Gidon knew how to sing "My Bonnie Lies Over the Ocean."

A year after we visited Prague, Gidon and I took another trip together, this time to Brooklyn. Naturally, Gidon was amazed by how different everything was. Seven decades had passed; it was like time travel. This was nothing like the Brooklyn Gidon immigrated to in 1948. Nothing. This was not here. That was not there. Monkey butt.

That's what I say to Gidon when he tells me something for more than the twentieth time. Monkey butt. Monkey butt. That is our code for "I love you, but you've said this before many times."

Being elderly means you have a lot of memories but fewer people who appreciate them to share them with. I knew this would happen to me, too, someday, if I lived long enough. I made a mental note to teach my kids the "monkey butt" code.

As we stood outside an ordinary-looking apartment building on East 21st Street in Flatbush, the building that Gidon and his mother first lived in, Gidon launched into "My Bonnie Lies Over the Ocean" to demonstrate for me, once again, that this was the limit of his English language at one time.

No one paid any mind to Gidon's singing; the streets were busy around us, and people went about their day without a passing glance. There was the usual CVS, several pizza joints, used clothing stores, and the aroma of spicy Caribbean food.

Gidon pointed up at the third floor of a building and told me that he and his mother stayed right there, in a small room next to the kitchen. It must have been cramped in the flat. It must have smelled like close spaces and cooking. It must have sounded like the shouts and beeps and honks from outside. It must have been noisy inside, too. Flora, Gidon told me, especially liked to watch boxing on television.

Televised boxing was all the rage in the 1940s; it was cheap and easy to produce. I could imagine the tinny sound of the crowd roaring in the background. I could imagine that Europe must have seemed for Doris and Gidon like another distant world.

Gidon and I stayed at the beautiful Brooklyn brownstone of our hosts, cousins of Gidon's late wife, Susan. I could see the family resemblance among Susan's grown children and her cousins. The family regarded Gidon with great affection; he was, after all, a connection to Susan, who died too young. But it was more than that; there was genuine love here. And history. This family was very much like Gidon's family in Israel—or maybe it was vice versa. They were articulate, artistic, musical. We enjoyed a family concert around the piano.

After everyone went to bed, I read aloud to Gidon about the past few days of events that I had both written and added and edited from his journals.

> **GIDON** "School was already out for the year because it was summertime. So I would go to a lot of movies. I saw *Batman* and *Superman*. I could not understand what was going on. I did not understand the language. This is America? People can fly? Go through walls? Finally, I spoke to Leonie and asked, '*Was ist das?*'"

"Hold on. Stop right there," Gidon said. "I don't think I would have asked her in German." I reminded Gidon that I was reading aloud from his own work. He frowned. "No, it must have been German. I didn't speak English yet," he said. "Keep reading."

> **GIDON** "I spent a lot of afternoons going to Prospect Park to watch the kids play. They threw this crazy-looking ball. American football, I think. None of these games I knew how to play. But one day I noticed some kids playing what Americans call soccer so I stood behind the goal and every time there was a goal or they missed the goal, I would run, get the ball, and kick it back to them because this is the game I knew. Finally, after an hour or two, one of the kids—an older kid, their counselor—saw me and asked me to join them."

When I thought about that skinny kid standing there hoping someone would ask him to join the game, I could have wept. My reaction surprised Gidon a little bit. It pleased him, too. He *was* a sad and lonely kid who was standing there, hoping to be included, when Gidon allowed himself to really think about it. He was so accustomed to telling his story as a series of events, often very detailed but usually lacking in any emotion other than a kind of stolid enthusiasm or matter-of-fact displeasure.

"I was very lonely," he admitted.

It turned out that the kids who invited him to join them were in the HaShomer Ha'tzair Socialist Zionist Jewish youth group. It wasn't the same group Gidon had been involved with in Karlovy Vary, but still, Gidon was overjoyed to have made new friends.

 GIDON "They invited me to their club the next Friday, and I went there for *oneg Shabbat* and folk dancing. I was so happy. We talked about Israel. Soon we will have a country and kibbutz and everything, they said. It was really a revolutionary state for me to be once again with kids and people who were Americans but were speaking about maybe going to Israel and what's happening there. I also learned things about being Jewish that I had not known. Even though I had been a Jew in a concentration camp, I had very little knowledge about what it is to be Jewish."

"You didn't say anything about the Good Humor truck," Gidon said. "Or stickball. I had no idea how to play stickball. You had to use a broomstick, and we played between buildings. We sometimes broke a window."

I reminded Gidon that I was reading his memories. How could I mention something if he didn't write about it?

"Okay, let's talk about the Good Humor truck, then," I said. "How much was ice cream?"

Gidon grinned and began to sing, "My mom gave me a nickel

for a pickle, a pick-pick-pick-pick pickle, for a nickel! My mom gave me a . . ." He paused. "I forget the rest."

The tune about the pickle that Gidon remembered turned out to be from a song released in 1950, called "Choo'n Gum," which goes, in part, like this:

> My mom gave me a nickel to buy a pickle
> I didn't buy a pickle, I bought some
>   choo'n gum
> Choo, choo, choo, choo, choo'n gum.
> How I love my choo'n gum
> I'm crazy over choo'n gum

I informed Gidon that, thanks to Google, I had discovered that the song came out in 1950; he must have heard it in Canada, not Brooklyn.

Gidon just laughed. "Anyway, I thought it was about pickles."

To learn English, Gidon went to night school. He was the youngest kid in the class; it was mostly for adults. In fall 1948, he was put in sixth grade. Once again, as was the case in Karlovy Vary in 1945, Gidon was older than the other kids. He had a lot of catching up to do. And now he was trying to catch up in English. Gidon must have adapted very quickly; after only half the school year, he was put in seventh grade and, later, eighth grade. But he struggled socially.

GIDON "I felt very strange, very isolated. I did not have friends because I couldn't speak English. In school, I was sort of an oddball. There were parties. They never invited me. I just remember the kids said, 'Oh, we went with this girl or that girl.' You know, like teenagers do."

Yes, like teenagers do. Oh, what a lonely boy. At least Gidon could sometimes hang around with cousin Leonie's eighteen-year-old son, Ted, who was "both tall and very fat" by Gidon's description. He had "a model airplane hobby" and took Gidon out to fly his planes in Prospect Park.

"Some planes flew and never came back," Gidon explained. "Flora went crazy about it. 'How can you spend so much money on all these little motors and lose them?' But," Gidon went on, "sometimes he kept them on a wire, and they just flew around in a circle."

Gidon told me that Ted shared a room with his mother, Leonie, and that their room was crammed with balsa wood model airplanes hanging from the ceiling, decorating every wall. Both Gidon and Doris thought this so strange—such an expensive hobby—and stranger still that Leonie shared the room with Ted. I pointed out to Gidon that the room he and his mother stayed in was probably Leonie's room before, and that she'd moved into her son's room to make space for them.

This had never occurred to Gidon. Suddenly, he felt chagrined. But that's how memory works, doesn't it? Only as good as our awareness at the time? Trapped in amber until something pierces it.

It was hot—a glorious late spring—and, I noticed, much noisier than our home in Israel. Sirens blared, police cars whooped, and airplanes buzzed overhead. Gidon and I made full use of our time; after we toured Brooklyn, we headed to Manhattan and went to the New York Public Library's main branch on 5th Avenue, which Gidon had never seen before. Gidon wasn't interested in going to the Algonquin, where I generally liked to absorb the greatness of some of my favorite writers, so instead, we lounged in Bryant Park. We watched people play bocce and jostle each other during the busy lunch hour. We apparently had missed the American phenomenon of "poke bowls," so we ordered some and ate outdoors. Gidon was not a fan; there weren't any potatoes.

Later, we went to Broadway to see *Network*. Gidon was not familiar with the Paddy Chayefsky film version starring Faye

Dunaway and William Holden, nor did he know who the actor Bryan Cranston was or anything about the television show *Breaking Bad*. This happens to us sometimes, with our age difference. We have different cultural touchstones. Despite my doubts, Gidon came away from *Network* thoroughly entertained, talking delightedly about it over Cuban food at a nearby restaurant, which, thank God, had potatoes on the menu.

The next day, we toured the 9/11 museum in grim silence. It was beautiful. And heartbreaking. Afterward, I made plans to meet a childhood friend for a rare visit. Gidon decided to do his own thing, which was just as well; I didn't think he would appreciate the marvels of the Lush store.

When we met up again, Gidon had walked something like ten city blocks, bought a hotdog, and argued with the guy about the price. I reminded Gidon that we were not in Israel—that in America, prices are not negotiable. Gidon remarked that the hotdog wasn't that great anyway.

Back home, I noticed a photograph of Gidon, his mother, and father, all of them splashing on the shore of the Vltava River in Prague. Gidon looked to be about three years old, and despite the coming storm, both his parents were smiling brightly. His father was wearing one of those male bathing suits from the 1930s that look oddly embarrassing to us today.

"Wait," I said, turning to Gidon, "I thought you said your mother didn't like you to swim? Remember? You wrote that about your trip over to Brooklyn."

"Yes, but that was the last time she let me in the water," Gidon said bitterly. "You know, she never once told me she loved me."

"Monkey butt."

Gidon's grandmother Alice Neubauer Samish with her daughter, Doris. (1917).
Alice was transported from Vienna to the Izbica ghetto in Poland in March, 1942. In November
1942 the ghetto was "liquidated." Victims were shot in the forest and buried in mass graves.

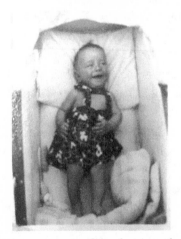

Gidon, about six months old, and about $2^1/_2$ years old

L-R: Gidon's great-grandmother Rosa Samish, her son, Gidon's grandfather, Fritz Samish, Doris (pregnant with Gidon), and Ernst. (1934)

L-R: Theresie Löw, her son Ernst, Gidon, and his grandfather, Alfred Löw. (1938)

Ernst, Doris, and Gidon in Prague. (1939)

Ernst Löw's application for an exit visa. (1941)

Above: Gidon's grandfather Fritz, his 2nd wife Elsa, and their son, Heinz. (approx. 1941)

Right: Gidon after liberation. (1945/46)

Above: Gidon and his camp counselor, Ruth, in the Krkonose mountains of Bohemia. (1947)

Gidon and Doris in Brooklyn, New York.
(1948)

Doris and Jus, Toronto, Canada. (1950)

CHAPTER 11
GRACE STREET

After being in Brooklyn for just one year, in 1949, Doris decided to leave for Toronto, Canada, to marry Jus, the man with whom she had developed a relationship after the war while they were in Karlovy Vary. Gidon experienced yet another dramatic change in a life marked by upheaval.

With no relatives in America, Jus had applied to immigrate to Canada, where he had a good friend from before the war, Frank Kohn. Frank was married to Gidon's father's first cousin, Paula. Small world, but then Karlovy Vary was a small town. On his immigration application, Jus said that he was Frank's brother and, although their surnames were different (Cohn versus Kohn), the Canadian immigration authorities bought it, and Jus moved in with his "brother" and began work at a textile factory. In their new ad hoc postwar family, Jus, Doris, and Gidon stayed with Frank and his wife, Paula, for several weeks before they rented their own place on College Street in downtown Toronto, above a kosher butcher shop. Doris began to work at a millinery factory. Gidon started eighth grade at Grace Street Public School, and although he was already a studious apprentice of adjusting to new circumstances, the move was difficult for him.

GIDON "You have to remember, I was fourteen years old. Once again, my heart fell to my toes. Here I was in a club in Brooklyn, making friends and just beginning to feel at home, and we were leaving again. I was hoping that for once, I would have a home, a family, and even a father. Little did I know that these two, my mother and Jus, two deeply emotionally injured souls, would have a very hard time working and talking things out between them. At that time, five to ten years after the war, survivors were not encouraged to speak about what we had endured, and we didn't know how to process what had happened to us, to our families, to millions of Jews. As a child, I even lacked the language to express what had happened and how to deal with it. There was a great deal of tension and arguing in our home, which for me was horrible."

An awkward adolescent, Gidon was in his second new country in the space of eighteen months, living with a stepfather with whom his mother's silence, moods, and anger made bonding difficult. His new family was struggling to make ends meet, and Gidon worked from four to six every afternoon after school five days a week and all day on Saturdays in addition to doing the many school activities that he threw himself into. ~~He was eager to get out of the house.~~

Gidon lined out that last sentence and scrawled on the side of the page: "He did manage to save up enough money from his work, after one year, and bought himself a Raleigh bicycle, of which he was very proud! He was eager to spend as little time as possible in the house, and the bicycle helped him to do so!"

 GIDON "I got an after-school job, at Seaman's Fish and Food Store, making eight dollars a week, stocking the shelves, cleaning the store, and stacking the frozen fish for smoking. After a year or so working for Mr. Seaman, when a shelf fell down on me, he gave me a raise to ten dollars. I would also do deliveries, especially on Saturdays, and earn a bit more from tips. Later, I went to Central Technical high school, and I took part in the school chorus, and was active in sports, especially in training for the 100-yard dash and football. At Central Tech, we learned various trades, such as auto mechanics, carpentry, electronics, plumbing, and so forth, together with math, history, literature, chemistry, even algebra, though the level was not always very high. And it was possible to learn something, especially when, from time to time, we had a good teacher, and in this, I was quite lucky. I had a wonderful literature teacher. I remember his name to this day: Wally London. He had been a professional football player with the Toronto Argonauts and got hurt, and started teaching. He made us understand and, to some extent, even love poetry. We had to learn two hundred lines by heart in order to pass his class, from one of Shakespeare's plays. I chose the speech by Anthony, from *Julius Caesar*, and can recall part of it to this very day."

Gidon put down his spoon and dramatically leaned back in his chair. We were eating soft-boiled eggs in the kitchen.

"Friends, Romans, countrymen, lend me your ears. I come to bury Caesar not to praise him . . ." There was a long pause. Gidon shrugged. "I forget the rest."

I asked Gidon whether he chose this speech or whether it was assigned. He explained that there were a few speeches the students could choose from. So, why this one? I imagined young Gidon relating to a powerful statesman, swathed in a toga, bedecked with a crown of olive leaves, gesturing dramatically. Being powerful. Being heard.

Gidon interrupted my train of thought. "It demonstrates how words can change people's perceptions of events!"

Was I trying to eke something out of Gidon that wasn't there? I didn't know the entire speech myself. Only the first line. I realized though, and not for the first time, that there was a performative aspect to Gidon. He's a ham. That's why he liked the speech and why he likes it still. ~~He loved attention.~~

Gidon amended this sentence: "He loved attention *and* also to be different!"

Only a couple of months after arriving in Toronto, Gidon sought out the meeting place of the Jewish Zionist youth group he'd gotten involved with in Brooklyn, HaShomer Ha'tzair.

At the time, there were fully thirty different streams of Zionist youth groups, with an array of socio-political ideologies —right, left, and center—that spanned the various Jewish denominations from Orthodox, Conservative, and Reform to interfaith, pluralistic, and humanist. Over time, incidentally, these youth groups shifted to political parties that would shape Israel and give the modern state many of its more prominent leaders. HaShomer Ha'tzair (the young guardians) was most decidedly on the far political left and was the movement that was most energetically committed to creating a revival of a Jewish nation founded on the egalitarian principles of socialism. For the members of HaShomer Ha'tzair, being in America or Canada was only a way station before their true destination: Israel. Gidon had found his tribe, and the movement found in Gidon an enthusiastic participant.

 GIDON "Every week, after work, I attended HaShomer Ha'tzair meetings. We had educational programs on topics connected to Jewish history, the Zionist movement, Plato's Republic, communism, capitalism, socialism, and Israel.

There were also lots of cultural activities, lots of singing—sometimes through the entire night—and lots of Israeli folk dancing. Much—or, rather, all—of my free time after work, I would spend at our club. After a year or so, I was given the responsibility of being in charge of maintenance and heating the meeting place, and this was very demanding, so I spent even less time at home."

Gidon was living two lives: one in a home that he desperately wanted to leave and one as a valued member of a movement that promised him that, with hard work and determination, he could go to sunnier climes and be an essential part of a family that needed him. At home, things continued to deteriorate.

GIDON "One day, I had a terrible fight with my mother and decided to not finish my last year of high school, so that I could go to work and pay my mother rent for the room I was living in. In school, they were a bit shocked because I was doing well, and had only four months to the end of the year and a diploma. But I just could not stand it any longer and wanted to be as free as I could of my dependence on my mother."

It wasn't that Gidon didn't think about the future when he made the rash decision to drop out of high school; he absolutely was thinking ahead—in a straight line that ended in Israel.

GIDON "HaShomer Ha'tzair was committed to Israel, and specifically to a kibbutz. I completely adopted that commitment; for me, it was unshakable. It became crystal clear to me that I would live on a kibbutz in Israel. My first job after stopping school was with a dental company delivering false teeth to dentists all around Toronto, and I really got to know the city and a lot of dentists all over town. Then one day, I gently backed into a Lincoln Continental, a very fancy vehicle, and that was the end of that job. Then, my second job was putting up prefabricated garages, once again all over the city. This was truly a hard job for two main reasons. To get to the site of the new garage, I used public transportation, and, often, I traveled for an hour or more to get there. Secondly, this was in the winter, and it was very cold, so cold, in fact, that at times nailing on the roofing, if I missed, and hit my fingers, I didn't even feel it because they were numb."

This willingness to do anything was classic Gidon. But this image of a slight, Czech boy with an accent, no father, and few friends, living in a lonely home riding the bus and pounding nails in the freezing cold made my heart hurt. For Gidon, staying busy and working hard were coping mechanisms. They still are. Even in his mid-eighties, he delivers flowers several times a week (he likes the extra pocket money) and climbs flights of stairs as he does. Sometimes, if it is a holiday, I go with him so he has a copilot and helper. He works for three brothers: Yankele, Itzhak, and Avram. Each owns his own florist shop in our predominantly Iraqi neighborhood. The brothers are accustomed to occasionally seeing me in the car, and they chuckle about how Gidon had a woman. *Ha isha shel Gidon*, they call me—Gidon's woman. Most of the deliveries are for Yankele, who usually leans in the car window, a cigarette smoldering in his mouth, and shoves the flowers at Gidon. Then the argument begins over how much Gidon should be paid. This typical Israeli interaction lasts less than thirty seconds. It evolves from an argument to a shouting match, with accusations of one man trying to ruin the other man's life, and then Gidon wins, Yankele grins and off we go.

"I actually am sure," Gidon added, speaking of himself in the third person, "Yankele respected and liked Gidon, as did the two other brothers."

CHAPTER 12
A MAN TO TILL THE SOIL

It was the 1950s, and cultural and political events were exploding all over the world, events that continue to shape our world today. But Gidon had tunnel vision. It's as if he was on his own island like Tom Hanks in *Castaway*. He didn't write anything about movies or music of the era. He didn't mention Sputnik or the Korean War or color television. Oddly, for a person so immersed in the ideas of socialism, Gidon made no mention of Fidel Castro, J. Edgar Hoover, or the execution of the Rosenbergs, although he did mention McCarthyism, obliquely:

> **GIDON** "There were parents who heard that we were a socialist/Zionist movement, and they refused to let their son or daughter come to our Oneg Shabbat and/or camp. Even when we went to their homes and explained to the parents that we teach the kids to help each other, to share, to treat the girls in the group as equals, to be fair, to work together rather than compete, when they heard the word 'socialism,' that made us 'pink' or 'red' or whatever. This was a very trying period for us. One

week, I would have ten kids show up for an activity; the next week, only five would come. It was very difficult. It felt as if we were under siege. And in a way, we were. Sometimes the parents even refused to see or speak to me. An atmosphere of fear prevailed."

Ten years went by. Gidon had started school, dropped out of school, moved out of the house, and worked at odd jobs. He hiked, he camped, he sang and danced, and he wholeheartedly embraced the ideology of Socialist Zionism. He spent a year in Chicago helping to rebuild the youth group community, which had slowly petered out. He spent a year on a kibbutz in upstate New Jersey. He attended a four-month-long animal husbandry course at Rutgers University. He was very busy, it seemed to me, doing everything but having any kind of a personal life.

"No, but seriously, I don't get it," I told Gidon, continuing a discussion we had been having for several days. "All you wrote about during your time in Canada was HaShomer Ha'tzair. What about sex, drugs, and rock and roll?"

Gidon looked at me blankly. I was thinking in American cultural terms again. It was the early 1950s: What about James Dean or Elvis? What about teenage rebellion? I peppered Gidon with questions. "Didn't you have friends who weren't in HaShomer Ha'tzair? What about in school?"

"No."

Why? I mean, he got candy after school, right? Was it because what he had seen was so terrible that he grew up too fast? Was he shy? Did he see the other students as silly or naive?

"No."

I was thoroughly confused. Why didn't Gidon write *anything* of a personal nature about the decade between arriving in Toronto and his immigration to Israel in 1959? He wrote pages and pages about the activities and doctrine of HaShomer Ha'tzair, about the folk dancing, about camping, about training farms and animal husbandry, but honestly, didn't he have a girlfriend?

Gidon gave me a leather notebook, a kind of album of memories from the period. In it, I was able to find some clues. On a piece of paper, written in English in tiny writing with a fountain pen, is a poem titled "Prophet Peter." It's a hilarious ode to Gidon.

"His mission was upon the earth, to make God's children neater." And, "So happy birthday, Gidon, dear, and courage in your fight. Believe me, though, we all are slobs, at least we know you're right . . ."

Gidon's friend referred to him by both his birth name (Peter) and his new name (Gidon). He didn't remember exactly when, but it was at some point during his time in Canada that Gidon changed his name from the most decidedly un-Jewish Peter, given to him by his secular family—who identified with their surrounding Czech culture—to Gidon, a name from the Hebrew Bible.

In the original Hebrew, by the way, Gidon is spelled גדעון. See that crazy-looking letter, the third from the left, the "ע"? That is a letter in Hebrew called "ayn," a strange, back-of-the-throat guttural sound, and it is almost impossible to translate that into any other language outside of Arabic, which shares the letter and sound. Over time, thanks to the gymnastics and mobility of language, most names from the Hebrew Bible are pronounced differently than they were originally. "Rachel," which English speakers would pronounce "Ray-chel," is, in its original form, "Rah-hel," for example, and "Samuel" in Hebrew is "Shmoo-el."

This name-changing thing was common practice in Israel in the aftermath of the Holocaust and in the early stages of building a new country. It helped to create a new, distinctly Jewish, Israeli identity. David Ben-Gurion, for example, was formerly David Grün. Golda Meyerson became Golda Meir.

In Gidon's scrapbook, there were postcards that Gidon sent

his mother (and obtained after her death) from his counselor training experiences for HaShomer Ha'tzair in Chicago and in Liberty, New York. There was a short note from Mrs. Beccum, his teacher at Grace Street Public School, dated 1950, in which she wished him luck at the end of the school year. There were a couple of notes, dated 1948, from friends in Karlovy Vary saying goodbye, I presumed. They were in Czech, and I could not make them out. There was a note from someone named Tom Simon that said, "Roses are red, violets are blue, someone stinks, maybe it's you." No date. Another note: "Dear Peter (anteater), I have just one saying, 'When you get married and have twins, don't come to me for pins.'"

Among the papers was a memorial pamphlet about another young member of HaShomer Ha'tzair Yoel, who died unexpectedly in 1955 at the age of eighteen. Someone named Eugene eulogized him:

> "People who do not know HaShomer Ha'tzair insist that in the kibbutz society personalities are lost. How far from the truth this is! Was there anyone who has not encountered Yoel's unique character? . . . If I ever needed the kindness of your voice and the comfort of your presence, Yoel, I need them now. I know you would put your arm on my shoulder and speak gently, quietly. And you would not talk of misery and death, but of life and creation."

I asked Gidon if anyone in HaShomer Ha'tzair knew that he was a Holocaust survivor. "One or two," he said. "But it wasn't talked about." Did anyone at school know? He shook his head .

The memorial pamphlet was neatly typed, and the cover was well designed with a photo of Yoel. So it was odd that the back page looked to be a fragment of something else.

"One May day in 1948, in the middle of the burning battle, a state was declared; the State of Israel. The new state is weak but full of strong ideals. Days go quickly by; much has been done; the sands of the Negev have become fruitful; the swamps of the Galil have been drained, but the awakening of the land is still coming. On Mt. Carmel, a mount from biblical times, a new structure grows up; a school for progress and knowledge. On a hot day a caravan passes the fields not far from Haifa and from the caravan emerge sabras dressed in traditional working clothes. They arise and build a new land, and thus is built the new Kibbutz Hachorshim. The members of the new kibbutz are faithful to the ideals of the new land. The land builds itself, but there are many difficulties in the development of a new country; the Arab is still a second-class citizen without rights in his own land. On the credit side, much has been done. An Arab youth movement has been established to go hand in hand with the progressive Jews. Eight Arabs have already been seated in the Knesset. There are people today who look at Israel today as a reformist party in coalition with reactionaries who oppress the Arab minority. This is a misconception. Governments come and go, but the true essence of Israel lies in the Jewish farmer, the Arab worker, the immigrant, and the Jewish worker. This is the main factor of Israel. We, the progressive Jews in America, greet the people of Israel as they strive for peace and libert—"

And there it cut off. I got the picture, though. This was the mantra and vision. This was what Gidon and his HaShomer Ha'tzair friends thought about morning, noon, and night.

Joseph Trumpeldor, one of the early icons of the Labor Zionist movement, described a Jewish pioneer:

> "What is a pioneer? Is he a worker only? No! The definition includes much more. The pioneers should be workers but that is not all. We shall need people who will be 'everything'—everything that the land of Israel needs. A worker has his labor interests, a soldier his *esprit de corps*, a doctor and an engineer, their special inclinations. A generation of iron-men; iron from which you can forge everything the national machinery needs. You need a wheel? Here I am. A nail, a screw, a block?—here take me. You need a man to till the soil?—I'm ready. A soldier? I am here. Policeman, doctor, lawyer, artist, teacher, water carrier? Here I am. I have no form. I have no psychology. I have no personal feeling, no name. I am a servant of Zion. Ready to do everything, not bound to do anything. I have only one aim—creation."

Was Gidon only a nail, a screw, a block? Or was he a true believer, to the extent that he didn't have much of a personal life outside of HaShomer Ha'tzair? Gidon had been thoroughly indoctrinated. He recognized that now, and he was painfully aware of other opportunities that he missed along the way.

> **GIDON** "I gave up becoming a motor mechanic, because I went during the summer months to camp where, for three to four weeks, we would live together as a group, developing a longing for Israel and communal living. This dream was not something I was prepared to give up. My working as an apprentice demanded five full years of

apprenticeship, including all the summer months, and without that, there was no chance to qualify and get a license. I also started ballet dancing and loved it, but, once again, I had to choose: ballet or HaShomer Ha'tzair. I also dreamed of learning tap dancing. Not having the cash for shoes or lessons, I took some old shoes of mine and nailed some metal tabs onto them, but who would teach me? I loved Fred Astaire and Gene Kelly, so I just tried on my own!"

Gidon has six grown children: two daughters and four sons. In each of his sons, Gidon sees an aspect of himself that he might have been, had things gone differently. One son, with a Ph.D. in neurobiology, Gidon sees as the intellectual, more sophisticated self he might have been had he studied at university. In another son, Gidon sees the confident, athletic, outgoing person he might have been if he had been taller and more handsome. In another, he sees the dancer, choreographer, and artist that he had in his soul but didn't have the opportunity to nourish. In the other—his eldest—he sees a wise, playful, grounded father. Of Gidon's two daughters, one is a reassuring yoga teacher and therapist, and the other an assertive, expressive architect. These are all aspects of Gidon that "would have, should have, and could have been" as Gidon puts it.

Today, Gidon's eldest son, Yanai, lives on one of Israel's most storied and successful kibbutzim, Kibbutz Mishmar Ha'Emek, in the Jezreel Valley. In fact, Yanai and his wife raised all four of their children there. Mishmar Ha'Emek boasts a large, newly renovated dining hall, a beautiful pool and recreation center, an auditorium, and about 1,250 residents. It is one of the few kibbutzim in Israel that has not yet been privatized. It's the real deal, in other words. For years, the work of Mishmar Ha'Emek was agricultural. Now, they produce the future: plastics. Six

Knesset members have hailed from Mishmar Ha'Emek, although in Israel, just about every kibbutz, regardless of whether it ultimately lasted, is storied and boasts influential alumni. Ask almost any Israeli, and chances are that they have or have had family members connected to a kibbutz at some time, in some way.

Kibbutz: The very concept is the ideological center of the many spoked wheels of Zionism. I am embarrassed to admit that, until I lived in Israel, I had always imagined the kibbutz as a kind of hippy Israeli commune where Jewish kids in the 1970s and '80s went to get in touch with their roots by learning folk dances and picking fruit. Um, not exactly.

A kibbutz, pronounced, by the way, "kib-bootz," and, in plural, "kib-bootz-eem," is defined as "a community, usually a village, based on a high level of social and economic sharing, equality, direct democracy, and tight social relations."

Zionists weren't the only ones committed to new, utopian ideals of socialism and communal living; dozens of other similar communities came into existence all over the world, with varying versions of socialist ideology, ranging from religious to political to anarchism. But in Israel, the kibbutz was the cornerstone of the new state.

In 1927, the United Kibbutz Movement was formed, helping in both pragmatic and organizational ways kibbutzniks achieve their goals. While the kibbutz movement was instrumental in serving as a mechanism for state-building in Israel, ideologies still differed. The majority of kibbutzim were secular and, depending on the founding members, emphasized various aspects of not just Zionism and socialism but also of communal sharing and living. Despite these differences, or maybe because of them, a new identity and culture were being born—that of the Israeli. The value of hard work, communal living, and resolute unity in the face of challenges deeply informs Israeli culture and society to this day.

The first kibbutz in Israel, Degania, was founded in 1909,

near the southern end of Lake Kinneret (also known as the Sea of Galilee). The land was purchased with the help of the Jewish National Fund, and the first kibbutzniks were mainly from eastern Europe. These were to be "the new Jews," hale, hearty, strong, agrarian. Kibbutzniks would go back to their roots, to their connection to the land. They would upend what Zionist Ber Borochov called the "class pyramid," created when restrictions against Jews from owning land in Europe left a paucity of Jews with the skills of workers and farmers needed to build a new country—the base of the pyramid. Rather, Jews had portable skills, like those of doctors, accountants, lawyers, or other professionals—the top of the pyramid. To build a new country, this had to be changed. More farmers, fewer accountants.

There was a painfully steep learning curve for the early kibbutzniks. Animal husbandry, agriculture, self-governance, and collective living were not skills acquired overnight. All means of production were communally owned: combines, tractors, fields, orchards, and workshops. All services were communally seen after: the kitchen, laundry, washrooms, and even care and education of the children. One of the most controversial aspects of kibbutz life was the children's house: where the children slept at night and where they were watched over and educated by other kibbutz members during the day so that the kibbutz could be as productive as possible—for both genders. The children spent time with their parents in the afternoon and evening, having dinner and playing games for two to three hours before retiring back to the children's house. Kibbutz children lived in this way from birth onward; this continued through the 1970s when kibbutzniks began to shift away from this level of collective living and wanted to have their children sleeping at home with them.

In 1957, Gidon spent a year in Hightstown, New Jersey, where HaShomer Ha'tzair had the only training farm in North America. The aim was to send the graduates to a kibbutz in northern Israel, called Kibbutz Ha'Zorea. It had been founded about twenty years earlier in 1936 and was struggling, and it needed an influx of young, trained, committed kibbutzniks. It was time to put into practice all the ideas Gidon had studied for so long.

 GIDON "We owned and ran a commercially viable farm in Hightstown. It was quite revolutionary. We learned everything from milking cows, plowing fields, raising chickens from start to finish, pruning apple trees, and just living together, cooking, shopping, even ironing our clothes. Everything involved in running an efficient enterprise. It was a kibbutz in a miniature form. It was like living in another world. We were short on manpower, refusing to hire pickers for ideological reasons, so every weekend, groups from our nearby branches in New York helped pick the apples in the orchards. After the apple-picking season concluded, I was assigned to the *refet*, the cow barn. This was a world that I knew very little about. I took out some books from our library and started to learn, besides the practical part, of working in the barn and learning everything, from milking the cows, feeding the calves, and even helping the cows at calving time. I loved it, though it was very hard work. By the end of the year, we were all looking forward to starting our new lives on kibbutz and Israel. We packed, we went for medical checkups, saw the dentist, and visited friends and family. In November of 1959, I got on the boat, the *S.S. Zion*, an Israeli vessel of the Zim line, and sailed to the Promised Land. My mother and even Jus, my stepfather, and my cousin John and family came to the port to see me off. It was really very moving, especially for me. Once more, I was passing the Statue of Liberty, this time on an Israeli ship, and sailing eastward, eleven years after I landed on these shores."

The true adventures of Gidon Lev were only just getting off the ground.

CHAPTER 13
THE NEW JEW

Gidon was headed to another world. He had learned much about Israel, but he could not have imagined life in the actual Middle East.

Mostly, when we think of the Middle East, we imagine the sandy landscapes of the Saudi Kingdom, the United Arab Emirates, Kuwait, or Iraq. In political and economic circles, the Middle East is often referred to more broadly to include North Africa, using the acronym MENA (Middle East, North Africa). Israel is in what used to be called "the Levant," a slightly archaic term that means "rising." The Levant is made up of the Eastern Mediterranean countries of Israel, Jordan, Lebanon, and Syria, and here there are seriously deep roots and history in most every epoch: The Stone, Bronze, and Iron Ages, and the Roman, Byzantine, Early Muslim, Crusader, Mamluk, and Ottoman periods. Then came the British Mandate and Israel's War of Independence in 1948.

But Gidon was not thinking in terms of epochs; he was thinking in terms of the excitement of starting a new life.

GIDON "The ship, the *S.S. Zion*, was packed with immigrants, to Israel mostly, but not only. We were young, energetic, enthusiastic youth. We danced, we sang, we discussed everything and anything from free love to equality, to utopia, and socialism versus democracy. It was a sort of free-for-all. This was the brave new world we were going to, as the saying goes: 'To build and be rebuilt' (*Livnot u-le-hibanot*). It was the voyage of our lifetime. After a brief stop in Naples, we got off the boat for a few hours, and a few prostitutes tried to proposition us guys, with not much luck."

"Not much luck?" I asked Gidon with a slightly embarrassed laugh. I wasn't sure I wanted him to expand on this.

"We were scared of them," he replied. "Honestly."

I imagined this group of nerdy, soon-to-be kibbutzniks, fresh off the boat, with dreams of helping to build a new country, faced with several Sophia Loren look-alikes, down on the docks trying to hustle some business.

"What did they say?"

"Oh, you know, 'Come here' . . . 'We'll do this' . . . 'We'll show you that.'"

The ship that Gidon and his friends sailed on, the *S.S. Zion*, was built in Germany in 1956 and given to Israel as part of reparations paid by West Germany to Israel. Negotiations for reparations from Germany to compensate for "Jewish material losses" totaled about US$1.5 billion in 1952, which is something like US$14 billion today.

The subject of reparations was hotly debated in Israel, with many feeling that to accept repayment from Germany would demonstrate, in a way, a willingness to forgive the Nazis for what they had done. Most of the reparations paid to Israel over fourteen years were plowed into Israel's infrastructure and economy: equipment, factories, and ships. Israel needed this economic injection to get its new country on its feet. Despite those funds, intense debate about the relatively small payments that Holocaust survivors received personally remains. Today, Gidon receives about $650 per month from the German government.

In Israel, the three largest cities are Jerusalem, Tel Aviv, and Haifa, the latter of which is a major port in the north. Built on the rolling Carmel Mountains, Haifa sits about 90 miles from the Lebanese border, as the crow flies.

Haifa is where most passenger ships arrive in Israel (the other, more southerly ports are more industrial in nature). Not that Haifa is not also a busy industrial port, with towering cranes and stacked cargo containers. In November 1959, the *S.S. Zion* docked in Haifa with Gidon Lev on board.

 GIDON "At the Port of Haifa, everybody was up on deck, and we were so excited, pointing out the mountains of the Galilee in the distance. I couldn't really see them; I felt so overwhelmed by just getting there. The idea of finally arriving—after something like ten years—at a place that you've been talking about and learning about, singing and dancing about . . . and then it becomes a reality. The most surprising thing was the crowds of people waiting and waving at us. Once we got off the ship, somebody came up to us and asked us if we were the group going to Ha'Zorea, and we said, 'Yes, yes, yes, we are! We are the group, yes!' A truck pulled up, not a big one, and we all got our things and piled into the truck, sitting on benches in the truck bed."

It is only about 14 miles inland from Haifa to Kibbutz Ha'Zorea, so the ride would have taken about half an hour. What a journey that must have been for Gidon! We travel to this part of Israel quite a lot, Gidon and I, since he has such history in the northern part of the country. He frequently remarks on how different things are today than they were then.

"This whole road is new," says Gidon, gesturing broadly in the general direction we are heading. "It was nothing like this when I first arrived."

"Monkey butt."

Over two million years ago, the broad, fertile Jezreel Valley, also known as Emek Yizra'el, was connected to the Mediterranean Sea. That is, until the Jordan Rift rose, closing the channel.

The lowest point of the Jordan Rift Valley is the famous and slowly disappearing Dead Sea. As the word *rift* might suggest, two tectonic plates rub against each other here. The Golan Heights and all of Jordan are part of the Arabian Plate, while the Galilee, West Bank, Coastal Plain, and the Negev, along with the Sinai Peninsula, are on the African Plate. Eons ago, there was a massive earthquake in this region, and there will be again. This is convenient, perhaps because Armageddon, or as we say in Hebrew, *Har Megiddo*, is located in the Jezreel Valley. Armageddon is the translated, differently pronounced version of the original name. "Har" means mountain. "Meggido" is the name of the place itself, which is a rather amazing *tel*—which is something that looks like a hill but is really several layers of civilization built on top of one another over thousands of years.

In 1457 BCE, the army of Pharaoh Thutmose III and their thunderous chariots fought the Battle of Meggido against a coalition of Canaanite vassal states in this now peaceful, agricultural valley. It's hard to imagine such a chaotic scene in what looks very much to me like the Sacramento Valley in California.

There usually are several archaeological digs happening all over the Jezreel Valley at any point in time. (All over the country, I should say.) You cannot walk 10 feet without tripping over a Canaanite jug. (Or so it seems to me. Not that I've ever found anything.) In the biblical era, the Jezreel Valley was the lands of the Hebrew tribes of Manasseh, Zebulun, and Issachar. In fact, it is in this valley that the biblical story of Gideon played out.

In this story, Gideon is a typical biblical hero of the time—an unwitting man who receives a message from an angel of the Lord, who reportedly said, "The Lord is with you, you mighty man of valor!" After asking the angel to prove that God said this, the angel demonstrates so by having fire shoot out of a rock and then by wetting and drying a fleece. Gideon takes up the task set before him: to destroy a pagan shrine to Baal and destroy a Midianite village. I liked this story of the biblical Gideon; there was something about Gidon that reminded me of Gideon, but maybe even more so of Don Quixote: merry, a bit kooky, with great intentions, always headed toward adventure and sometimes tilting toward windmills.

In November 1959, bouncing along in the back of a truck, twenty-four-year-old Gidon was headed toward a challenging new adventure and the beginning of a whole new life.

 GIDON "I remember the intense feelings as we drove into the Jezreel Valley, which for years had been just a huge swamp and was now one of the most fertile valleys in the land of Israel—a sort of breadbasket for the entire country, providing fruits, vegetables, wheat, cotton, sunflower seeds, and the famous melons. It was a wide valley with mountains on the right and fields and the hills on the left and a tell right in front of us. We didn't know what a tell was yet; we found out only afterward. When we arrived at the entrance to the kibbutz, it felt like a dream come true."

Gidon was part of the second attempt to revive Kibbutz Ha'Zorea with an influx of trained, motivated, excited new kibbutzniks. The first group, a year earlier, hadn't worked out so well.

 GIDON "We were to boost the population at Ha'Zorea and help to diversify the social and cultural fabric there. The founding members were from a German youth movement known as 'Werkleute' and the 'Blau-Weiss' rather than the much larger HaShomer Ha'tzair youth movement. Most of the founding members were academics, some with degrees, and almost all with at least some university education. They truly knew very little about agriculture and manual labor, so their first years in Israel and establishing a kibbutz were tough. It is almost a miracle that they managed to do it. When we arrived, we were, on the whole, warmly received, though with some skepticism, mainly because the group that had come from America the previous year turned out to be a very difficult lot. Some of the people in that first group were problematic individuals. It took us, the new arrivals, a while to change the mostly negative attitudes of the kibbutz members toward us, something that was not so easy to do!"

One of my favorite photos of Gidon was taken only months after he had arrived in Israel. He is on a tractor, and he looks back toward the camera, confident, smiling. The sun shines on his face, his sleeves are rolled up, and he seems like the king of the world. Gidon had pulled a new, empowered identity over his shoulders like a protective, warm sweater. It was a perfect fit. No longer the malnourished boy in a concentration camp, or the shy, friendless immigrant in Brooklyn, or the delivery boy with numb fingers in Canada, the new Gidon was a sun-bronzed, muscular, important part of a hardworking kibbutz.

 GIDON "At first, I worked with the grain elevators. I learned not only the various grain mixtures to prepare—for the cows, calves, chickens, pigs, and sheep—but also how to calculate the nutritional value of these mixtures, and where and how to deliver them. I learned to drive a tractor with a grain delivery bin, to back it up carefully, add exactly the right amount to each grain bin, and how to unload and stack hundreds of sacks of grains into sometimes 20-feet-high stacks, so that they would not come crashing down on our heads. It was hard work, but I liked it. I also loved the Purim celebration; it was an almost all-night festival that involved the entire kibbutz. Weeks before the date, groups formed themselves—such as the orchard workers, the kitchen staff, the laundry group, the cowshed workers, and many more—each performing a skit based on the theme chosen that year, with music, costumes, and lighting. The productions were creative, funny, and entertaining. Of course, there was a lot of food and drink as well. That did make us feel really happy and good."

But life was not perfect. "I did feel quite lonely at times," Gidon admitted. "Being alone on the kibbutz, friendship and companionship were not that easily found."

> **GIDON** "I remember being given a 'lift,' a sort of large wooden box (used as a cargo container for shipping), with a roof on it, standing on six cinder blocks on a hill overlooking the Jezreel Valley. It was a fantastic view, but also very lonely. At night, little mice would come to visit me, and at times lizards, too, were my companions."

Though many of the kibbutzniks on Ha'Zorea spoke English (and German), the real key for Gidon's new life was learning to speak Hebrew. An ancient Afro-Semitic language that bears— and I cannot stress this enough—absolutely no resemblance to English, Hebrew looks like this:

עברית היא שפה עתיקה. לאנשים מסוימים קשה ללמוד אותה.
אני חייבת להשקיע יותר בלימודיי

For you non-Hebrew readers, that reads: "Hebrew is a very old language. It is hard to learn for some people. I should study harder."

In 1948, the new country of Israel had a huge challenge: immigrants were arriving from all over the world, and most of them did not speak Hebrew. Hebrew had been, heretofore, mainly the language of religious study, of liturgy, and of the Bible; it was a sacred language, not one that most Jews spoke in the modern age. Instead, Yiddish, a delightful and mysterious combination of several languages (most notably Hebrew and German) was the most common language spoken among Jews living in the diaspora (i.e., Jews living outside of the region, which was the vast majority at the time). When the new State of

Israel was founded, the question was what the official language would be: Yiddish or Hebrew. Some argued that Hebrew should remain the language of prayer and that Yiddish should be the language of Israel. Others argued that Yiddish was the language of exile and that Hebrew should be the new national language. Hebrew won out. The question then became one of what to do with all the immigrants who couldn't use the newly revived ancient language of the Jews.

Intensive Hebrew learning programs were funded, variously, by municipalities, the Israeli Ministry of Education and Culture, and the Ministry of Immigrant Absorption. The Ulpan program, as it was known, provided five months of Hebrew language lessons for new immigrants.

This program still exists today; in fact, when I came to Israel in 2012, I enrolled in Ulpan. It's not exactly required, but it is subsidized by the government and is a robust national program. The Hebrew alphabet has twenty-two characters and reads from right to left. I thought that this, like driving on a different side of the road, would be the stumbling block, but it wasn't the biggest problem for me. It was the aforementioned zero resemblance to English. I found it notable that, in Hebrew, there are no upper- or lowercase alphabetic characters. In written Hebrew, in other words, nobody can hear you scream. Israelis tend to make up for that with emphatic speech.

Gidon readily learned Hebrew, not only because he already spoke three languages when he arrived in Israel (German, Czech, and English) but also because he has a knack for languages. Perhaps even more importantly, because absolutely nothing was going to slow him down. If Gidon had had to learn Latin, too, he would have done so. Of that I have absolutely no doubt. *Nolite te bastardes carborundorum*, as Margaret Atwood would say.

 GIDON "Luckily, Ha'Zorea was running an Ulpan where young people came to learn Hebrew and work half a day on the kibbutz. Many were from America, but some were also from other countries around the world, and not all were Jewish. They were chiefly attracted by the idea of kibbutz living. I started teaching them Israeli folk dances and began to make some good friends. When the Ulpan group would go on trips to see the country, I usually joined them and, more often than not, helped out in carrying supplies or climbing down steep cliffs, such as the one above the Kineret (the Sea of Galilee) near Tiberias, where the remnants of the revolt against the Romans had holed up, hewing deep caves, cisterns, storage caves, and hidden paths and steps. It was fascinating, and Mordecai Tel-Tzur, the Ulpan teacher and guide, made it all very understandable. This particular trip was really special, not only because of the difficulty of the climb itself, but we ended up on the shores of the lake and had a wonderful swim and picnic. I loved these trips, not only because of the friendships I made but because I learned so much about this country of ours."

Gidon was absorbing more than the geography, history, and culture of kibbutz life; he was adopting the spirit of "the New Jew" and the zeitgeist of the new Israel. To most Zionists at the time, religion had failed the Jews. Where was God during the Holocaust, they asked? A new attitude was needed: a spirit of nationalism, pride, cultural identity, and strength.

"The state," Chaim Weitzmann, the first president of Israel, said in 1947, "will not be given to the Jewish People on a silver platter."

By 1959, the year Gidon departed for Israel, the Suez Canal Crisis of 1956 had come and gone, setting the stage for further conflict between Israel and Egypt. David Ben-Gurion was the prime minister of the country. Four Russian-made Egyptian MiG-17 jets entered Israeli airspace only to be driven away. And Israel marked its first-ever official Holocaust Remembrance Day. If Gidon was nervous about any of these events—or about what might occur in the coming years—he hadn't written about it.

CHAPTER 14
NAHAL

In 1960, John F. Kennedy announced his candidacy for the Democratic presidential nomination, the Aswan dam began construction in Egypt, France tested a nuclear bomb in Algeria, and the United States announced that yet more U.S. soldiers would be sent to Vietnam. President Dwight D. Eisenhower signed the Civil Rights Act, the Belgian Congo received its independence from Belgium, Niger became independent from France, and Typhoon Mary killed sixteen hundred people in China. Adolf Eichmann, one of many Nazi war criminals living in hiding in Buenos Aires, was kidnapped by four Mossad agents and brought to Israel for trial, and that same year, Gidon Lev reported for duty in the IDF, the Israeli Defense Forces.

Israel has a conscription army, which means that all citizens, male or female, are obligated to serve starting at the age of eighteen: three years for men, two years for women. Not all soldiers are in combat units. As with any army, there is a plethora of other duties to fulfill, ranging from intelligence to training, clerical support to transportation to coordination, as well as National Service positions. There are exceptions made for Arab-Israelis, who are not obligated to serve, and there are Israelis who can refuse to serve for religious or other reasons, but they are few and far between. In Israel, there is a bit of a stigma around not serving, and indeed, half the population in Israel has served in the military in one function or another. After their regular service is over, Israelis are then part of the reserves (*miluim*, in Hebrew, pronounced "mil-ooh-eem") and must be available for emergency call-up and, barring that, must serve thirty-six days each year until age forty-five. Up until 1986, the age was fifty-four; the downward shift is a reflection of both the shifting nature of warfare and the increased population in Israel. Currently, there is an intense debate in Israel about whether the Haredi (ultra-orthodox) should be required to serve. More and more, Haredi Israelis do serve, but a large portion of them believe they should not have to because they instead serve Israel through prayer and study. This does not go over well with the general public.

Israel's army isn't the largest or the most powerful in the world, but it is considered the world's most agile and experienced—and with good reason. Since the IDF was created in 1948 from a group of smaller militias, it has engaged in more than twenty-three major operations. The Mossad, the Israeli secret service (equivalent to the CIA in the United States), is one of the most respected and feared intelligence agencies in the world.

A first-time visitor to Israel might be a bit taken aback to see soldiers with submachine guns slung over their shoulders, casually walking down the street, or on the bus, at the mall, or in cafés. It took me a while after moving here to realize that this wasn't because these soldiers were guarding the train or the café, or that some kind of danger was imminent, but rather because these soldiers were *en route* from their base to their home or vice versa. Israel is a small country, and army bases, large and small, are a common sight. There's a base not far from where Gidon and I live, in fact, and it isn't unusual for us to overhear shouts and singing drifting over the rooftops.

If the kibbutz movement was one major influence on the

culture, outlook, and personality of Israelis, the IDF was another. Though Dan Senor and Saul Singer's seminal book, *Start-Up Nation: The Story of Israel's Economic Miracle*, is primarily about technological innovation and its attendant economic impact on the region, the book also points to the IDF's considerable impact on Israeli culture.

"Israel is arguably the only modern country," Sebastian Junger writes in *Tribe, On Homecoming and Belong*ing, "that retains a sufficient sense of community to mitigate the effects of combat on a mass scale."

Because Israel has existed with the backdrop of war and conflict on and across its borders since 1948, cooperation, swift decisions, less formal social hierarchy, questioning authority, and what Israelis call *combina* (i.e., making do with what is at hand) have imbued themselves into the Israeli personality. Israel's social resiliency, which is a measure of how well a society copes with stress and even hardship, is thusly elevated. The social glue, if you will, is quite palpable in Israel. It's the ongoing conflict between Israel and the Palestinians, yes, but it's also due to the size of the country. When it's night in Israel, it's night for everyone. When it's hot in Israel, it's hot for everyone. When the country is under attack, everybody must deal with it. Israelis cannot hold one another at arm's length; they don't have the luxury. At its narrowest point, the country is 9 miles wide. Imagine that. The military is very much woven into everyday life, and its ethos is deeply embedded in Israeli society.

Thus, when it came time for Gidon to show up for duty, he jumped right in for all it was worth. Luckily for him, he was part of the Nahal Unit, which had been established in 1948 to allow kibbutz members to serve in cohesive units and combine military service with farming. The Nahal had another objective, which was to ensure that kibbutzim were protected by trained soldiers on all of Israel's borders.

GIDON "At the advanced age of twenty-five, I found myself at the Nahal 'boot' camp—called 'base 80'—in an area about 35 kilometers south of Ha'Zorea and almost totally planted with citrus groves, the smell of which penetrated the camp. The Nahal battalion was almost entirely made up of young people: boys and girls from the various youth movements and the Kibbutzim, plus groups from the Israeli scout movement. It was somewhat bewildering for me, of course.

Everything we did had to be done to perfection and in a specific time. For me personally, this was not so hard, but there were others who could not cope, and we quickly learned that it is to our advantage to help them, whether that be making their cots, filling their water canteen to the top with water, or other responsibilities. Punishments were dished out not so much to the individual, but rather to the entire squad or tent. (There were ten of us in each tent.) Together with all that, we received four hours of Hebrew lessons for the first three weeks, given by mostly pretty female army teachers. For me, this was wonderful, because it really helped me to start speaking and reading this new language and, besides, it was sitting in a class instead of running, crawling, and doing drills!

One of the crucial activities from the first day on the base was running. We did this in platoons— each platoon numbering about thirty-five to forty recruits—and we needed to help those that had a hard time and lagged behind. Sometimes, we literally had to carry those that were just too exhausted! I very quickly learned that I would do the best if I stuck up front, close to the commander that led the troops. As our stamina increased, we all started singing all kinds of songs, and I taught my platoon the song 'Michael, Row Your Boat Ashore,' with me or someone else calling out the words and rest answering 'HALLELUJAH!' By the end of the three months in basic training, the entire base was singing this song, which really made me happy. It was my little contribution to this macabre way of living.

In my tent and platoon, most of the boys were Brazilians from Kibbutz Givat Oz, about ten kilometers east of Ha'Zorea and on the very border of the 'West Bank,' at that time ruled by Jordan and the Jordanian army. Jenin was the closest Arab city over the border. Givat Oz was a kibbutz first settled by Hungarian Holocaust survivors and now had been joined by a large group from Brazil. Most of them spoke little Hebrew—but a lot of Portuguese. Over three months, I picked up a few Portuguese words. In general, peace reigned in the area. When there was infiltration by the Palestinians, it was mainly to steal equipment, livestock, or produce grown in our fields."

These cross-border infiltrations began in the 1950s and were conducted by what is called fedayeen, Arab guerilla fighters organized into and sponsored by several factions. The earliest fedayeen were primarily mercenary but ultimately banded together to push for a Palestinian state by whatever means necessary. The early beginnings of these raids were largely tit-for-tat, but the movement began to evolve significantly in the 1960s toward Palestinian Nationalism; Gidon's two-and-a-half-year period of service, from 1960 to midway through 1963, was just ahead of this wave.

GIDON "One of the most significant events in basic training was, of course, receiving our rifle, which was the FN 5.56 caliber, a Belgian-made weapon. It was not too heavy, had a light kickback, and we learned to clean, take apart, put it back together in record time. By the time we finished our training, we could do it with blindfolded eyes. The rifle became an integral part of our body, we walked with it no matter where we went, to the loo, to breakfast, to any and all activities—including, of course, running. We slept with our rifles, and it was never ever farther away from us than one step. Each gun has a serial number, and we learned it by heart, and since all the rifles were the same, we devised ways of identifying our personal weapon. I had brought a bit of black tape from Ha'Zorea and used it to mark my weapon. We spent hours cleaning it and, if during the daily morning inspection the slightest speck of dirt was found, it meant no after-lunch rest, because there would be another inspection just before going out for the afternoon training and more cleaning to be done! There were times, I recall that I felt hopeless and frustrated, as did many of us.

When basic training ended, we were new soldiers in the Israel Defense Forces. We had overcome many hardships, learned to camouflage ourselves in minutes, dig personal trenches, crawl, shoot by day or night, walk silently and with utmost caution during night patrols, keep our personal weapon clean and ready at a moment's notice, and, most importantly, appreciate each other's strengths and know each other's weaknesses. Each squad (seven soldiers and commander) was like a close family. We really felt ready to defend ourselves with a great deal of confidence and motivation.

By the end of boot camp, sixteen or so soldiers were selected to continue training for the next level—to become squad commanders—and I was one of them. For me, this was a bit of a surprise. I hadn't expected it. I didn't think I was that good, but my commander thought otherwise. I was quite happy about this additional challenge.

We were given a week's rest—and sent home to our respective kibbutzim, which was really great. To rest, have good food and no pressure, what else could I want? Maybe a girlfriend?

It was hard to go back to the strict and rigorous army discipline, but on Shabbat evening, I got all my gear together, and Sunday at 5 a.m., I was on my way to Beer Sheva, our southern city on the edge of the great Negev desert. A couple of army trucks awaited to transport us and our duffle bags to an isolated base near the ancient Nabataean city of Shivta, very close to the Egyptian border post, called Nitzana.

For hours, we rode on these trucks till we got there. It was a small base then, surrounded by sand dunes, not a tree in sight. It certainly evoked a foreboding. We all asked '*This* is the training base for commanders?' There was only one concrete building that housed classrooms, a dining hall, a kitchen, and officers' quarters. Everything else was set out in the stark and barren sand. There were about fifteen large tents with concrete floors, and we were very quickly assigned a bed in one of the tents, given a sheet, two blankets, and a small pillow, and told to make our beds—'smooth like a baby's bottom'—and stand in rows of three in front of each tent. It was to be our first inspection. A sergeant and an officer appeared and went from tent to tent, and any bed not correctly made was overturned. This time I was lucky: Mine was okay. It became obvious very quickly that discipline was very severe. Of course, it was hot as hell there, and water was absolutely a matter of life and death so that we were told to keep our water canteens filled and with us at all times.

I was so tired that as soon as we had eaten our supper, and were told to go to our tents because at daybreak, we would start a new day. At 5:30 a.m., we woke up to the bugle call, put on shoes, pants, and out we went to do our morning exercises, starting with push-ups. After that, a quick-pace five-kilometer run. Then wash up and breakfast time, and our first lecture and orientation session with the commander of the base. I have never seen one hundred sixty guys sit so silently and listen so intently as I did that morning. It was truly impressive, and a bit scary, I felt.

We received a commander's weapon—an Israeli-produced submachine gun called Uzi 9mm —and learned to use other weapons, did countless push-ups, and ran daily. We learned topography, first in the classrooms, and then out in the desert on foot. In small groups of three to four, we were given a map and coordinates and sent out into the vast wilderness of the Negev to find what we were assigned, describe it, and return to base. The longer it took us, the less sleep we got. Sometimes we would go out at seven in the evening and get back only at two or three in the morning, and by 5:30 a.m., we were back up again. We trudged through the endless desert sand dunes for hours and hours, and, looking back on it today, I don't know how I survived at times!

We also trained in the use of other light weapons and continued doing a lot of running and cleaning our personal Uzi submachine gun, much smaller than the FN rifle, and used mostly in short-range, house-to-house combat.

Then, in the last month of our course at Shivta, we made camp in an area called Beit Guvrin, close to Jerusalem, close to the West Bank border, with very steep hills all around us. This was the final part of the rocky training course before we were to receive our commander's stripes. It was bound to be hard. For three weeks, we camped out in small, two-man tents, had a field kitchen and field toilets, and were constantly on the move. We did patrolling exercises and, using coordinates, located, described, and marked cisterns, landmarks, and abandoned houses. We rested, from time to time, under wonderful large fig trees that had lots of fruit, so we ate figs relentlessly. The problem was that many of us got the runs, and where would we relieve ourselves, if not under the same trees? So it was like stepping into a minefield of human excrement. Thus, we lost our shaded resting places.

As soon as the evening sun gave us respite from the ever-present heat, each platoon (about thirty soldiers) was assigned to carry out a hit-and-run operation (with blank cartridges) somewhere deep in the steep hills. Under the command of one of our officers, we carried out a surprise attack on an imaginary reinforced enemy stronghold. There were always 'injured' fellow soldiers who had to be put on stretchers and carried back to base. Because I was fairly small and light, I was a favorite 'injured' target, and it was painful to be taken over the shoulder by one of the guys! I learned to keep my distance from the commander because it was he who ordered, 'Lay down! You are injured!'

The day we finished this part of our training after three long weeks, we loaded up all our equipment onto the trucks and climbed up onto them, each one of us exhausted. Of course, all of us fell asleep on the long ride back to Shivta, and after a good meal and a warm shower, it felt good to be home! Finally, at the end of our course, we were given our stripes and had a great party. Actually, it was on the very night that Maccabi Tel Aviv beat the CSK Moscow in the European basketball champions for the first time ever! It was quite a party, and we were all together with our commanders and officers.

After that, all those who volunteered for the parachute unit left the base, and the rest of us were given new assignments to various units all over the country. I was quite happy to be sent to a platoon in the north, on the Lebanese border, to Kibbutz Yiftach, as the second-in-command. The detachment was commanded by a sergeant by the name of Yoyo, a very amiable and easy going guy who had another three months to go before his release from the army. The entire platoon, both male and female, was a group made up of *Tzofim*, (the Israeli scouts movement) and they were a great bunch of people.

This border, at the time, was quiet and peaceful. We could walk all the way to the border post that separates Lebanon from Israel, without any fear or much hesitation. We could see the

Hermon Mountain and its snow-capped peak, the highest in this region.

We worked, did guard duty at night, and had a very rich cultural life, which was greatly appreciated by the members of the kibbutz. They were very short of manpower, and our thirty-five or so platoon contingent made a serious contribution to all aspects of kibbutz life. For the first time in my life in Israel, I saw and tasted the wonderful McIntosh apples that the kibbutz was growing in their huge orchard.

We were known as Nahal Unit 902, and we were spread out over about ten different kibbutzim on the border throughout the north. The Syrian border was the most problematic because, from time to time, snipers would shoot at us or artillery would lob mortars down on us from the Golan Heights."

Reading all of this, editing Gidon's writings for clarity, I suddenly felt a bit guilty about my "monkey butt" policy. Gidon had run, guarded, crawled, lugged, carted, sweated, mapped, slept, and bushwhacked over most parts of this country of Israel. Of *course* every hill, every wadi, and every river had meaning and memory for him. I also was reminded not only of how Gidon became so intimate with the geography of Israel but also why he makes a first-rate camping companion, were it not for his habit of charging off the designated road into areas not strictly legal for camping. But that's another story.

CHAPTER 15

BIG HARD SUN

It is time for us to have the talk about *hamatzav*, or "the situation," which is how Israelis refer to the, well, situation between Israelis and Palestinians. You may have seen news about this ongoing conflict on television, represented by images of a smoking crater where a building once stood, women keening and wailing, a burning bus surrounded by flashing lights and ambulances, a graffitied concrete barrier wall, or young Palestinian men wearing black-and-white checkered keffiyehs, hurling stones or Molotov cocktails at Israeli soldiers. You've probably seen footage of Israeli bulldozers tearing down Palestinian houses or Israeli tactical teams dressed in black busting down the door of a Palestinian home. Israel and its heartbreaking, seemingly unsolvable problems show up on television news with dismaying regularity.

During the war between Israel and Hamas in 2014—Operation Tsuk Eitan (Protective Edge)—while air raid sirens wailed outside and missiles fell in Gaza, there was another war, but this one was online. My Facebook feed was filled with fusillades of angry words and memes showing Israelis as evil oppressors or of Palestinians as bloodthirsty terrorists. These divisive memes and posts were so intensely ugly and one-sided that I was shocked. I found myself bridling and feeling defensive. When I engaged and asked people questions about what they had posted, I was very often met with combative words, hostility, and accusations of being either a warmonger or a self-hating Jew. Those advocating for peace were anything but peaceful. What I found even more despairing was the dearth of knowledge about the conflict between Israel and the Palestinians, paired with a conviction that weighing in was somehow necessary as some kind of armchair activism. I realized that while the conflict between Israel and the Palestinians is a famous (or rather, infamous) one, many people don't know about the roots of the conflict and how we came to this pass.

For Jews, returning to the land of their ancestors, a land they never forgot or abandoned in their longings, was a historic inevitability. Throughout the centuries of exile, Jews continued to return to the land, though in small numbers. There was no Jewish identity and no Judaism without the land of Israel. Jews around the world felt indigenous to the land from which they had been expelled, and to which they believed they would one day return. Zionism—a mechanism to make this dream come true—became a political movement as a response to rising violence against Jews—particularly in Russia—in the late nineteenth century.

The First World War lasted from 1914 to 1918 and caused the fall of the Ottoman Empire, which for centuries had ruled over countries that we today call Lebanon, Israel, Jordan, Turkey, and parts of northern Syria and southern Iraq. After the war, the French and the British divided up the former Ottoman Empire, with Britain controlling "Mandatory Palestine," which was comprised of what is today Israel, Palestine, and Jordan. France controlled the remaining territories.

After the devastation of the Holocaust, many of those now stateless Jewish refugees who managed to survive sought refuge in Mandatory Palestine. For Arabs, the Jews weren't "returning" but invading. They saw their historic role as denying an invader any part of the land they felt belonged to them in its entirety. *We've seen occupiers come and go*, they said, *and the Jews, too, will one day be forced to leave.*

The British tried to maintain equilibrium over Mandatory Palestine but a sporadic guerilla war, with Arabs fighting Jews and Jews fighting the British forced their hand. They needed to cut their losses and extract themselves from an increasingly chaotic situation.

Subsequently, the United Nations voted for a two-state partition plan in 1947, dividing Mandatory Palestine between the Palestinians and the Israelis. The surrounding Arab nations refused to accept the international community's decision and, when Israel proclaimed its independence in 1948, declared war. Israel galvanized, fought back, and took extra territory which it later relinquished to the Arab countries. In 1967, as Arab countries once again attacked Israel with the intent to destroy it altogether, Israeli forces captured east Jerusalem, the Gaza Strip, the West Bank, the Golan Heights, and the Sinai. This time Israel decided to maintain control of the territories as security buffer zones but has since returned the Sinai and uprooted its settlements and soldiers from Gaza.

Over the decades, Palestinians developed a yearning for national identity, autonomy, and political cohesion. As they struggled to do this, desperation and anger arose, and some turned to spectacular violence and terror.

Palestinians say that Israel expelled seven hundred thousand Palestinians in the 1948 War. Israelis say that some were expelled during the fighting but many fled. And Israelis note that the Arab world expelled almost a million Jews. Today there are over a million Palestinians who are citizens of Israel, and almost no Jews left in the Arab world. Very many agreements on both sides were broken, promises were made, and betrayals and violence occurred over and over again. There have been ongoing clashes and intifadas (uprisings) ever since. This cycle has woven itself into a dense tapestry of distrust, injustice, and pain.

Both sides, the Israelis and the Palestinians, have been acting out of a sense of justice and being faithful to their reading of history. They feel they have no other choice.

~

Countries have collective narratives—stories about themselves that they relate over and over through national anthems, textbooks, art, culture, and history books. We tend to exalt the versions that reflect positively on us and skim over or simplify those that do not. In America, the prevailing narrative is one of rebellion: We dumped the goddamned British tea right into the Boston Harbor! Later, as cowboys and outlaws, we conquered the wild, wild west. Today, in America, we are only beginning to come to terms with the enormous flaws in our history as we have been taught it.

The history of Israel's War of Independence was as familiar to Gidon as the stories of the *Mayflower*, the pilgrims, and Thanksgiving were to me.

 GIDON "Once this tiny Jewish state was born, all the Arab states surrounding this ridiculous little sliver of land categorically and emphatically rejected it even before Israel declared its independence. Instead, they opened five fronts with their armies. In the south, the Egyptians; in the east, the Jordanians; in the north, the Syrians and the Iraqi army set out to attack; and, even in the northwest, the Lebanese set about to attack. The only border safe from attack was the Mediterranean Sea, into which the Arab armies, their leaders, and generals planned to push us in. I think that the Arab armies, with their overwhelming manpower, arms, tanks, and artillery, were sure that within days, perhaps weeks, there would be no talk of a Jewish state called Israel. And they had good reason to believe so. They were exceptionally confident and arrogant, forgetting one major fact, which was that the Jews living at that time in Israel had nowhere to go. That would be the end of the dream of a Jewish state. And in that kind of a situation, each soldier, each house, each trench becomes an unconquerable bulwark. There were many instances where the commanders of the Arab armies used loudspeakers to tell the local Arab citizens to leave their homes and stay out of harm's way because they would come back.

It is important to know that Israel had a very small army (mind you, well trained), few arms, no tanks, hardly any artillery, and very limited amounts of ammunition. It was committed, it was determined, it fought fiercely; its very existence was on the line! On top of all that, the minute hostilities commenced, the world called for an embargo on arms to the Middle East, which essentially affected Israel but not the Arab nations fighting it; they were simply too large and spread out to enforce such a dictum on them. I am really proud of the fact that the only country that came to Israel's help was the country of my birth, Czechoslovakia. Clandestinely, by night and day, they flew in planeloads of Czech rifles, ammunition, and even some light machine guns to a small airport in the Jezreel Valley, so we could somehow defend ourselves.

So, yes, the Arab armies lost the war, but for us, it was a miracle! We held them at bay, we managed to push them back, and we took control of much more territory than the U.N. had allocated to us in the first place. Perhaps had the Arab nations been prepared to meet and sign a peace agreement with us, much of the territory we captured would probably have been returned to them. But they were and are a proud people, and in that war, they were humiliated and were not prepared to recognize us here in the Middle East. Mind you, we did sign peace agreements with two of our neighbors, Egypt and Jordan, thanks to Anwar Sadat of Egypt, Hussain of Jordan, and Begin and Rabin of Israel. However, we remain in deep conflict with our closest neighbors the Palestinians, and that must be resolved not just for them (the Palestinians), but also for us, and our existence as a free Democratic state of the Jewish people and all its citizens."

For Israelis, the 1948 War of Independence was like a miracle, and this impossibility—this unlikely and amazing outcome—whether it be divine or human, informs the Israeli identity today: a people who exist in a hostile world against all the odds. If the ideology of kibbutz and service in the army are two pillars that make up the Israeli identity, the third pillar is that Israel has to defend its existence every day.

But what was a miracle for the Israelis, was a *Nakba* for the Palestinians—a catastrophe. Palestinians have absorbed a different version of events, one from their perspective. A chronology of catastrophe, displacement, and victimhood is shared by the Palestinians and the Israelis in tragic ways that have strengthened and reaffirmed each narrative for decades.

In *Letters to My Palestinian Neighbor*, Yossi Klein Halevi writes:

 "We need to challenge the stories we tell about each other, which have taken hold in our societies. We have imposed our worst historical nightmares on the other. To you, we are colonialists,

Crusaders. And to us, you are the latest genocidal army seeking to destroy the Jewish people. Can we, instead, see each other as two traumatized peoples, each clinging to the same sliver of land between the Jordan River and the Mediterranean Sea, neither of whom will find peace or justice until we make our peace with the other's claim to justice?"

Gidon had written very little about the tumultuous backdrop of Israel's history, conflict, culture, and politics, choosing instead to focus on his life. It wasn't that he didn't *have* opinions about these things, mind you, or experiences with them; he just hadn't focused on them. This, in retrospect, was something that Gidon wanted to change. It wasn't too late. Now was the season of our activism.

Gidon and I found ourselves with several other people, mostly women, riding in the back of a tour van down a bumpy road in the West Bank. We were on our way to Qalqilya to see one of the hundreds of checkpoints that lace through and around the West Bank. The tour was organized by Machsom Watch (Barrier Watch), a volunteer nonprofit group led by Israeli women who are peace activists with a mission to monitor activities, bear witness, and agitate for justice at checkpoints and in military courts in the West Bank. Machsom Watch also provides opportunities for Israelis and others to see for themselves the impact of the checkpoints at the barrier wall.

The barrier wall wasn't always there. It was built during the Second Intifada, which began in September 2000 and lasted until 2005. The Palestinian intifada (or, uprising) took the form of suicide attacks on buses and in cafés, claiming the lives of more than one thousand Israeli men, women, and children—as well as the lives of an estimated three- to four thousand Palestinians, both combatants and noncombatants. The senseless deaths on buses, in cafés, and at shopping malls were not the only consequence of a yearslong wave of suicide bombers —it's called *terrorism* for a reason. Countless Israelis and Palestinians were traumatized, and some were maimed for life. The Second Intifada destroyed any shred of hope, trust, or empathy that Israelis had struggled to harbor.

The Israel of Gidon's younger days did not have the checkpoints or barrier wall. To say that he was disillusioned that the Israel he had loved and had been a part of building had erected military checkpoints is an understatement; Gidon had been busy raising a family and hadn't really taken the time to stop and consider the implications. But he had lived through the terror of the intifadas that took the lives of so many, including people he knew. He felt conflicted and deeply saddened. Later, he wrote about our experience.

 GIDON "I must say here, clearly and loudly, I have come away horrified! There are Arab villages that are totally fenced-in, with only one exit and entry gate. It so reminded me of Térézin. I found it hard to believe that we Jews are doing to others the very thing we suffered from for generations, even before the Holocaust. Not for one minute can I justify our ruling over another people. That was not, and is not, and never will be my reason for coming and living here in Israel! What I saw in the central part of the West Bank is sheer madness, debilitating, unfair, and, in the end, self-destructive! The worst aspect of this situation is that it is, for the most part, demoralizing for our own soldiers, and that is self-destructive. I am old and have, I believe, done my part for the State of Israel, but my children and grandchildren deserve better."

A few weeks later, Gidon and I attended the Israeli-Palestinian Memorial event in Tel Aviv, sponsored by Combatants for Peace. Side by side with more than eight thousand people, Gidon and I reveled in the emotional speeches and heartfelt calls for peace made by both Israelis and Palestinians. During a rally in Tel Aviv to memorialize the 1995 assassination of Prime Minister Yitzhak Rabin by a right-wing Jewish extremist, Gidon was front and center, proudly holding a sign protesting Benjamin (Bibi) Netanyahu. He was activated, all right.

The pride and accomplishment Gidon felt about his role in helping to build Israel was earned honestly, but it was uncomfortable to consider the outcomes we live with today. So many things should have and could have been done differently. The question becomes "What can we do today to make things better?"

One day, Gidon and I drove past a giant billboard urging Israelis to cast their votes for Prime Minister Benjamin Netanyahu in the second election in less than a year. Politics in Israel were boiling over once again, and peace looked even further away than ever before.

"I'm going to write something on that," Gidon muttered darkly. I laughed.

Two days later, a can of spray paint appeared on our dining room table.

"Gidon, you can't be serious!" I imagined Gidon being bundled off to the police station. Then, a second later, I realized he would probably love that because then he could make an even bigger stink.

At three o'clock in the morning, Gidon donned his Batman hoodie (seriously, he has a hoodie with the Batman insignia on it), took the can of spray paint, and crept to the intersection with the billboard.

The next morning, as Israelis hustled down the sidewalk heading to work and soldiers streamed to a nearby base, I stood and gazed upon Gidon's handiwork. He'd crossed out one letter because of a misspelling, but his message was clear: "Enough, Bibi, go home!"

CHAPTER 16

ARCHAEOLOGY

After the near-total destruction of Jewish life and cultural
centers in Europe, American Jewry had become the largest
Jewish community in the world and had begun to integrate
successfully into American life. As suburbs blossomed on the
outskirts of cities, Jewish populations migrated with them and
began to forge new, more modern Jewish American identities
and traditions. Israel, a great source of hope and pride for
American Jews, with its kibbutz system of secular, earthy ideals
of communal and agrarian life, was an attractive destination for
many young American Jews who saw an opportunity to be a part
of history and join the movement of a renewal of Jewish life and
thought. New arrivals were an important part of kibbutz life,
injecting kibbutzim with fresh energy and enthusiasm. Sparks of
romance and disagreement flew as different personalities
encountered one another in such an intense, exhilarating
environment.

In fall 1963, a vivacious, redheaded American woman arrived
on Kibbutz Ha'Zorea. Naomi had come to Israel with her
identical twin sister, Paula, and the two decided to live on
different kibbutzim to foster more independence from one
another. While the two had grown up with Jewish

cultural traditions like celebrating Passover and Chanukah, theirs was a secular home. Naomi and Paula had heard much about Israel through a family friend and, after much discussion, decided to take a gap year ahead of college. They were part of a wave of American youth who headed to Israel in the 1960s to explore their Jewish roots.

The two energetic young Americans had come from the rural, foggy coast of northern California and were fresh out of high school. Being part of a kibbutz—which was such a radical social experiment—and being so far from home was strange and exciting. For Naomi, the culture of Kibbutz Ha'Zorea was quite an adjustment. The kibbutz, founded by the German Werkleute movement in 1936, was known for its "yekkes" ways: intensely ordered and disciplined. For Gidon, this environment was perfect.

One of Gidon's passions was Israeli folk dancing, which he had learned and taught in Canada and continued to teach at Ha'Zorea and for years afterward. He was a nimble dancer and loved the feeling of camaraderie and the raised spirits of the dance. Plus, it was a great way to meet young ladies.

"Though he had met and dated other young women, Gidon was smitten by Naomi's lively, open, warm, American personality." It was our read-aloud time. I glanced tentatively at Gidon, as I always do on sensitive subjects, to gauge his response.

"Say that I was *infatuated* with her," Gidon said from his usual spot on the couch.

Though he had met and dated other young women, Gidon was *infatuated* with Naomi's lively, open, warm, American personality.

I continued to read aloud:

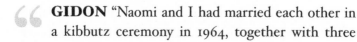 **GIDON** "Naomi and I had married each other in a kibbutz ceremony in 1964, together with three

other couples, and at the time, we felt very much committed to each other. But Naomi was young—only nineteen years old—and, though I was ten years older, I was still very closed-up emotionally, and really not able to take the leap of hope and trust that a loving marriage requires."

I stopped. "Gidon," I said. "This is not enough."
He looked at me questioningly.
"What about your courtship? Where did you meet?"
"I told you, on the kibbutz."
I knew exactly why Gidon had written so little about his early days with Naomi and yet so much about their parting several years later, but I wasn't going to let him off the hook. Excavations would be done. He shuffled to his office and rummaged at length through files and papers. A few minutes later, he returned and handed me a crinkled, handwritten page that had gotten lost in the shuffle. He didn't exactly describe a courtship *per se*, but he noted that, as a couple, they did a lot of hiking and exploring and even participated in a skit of *West Side Story* at Ha'Zorea's Purim festival.

Gidon wrote at length about how he and Naomi went to Masada, the legendary Herodian fortress in the Judaean Desert that overlooks the Dead Sea. (King Herod had four palaces in the Holy Land, and the one atop Masada was just one of them. The other three palaces were in Jerusalem, in the desert outside of Jerusalem and Caesarea, north of Tel Aviv on the sea.) Masada is an awe-inspiring sight, rising out of the desert like a huge mesa with commanding views for miles in all directions. It's a good place for a fortress. Masada is a fascinating archaeological site and the subject of much study, most famously because of the Roman siege of Masada, in 72 to 73 CE, during which the Romans built a ramp and a battering ram to finally access the

Jewish rebels who had fled to safety there. The Romans came up empty but were stirred when they gazed upon the bodies of the 960 men, women, and children who had killed themselves rather than be captured.

Today at Masada, there is an air-conditioned tramway that whisks visitors straight to the top. But that wasn't built until 1971. When Gidon and Naomi visited, they had to set off at 4 a.m. to avoid the heat of the day, bring plenty of water, and navigate the narrow and dangerous hike up the Snake Path, which gains 980 feet in elevation.

In the 1960s, there were extensive excavations in conjunction with Hebrew University and led by famed Israeli archaeologist Yigael Yadin, who also just so happened to be the former military chief of staff and the head of operations in the 1948 War. It was Yadin who greeted Gidon and Naomi when the two reached the top, no doubt breathless, sunburned, dirt-smeared, and sweaty. Yadin warmly welcomed the young couple, who were stunned to meet such a famous figure. Yadin then remarked on the weather, and assumed the two were part of the dig at the cistern. Gidon and Naomi nodded in the affirmative, sidled away to pretend to be archaeologists, and then melted into the dun-colored rocks along with everybody else. They spent a few hours looking around before hiking back down and camping under the stars near the lush waterfall and pools of the oasis of Ein Gedi, on the shores of the Dead Sea.

This is my favorite part of Israel, out in the desert with its jagged, shadowy mountains and hues of gold, taupe, peach, and heather layered over one another in endless shades. The dry heat feels like a weight on your head, which compared to the soupy humidity of the coastal plains in Israel, is a relief. The Dead Sea is the lowest place on earth, at -1,421 feet below sea level; subsequently, the air there is rich in oxygen. The lake is hypersaline, which means that it is so salty that you bob to the surface and stay there. When they say not to get even a drop of the water in your eyes, they mean it. Don't ask me how I know this.

The famous Dead Sea mud is not found just anywhere—only at particular parts of the lake. In other areas, you have to walk up to a quarter of a mile over desiccated mud and large stretches of crusty, white salt to reach the water's edge. I have found, through trial and error, that entering the water backward, behind first, and thinking of yourself as sitting in a chair is the best way to be in the Dead Sea, with its warm, silky water and stunning views of the Judaean Mountains on one side and the Jordanian mountains on the other.

In fact, the border between the two countries runs right down the center of the lake. At night, the glittering lights of small, Jordanian villages are visible, strung along the mountains and going down toward the water. In 1964, when Gidon and Naomi enjoyed their outing, the level of the sea was undoubtedly higher than it is today. For the past few years, the Dead Sea has been shrinking at an alarming rate and there are, resultingly, sinkholes on the roads that surround it, a subject of great ecological concern in Israel and in Jordan (and among the drivers of cars). For many years, there has been a plan to replenish the waters of the Dead Sea by connecting it to the Red Sea, which is about 100 miles to the south. This plan, however, would require the cooperation of the governments of Israel and Jordan, cost approximately $1 billion—no part of which Jordan was willing to pay—and has thus far not happened (although news of it turns up in the paper every couple of years with optimistic reports to the contrary).

Gidon and Naomi also traveled to the Negev Desert to see the craters in that sprawling, parched moonscape that occupies the majority of southern Israel. *Crater* is a little misleading, sounding more like a place where a bomb or meteor made impact; these craters were caused by erosion due to rising and falling geological rifts, ancient seas, and millions of years. Israel has one large crater, Maktesh Ramon, and two smaller ones. Standing on the edge of the 24-mile-long Maktesh Ramon is an almost spiritual experience. Hawks swoop and circle in the silent blue sky, and the jagged, ochre, rocky desert descends about 1,640 feet to the bottom.

It was here in the Negev, at one of the smaller craters, that Gidon and Naomi had an argument that was very emblematic of their relationship in many ways. Gidon had "misjudged the distance and hardship" and "hadn't brought enough water." Naomi, by then pregnant, was very upset.

"To put it mildly," Gidon scrawled on the side of the page. I could only imagine. I would have been pretty upset too.

Gidon tended to go on half-cocked wild goose chases; I'd experienced this myself many times already. I prefer to plan, to have information, to be prepared. Gidon likes to be spontaneous, to figure things out on the fly.

Gidon has a lot of ideas about how to do things that are different from my own and, possibly, that of many people. Call me American, but when I take a shower, I think of that as "me time" in the bathroom. One day, after Gidon had once again come into the bathroom, inquired about whether the water was hot enough, and asked whether he should start some laundry, and questioned whether I minded if he shaved, and reminded me not to forget to buy milk, my usual intense irritation was interrupted by an insight. It was so *obvious* why he didn't see "private time" as an actual thing.

I rushed to join Gidon in the kitchen, where he was examining a moldy piece of cheese he'd found in the refrigerator.

"Gidon, I finally get it. You lived in communal situations

most of your life. First the concentration camp, then in the youth group summer camps, then on a kibbutz, then the army, then raising a large family. No wonder you—"

"Living in a concentration camp is *not* a communal situation," Gidon corrected me, tersely. "We were crowded together twelve in a room, but we didn't *share* things. We fought for every inch of space. You had to take what you could get for yourself to survive."

Oh. Right. Another piece of the puzzle of Gidon Lev fell into place in my mind.

"This is fine by the way," he said, slicing off the mold.

I was beginning to understand Gidon differently; he may have projected a persona of cheerful haplessness, but he was extremely canny and shrewd. He'd had to be. He did what it took to survive, from being thrifty and hardworking to protecting his fragility with carefully curated truths. But don't we all try to protect the most sensitive places in our hearts, the secret zones, the murky places, inarticulate and mysterious?

When it came to his relationship with Naomi and the tragic direction it took, I understood why Gidon had not wanted to think more deeply about this period of time—it's painful to dig into the past. Back in 1964—the year they married—although Naomi and Gidon enjoyed a strong physical attraction and shared many outings and hikes, the tension between the two was already evident. Naomi's young, searching, independent spirit, coupled with this overwhelming new experience, crashed right into the rock-solid determination of Gidon, a fully committed kibbutznik. Naomi was trying to find herself by working in the nursery, orchards, and fields in a new country very, very far from home. Gidon was no longer a shy, out-of-place boy; he had become a focused, hardworking man not especially blessed with the sensitivity and emotional intelligence required in a marriage. Neither understood the past traumas of the other, nor did they discuss them. In that time and place, on a kibbutz, after the war, and just before the Swinging Sixties, looking back was not as important as looking forward.

Now, decades later, Gidon had the luxury of looking back, and I could see small changes in his emotional landscape as he did. He had done something quite courageous and transformative, really, in the process of writing this book. He allowed me to root around in and interrogate his memories. In his willingness to do that, he was revealing himself.

Yet still, for a person who joked about the yekke environment on Ha'Zorea, Gidon was most decidedly himself a yekke. His penchant for obscuring emotions in favor of details was formidable. Though I knew it was one of the most significant events of his life, I had to go through pages and pages of kibbutz and work details to unearth Gidon's writing about the birth of his first child, Maya, in 1965.

 GIDON "On the evening before Pesach (Passover), during the harvesting of the winter wheat, the entire kibbutz went out into the fields, including Naomi, who was due to give birth at any moment. I wasn't sure it was a good idea, but she was a hard worker and she insisted. On our way back from the fields, we stopped in the dining hall and went to the kitchen to fetch something to eat. I heard a scream 'OH, GOD! My water just broke!'

I got the kibbutz jeep, ran for the bag, and we were off to the hospital in Afula. The contractions were coming at five-minute intervals, and as soon as we arrived, the hospital staff took charge. They told me to go sit in the hall and not to worry. I was so excited, I could hardly believe it was happening. In the early hours of the morning of April 18, 1965,

Maya was born. A beautiful baby girl. It was a great joy for both of us, and I loved to participate in taking care of our lovely little baby. At that time, Naomi and I lived up on the hill, quite a distance from the baby house, so at night I would go down and change diapers and feed Maya the night bottle so that Naomi could get a good night's sleep. My mother came to visit us; it was her first grandchild, and I remember we went together to a lovely swimming place in Beit She'an Valley for a picnic. Babies under three months old weren't supposed to leave the kibbutz, so we snuck Maya out in a cardboard banana box."

CHAPTER 17
FROM SPARKS

~~It was yet another oppressively hot summer day when~~
Okay, hold on. Let's just get something out of the way. In the summer, temperatures in Israel range from Regular Hades to Super Hades to Ultra Bonus Hades. Summer starts in May and ends in September. So mostly, it's hot. Very, very hot. Israel is divided laterally, with the coastal side being very Mediterranean, resembling many parts of southern California. It is scrubby and dusty and green, with olive trees, palm trees, orange orchards, and brilliantly colored red, purple, and peach bougainvillea clambering over it all. The other side of Israel is what you probably already imagined: hilly and rocky, full of date orchards, and shimmering with heat reflecting in waves off a vast, scrubby landscape. At least the desert has dry heat. The coastal plain of Israel is so humid in the summertime that you have to shower twice a day or just hose off not to mention carry around handkerchiefs all the time.

Anyway, it was yet another oppressively hot summer day when Gidon took me to visit the kibbutz where he, Naomi, and Maya moved to in 1966 when Maya was just a baby. Kibbutz Zikim is nestled on the Mediterranean coast, about 6 miles south of the seashore city of Ashkelon, where archaeological digs have revealed carbon-dated evidence of a Neolithic settlement almost ten thousand years old. The city was once a seaport, wrested from the Canaanites by the Philistines (the archenemy of the Israelites). Eight miles north of Ashkelon lies another ancient Philistine seaport, today the largest seaport in Israel: Ashdod. This is said to be the place where the Philistines, having previously captured the legendary Ark of the Covenant in battle, then hid the cursed object until a plague of mice and epidemic of tumors beset them after which they promptly returned the Ark to the Israelites. Outside of Indiana Jones, maybe, nobody knows where it is to this day.

Established in 1949 by Romanian Holocaust survivors and members of HaShomer Ha'tzair, Kibbutz Zikim borders the Gaza Strip. The day Gidon and I visited, the barrier wall and buildings in Gaza City were just visible through the shimmering heat and thick smoke. As Gidon and I arrived at the kibbutz, firefighters were everywhere, trying to beat back the flames. Thousands of acres of land were burning throughout southern Israel as Palestinians in Gaza protested their terrible conditions by sending kites and balloons tied to rudimentary incendiary devices and flammable materials over the barrier wall to set the fields afire. In a cycle as regular as the seasons, the country was on fire once more. "Zikim," which means *sparks*, was aptly named. The name came from a quote by Alexander Pushkin: "From sparks shall come a flame." Pushkin had no idea just how true this could be, figuratively and literally.

As Gidon and I toured the quiet, smoky kibbutz, it was clear to me that the place had seen better days. The grass was lumpy and dry, and evidence of its nearness to rockets coming from Gaza was everywhere. Emergency bunkers dotted the kibbutz, where reinforced concrete protected communal buildings. While previously an agricultural kibbutz, today Zikim is semiprivatized and manufactures mattresses. The dairy where Gidon worked is still in full use, though, and we found our way to it by the pungent odor. I refused to get out of the car.

This was not the first dairy Gidon had taken me to. During such visits, he beamed with pride as he viewed the cows, calmly chewing their cuds or lined up at milking machines, while I tried to be interested, meanwhile thinking that this was gross, stinky, and inhumane. Be that as it may, whenever we are near a dairy barn in Israel, Gidon pulls over and wistfully takes it all in. Very often he is recognized and greeted with backslaps and shouts by barn workers who remembered him from his younger days on and off a kibbutz, as a dairyman and later as a milk tester of hardworking repute.

In 1966, when Naomi, Gidon, and Maya relocated to Zikim, the border between the kibbutz and Gaza was marked simply by signs; no fence or walls had yet been built. The kibbutz, established only seventeen years earlier, had planted avocado, mango, and loquat trees and built one of the most modern dairy barns in Israel. They also raised chickens for the local market. Because HaShomer Ha'tzair was so left-leaning, Gidon told me, Kibbutz Zikim was jokingly known as "the last outpost with a red flag before Cairo."

 GIDON "Naomi, little Maya, and I arrived there in the fall of 1966 as part of a group of ten members from Ha'Zorea to help Zikim add more cultural activities. The members of the kibbutz welcomed us very warmly and went out of their way to make us feel at home there. There was not a single area of this kibbutz's life that did not need help, and we had all come to do just that. Whereas in Ha'Zorea everything was well established, organized, and order ruled supreme, here in Zikim, everything was, to put it mildly, fluid. For example, let us say that Naomi was scheduled to work in the kitchen starting at 6:30 a.m. At 6 a.m., the work manager (*sadran avodah*—responsible for assigning work duties for the members) would rush to our room and inform Naomi that he was sorry, but so-and-so felt ill and couldn't work in the children's house, so she had to go help out there instead. True, this kind of a situation can happen any time and any place, but when this occurs very often, it is disruptive and causes a lot of tension among the members.

Zikim needed help in all areas of their communal life, be it in the workforce, administration, cultural activities, or social problems, and we readily tried to do the best we could. Within a week of our arrival, I started a weekly folk dance evening. Naomi and I both helped to plan and participate in cultural activities such as organizing holiday celebrations and Friday night *Oneg Shabbat* activities. For the two of us, it was challenging and felt as if we were starting anew, not only in general but also in our personal relationship, which took a turn for the better. We felt good and were happy."

After the War of Independence in 1948, kibbutzim bordering Arab land were reinforced and new ones established to help secure the borders. Zikim was just one such of these border kibbutzim, situated on the land of the depopulated Palestinian village of Hiribya.

"They weren't depopulated. They *fled*," Gidon interjected.

Here we went again with this argument. I asked Gidon whether it ever struck him as odd that the kibbutz was located on a former Palestinian village or whether the conditions in Gaza ever niggled at his conscience, with so many refugees crowded into a too-small space, so near to the bucolic kibbutz.

Gidon replied vehemently, "I came to this country almost sixty years ago, and my idea of a country and Zionism and socialism and democracy and equality was at the top of my beliefs. I had no qualms about going into the army. I felt, we got this piece of land, and I was prepared to defend and die for it."

"Okay, okay, okay," I said, weighing whether to dwell on the subject. I knew that Gidon is a liberal thinker, and I knew that he came by his point of view the way we all did: through life experience. I decided that it's not worth beating Gidon over the head about not just the larger picture between Israelis and Palestinians but also about the proximity of Gaza to Zikim and what he should have been thinking about or doing, according to me. It's so easy to judge someone else for their past actions, inactions, and/or views. I wondered what I was doing in that red-hot minute, to address the social issues of this time, of my time?

On Kibbutz Ha'Zorea, volunteers and college kids—Jewish or not—the practice of exchanging a temporary farming experience for room and board was not allowed unless they also signed up for the *Ulpan* (Hebrew learning) program. Zikim, however, did not have this requirement and was generally a more relaxed, socially engaging environment. In some cases, enduring, lifelong friendships were made. Gidon didn't know it yet, but some of these friendships would later prove invaluable to him.

 GIDON "Life in Zikim was less rigid, less constrained than it had been in Ha'Zorea. It was more relaxed, perhaps at times too much so! Our sweet little daughter, Maya, found herself in the baby house, together with three other babies her age (nine to eleven months old), and she seemed happy and content, with a very devoted and experienced baby nurse looking after her and the other babies from morning to 4 p.m. At 4 o'clock in the afternoon, having showered and cleaned myself up, I went to the baby house and brought Maya home to our room. If I was not able to do so, Naomi went. We spent the next three and a half hours together playing, taking walks, or whatever. It was the time to be together as a family, and we loved it!

From time to time, we even took walks to the cow barn, and Maya would help me feed the newborn calves, which hardly knew how to eat or drink their milk. After a few months, we so enjoyed the more relaxed atmosphere in Zikim, that Naomi and I decided to make it our permanent home, and we became full voting members of the kibbutz. I had my work cut out for me in the dairy barn, where I was in charge of raising the calves, while Naomi found her work in the expanding avocado, mango, and loquat orchards hard but rewarding."

One day, Gidon and I took a break from working on the book and went to Mini Israel, a kitschy theme park that boasts a walkable map of the country of Israel in miniature. By the look of the empty parking lot, we were not in for a treat. We trooped through the byways and paths, peering at Mini Haifa, Mini Acre, and Mini Jerusalem. The kibbutz section was big—probably the most developed—with tiny orange orchards and barns with mooing cows and little people dancing the hora. There were motion sensors so that music or other sound effects suddenly blasted out of the bushes; the tolling of bells, folk music, the call of the muezzin, even the *plonk plonk* of *matkot*, the Israeli paddle ball game played on the beach in Tel Aviv. Decked out in his Batman hoodie, Gidon was some distance behind me, peering like Gulliver down upon the country of his dreams, now rendered in chipped painted plastic and carved Styrofoam.

I thought, *How insensitive of me to have brought him here!* To view the country that Gidon fought so hard to live and be in, after all he's gone through, as a roadside attraction! How awful, yet how wonderful and weird this whole book must be for Gidon, to be walked back through his life like it was a theme park: the Holocaust Trauma, the Kibbutz World, the Marriage Experience, the Six-Day War.

I went to Gidon and took his arm. "Let's get going."

He looked at me brightly. "I am just amazed by this!" He pointed to the teeny model of Masada. "Look! The cistern is right there!"

After Israel's victory in the 1948 war, the mood among Arab nations surrounding Israel was one of vengeance. The loss had been a humiliation, and Israel's enemies needed to regroup. By way of exerting influence in the Middle East, the Russians supplied Egypt, in particular, with formidable arms. This habit of supplying arms to various and changeable allies for the purpose of geopolitical influence continues today. Obviously.

The first mission of the United Nations Peacekeepers was to send peacekeepers or "blue helmets" (or, as they are called in Israel, "smurfs") to Israel to watch over the border areas after the uneasy ceasefire of 1948. Their white UN jeeps remain a common sight in Jerusalem, in the Golan Heights, and on the Lebanese border today.

Tensions between Israel and Egypt in the 1950s and 60s were particularly tense. In 1956 Egypt closed the strategic Straits of Tiran, a much-needed shipping route for Israel that lies between the Saudi and Sinai peninsulas. On the same day, Gamal Abdel Nasser Hussein, the second president of Egypt, closed the Suez Canal to Israel.

The Suez Canal is 120 miles long and connects the Mediterranean Sea to the Red Sea. This does not sound particularly exciting until you realize that the canal shaved 5,500 miles off the usual trade route from Europe to East Asia, making unnecessary the journey over and around the African continent. A whole new world of efficient shipping trade was made possible. Built between 1859 and 1869 by the Suez Canal Company, the canal was jointly owned by French, Egyptian, and Ottoman interests, which mostly means a certain Saīd Pasha, an Ottoman statesman and politician. In 1869, plans were made to create a colossal neoclassical sculpture that also would serve as a lighthouse. Designed by French sculptor Frédéric Auguste Bartholdi, the sculpture would be of a robed woman holding a torch and was to be called *Egypt Carrying the Light to Asia*. Bartholdi's bid was not accepted. In 1886, the same statue, now called *Liberty Enlightening the World*, was inaugurated in New York Harbor.

The Suez Canal, meant to be an international shipping waterway, was often a problematic point of contention between the Egyptians, the French, and the British. In 1967, Nasser closed the Suez Canal to all shipping, in part by scuttling ships and stopping the dredging that was needed for its maintenance. This closure rocked the world economy and resulted in the stranding of a motley collection of fifteen shipping vessels hailing variously from the UK, Poland, Czechoslovakia, Bulgaria, France, Sweden, the United States, and West Germany.

In the Middle East, saber-rattling is a Kabuki performance, a battle of words, which occurs cyclically and is meant to assert leadership badassery by way of assuring the public that their enemy will not just be defeated but humiliated and destroyed— annihilated on a biblical scale—and that their blood would flow into the sea. I mean, it's *really* dramatic.

In *Like Dreamers*, Yossi Klein Halevi writes of the anti-Israel sentiment brewing all around Israel in the months and weeks preceding the Six-Day War of 1967.

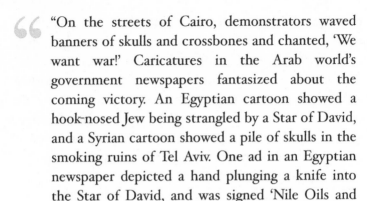

> "On the streets of Cairo, demonstrators waved banners of skulls and crossbones and chanted, 'We want war!' Caricatures in the Arab world's government newspapers fantasized about the coming victory. An Egyptian cartoon showed a hook-nosed Jew being strangled by a Star of David, and a Syrian cartoon showed a pile of skulls in the smoking ruins of Tel Aviv. One ad in an Egyptian newspaper depicted a hand plunging a knife into the Star of David, and was signed 'Nile Oils and Soaps Company'."

This was some serious saber-rattling, and it was backed by sobering evidence. Israeli intelligence indicated that Egypt, Jordan, and Syria were well-armed and massing on Israel's borders. Israelis were frightened: the army was on high alert and the reserves put on notice. The numbers of soldiers Israel could mobilize amounted to about 250,000, but Arab forces, combined, had double the amount of soldiers and three times as many planes and tanks. Israel would need a serious miracle to survive. In Tel Aviv, plans were drawn up to use parks and other public places to dig deep pits for the mass graves of the inevitable casualties of a devastating war. All reserves were called up. For Israelis, spring 1967 was a terrifying time.

> **GIDON** "In the early days of spring 1967, there was a definite feeling of doomsday approaching. The Syrians, in the north, on the Golan Heights, were moving more and more troops, artillery, and armor, and there were more incidents of sporadic shooting into Israeli towns and kibbutzim and the valley below Golan. The Jordanians, with their well-entrenched and highly trained (by British officers) army, lobbed mortars into Israeli-controlled West

Jerusalem. But it was Nasser's huge Egyptian army that posed the greatest danger to our existence. They were moving huge forces into the Sinai Peninsula, reinforcing their positions in the Gaza Strip, and were being supplied by untold amounts of armor, planes, and munitions by the Russians, who had their own geopolitical ambitions! All border kibbutzim were given instructions to reinforce their existing bunkers and to dig trenches connecting our living quarters to the children's area, the dining hall, the chicken coops, and other work areas. Volunteers arrived from the cities, and other kibbutzim, and it seemed like Kibbutz Zikim, was one large army post. Since our fields were next to the Gaza Strip, which was Egyptian territory, we were very vulnerable. It was made clear to us how vulnerable we were when, one night, four of our tractors were blown up in the fields."

"Whoa, trenches? Explosions? How were you not absolutely terrified?"

Gidon and I had just seen the Sam Mendes film *1917*, set in the trenches of the First World War. I couldn't comprehend that Kibbutz Zikim, quiet, rural, and peaceful as it is today, was actually in a war zone with trenches.

It was read-aloud time, but Gidon wasn't really paying attention. He stared grimly at the ceiling of our bedroom, his eyes carefully scanning while he held a red fly swatter shaped like a chubby hand. He looked like Albert Einstein, with his white hair tousled. He needed a haircut.

"THERE! No. THERE! Missed it. THERE! No." He was going to get this mosquito if it killed him. Fair enough: that little jerk had definitely binged on both of us. You'd think that if Israel could build a rocket to go to the moon, we also could have screens on our windows for the ubiquitous mosquitoes. Of course, the rocket didn't make it to the moon, so . . .

~

I couldn't imagine what it must have been like to live with such big threats so nearby. But then, everybody in Israel has a bomb shelter of one kind or another. Beginning in 1951, Israel began instituting a civil defense system. Residential buildings are required to have large bomb shelters on the basement level, spacious enough to pack in everybody in the building all at once. The shelter in the building where Gidon and I live is quite large —or it would be were it not illegally crammed with the extra stuff of ours and our neighbors, like suitcases, boxes of clothing, and scuba gear. The steel door to get into the shelter has a big iron handle that must be turned just so and bars that lock the door from the inside. There is a fresh-air ventilation system, a toilet, a sink, and even two showerheads. Israelis are accustomed to meeting each other on stairwells and in shelters in various stages of undress. Newer buildings have safe rooms, or *mamads*, which have reinforced steel doors, reinforced concrete walls, one steel-shuttered window, and a ventilation system. Israelis being Israelis, these rooms often double as offices, guest rooms, or playrooms.

Bomb shelters come in all manner of styles here. In the southern part of Israel, bordering Gaza, the bus stops are cupped by reinforced concrete, creating odd, hunched shapes along the road. Many kibbutzim have underground bunkers that initially look like either a huge pile of rocks or a badly designed concrete something-or-other with a loudspeaker attached to the top. The Dizengoff Center in Tel Aviv, a large shopping mall, has a nuclear bomb shelter in its bowels with enough room to shelter more than two thousand people. There are many such cavernous shelters underneath public buildings in Israel, reflecting the collective ability of a society to acclimate to war as a part of everyday life.

~

Smack. Got him!

Satisfied that he had eradicated our winged tormentor, Gidon explained to me that the trenches on Kibbutz Zikim were not nearly as elaborate as those used during the First World War, but that they were about as deep and lined with planks to keep from caving in. How backbreaking it must have been to build them, and in such sandy soil. I asked why the scars of the trenches were not visible when we had visited Zikim.

Gidon only shrugged. "Guess they were planted over." The grass was a bit lumpy in places, now that I thought about it.

GIDON "We all received emergency call-up codes, and by the 15th of May, we said goodbye to our families. I reported to my northern unit in Tsfat, just north of Tiberias. After receiving my army gear and meeting my reserve unit squad and company, we set out in a long convoy to the Syrian border in the north. Finally, we arrived at our assigned area. It was just north of Tiberias, near Lake Kinneret, where, a few hundred yards away, the underground pumps were supplying water to the rest of the country. Our assignment was clear: to prevent the Syrians from capturing this very vital area of the pumping station.

As soon as we arrived, we were given picks, shovels, and sledge hammers and, for the next two weeks, dug trenches, dugouts, and artillery launch positions. In this terrain, we dug through a bit of earth, but a lot of hard black basalt rocks. As a squad commander, I was overseeing this task, and every time I thought that we finally finished digging, another officer would arrive and make changes so we would have to continue to dig and dig again. Our hands were so covered with blisters that, if the Syrians had attacked us at that moment, we would hardly be able to squeeze the triggers of our machine guns or rifles to defend ourselves.

While we were digging in and strengthening our positions in the north, along the border with Jordan and Syria, up to the Hermon Mountains, Egypt expelled the U.N. from the Gaza Strip and closed the Tiran Straits (near the Red Sea), effectively shutting Israel off from any help and supplies it might get from the south. Egyptian forces were advancing in Sinai toward our border. It felt very, very claustrophobic and threatening— and it was! Then, in the early morning of June 6, 1967, we heard the news that the Israeli Air Force had taken to the sky and was attacking the huge convoys of Egyptian forces in Sinai. They were also going for the Egyptian airfields in Egypt itself and rendering them unusable. One can only imagine the tremendous relief and joy we all felt on hearing this news. This preemptive strike was most definitely the right way to go; otherwise, the very existence of the state of Israel was in danger.

The air force also attacked in the north and, together with the armored division and the infantry, made quick progress against the Syrians. Where my unit was dug in, we held our positions, expecting an imminent attack. The next night, we heard the rumbling of the tanks and other armed vehicles and thought 'Okay. Here they come!'

We were as ready as we could be, but nothing happened. At 5 a.m., just as the first light came in the eastern sky, we were commanded to get out of our trenches and start to advance down toward the Syrian border, which was just a few hundred yards away, across the Jordan River. Turns out, the noise we heard was the Syrians retreating from the valley below us. When we arrived at the Jordan River, the water was really turbulent. Some ropes were stretched across the river, and we were ordered to cross.

This was a disaster. We had never crossed or practiced crossing a river. We were to hold our weapons out of the water's reach, but that was next to impossible. Some of us not only fell and lost our weapons, but also our shoes or trousers. Tragically, a number of soldiers drowned. Had the Syrians just set up one or two machine gun nests across the river, they could have finished us all off with ease. Luckily for us, they had made a hurried retreat—both the army and the villagers—and we entered the village and army camp encountering no opposition at all. In the army camp, we found cases and cases of arms, boxes of ammunition still unopened, and even heavier weapons; it was amazing. Some, not very many, of our soldiers tried to do some looting, but were quickly stopped and even court-martialed! I found myself a pair of army pants, since mine had floated away in the waters of the Jordan River. To think back today that I and many others crossed the Jordan in our underpants isn't just funny, it's embarrassing!

There were some Syrian strongholds that did fight back and, in a couple of instances, caused us heavy losses. But, on the whole, it was not a difficult battle, and we made it all the way to Kunetra, the biggest town on the Golan Heights.

It became quite clear that this area was essentially a very large army camp, and the civilian population was mainly in the far north, and almost all Druze Arabs, not part of the Syrian entrenchment.

The fighting ended, and it turned out to be the biggest victory we had ever won, against three Arab armies. My thinking at the time was, 'Well, now that we have captured so much of their territory, hopefully we can use this as a negotiating tool and, once and for all, make peace and become an integral part of the Middle East.' How naive and foolish I was, looking back at the past fifty or so years!"

The war was a rout. Israel not only destroyed the Egyptian air force as it sat on the ground but also controlled the key territories of the Golan Heights and Sinai and, importantly, reunited Jerusalem. Israel also took control of Gaza from Egypt and began its occupation of the West Bank. Israelis were exhilarated and relieved. The war, it seemed to them, was an acid test: do or die.

When I asked Gidon about whether he was frightened during this time, he didn't recall fear, just implacable focus. This determined stance of defending a country despite a clear imbalance in arms was fueled by innovation, courage, and desperation, too. There was nowhere for Israelis to go except the clear blue sea, a place that their enemies repeatedly and graphically threatened them with. But it was not to be. Not this time. Once more, the table was already set for the next confrontation between Israel and its neighbors.

~

Gidon came back home from army reserve duty, and a few weeks later, he, Naomi, and Maya visited the United States to spend time with Naomi's family in northern California. Everything was changing. With the war over, the map of Israel had been fundamentally redrawn. Israel had captured Sinai, the Golan Heights, Jerusalem, and the West Bank up to the Jordan River. Israelis celebrated another unlikely victory. They were euphoric; it had been a very close call. For Gidon, the Six-Day War reaffirmed his belief in Israel and in his life there. But even the fragrant loquat and mango orchards of Kibbutz Zikim could not hide the fact that the stage was set for future conflict, not just for Israel, but for Gidon, Naomi, Maya, and now, a son, Yanai, born less than a year after the end of the war in May 1968.

CHAPTER 19
THINGS FALL APART

In 1970, E. M. Forster died, the Aswan Dam was completed in Egypt, and I started the first grade in a tiny rural town in northern California. The Who performed "Tommy" at the Metropolitan Opera House in New York, with one Met fan suggesting they change their name, for the day, to The Whom. The Ford Pinto was introduced, and Monday Night Football debuted on ABC. Egyptian president Gamal Abdel Nasser died and was replaced by Anwar Sadat. Joni Mitchell's "Big Yellow Taxi" was a hit, and late in June of that summer, Gidon was only days away from the most painful event of his life.

Hamelin Town's in Brunswick,
By famous Hanover city;
The river Weser, deep and wide,
Washes its wall on the southern side;
A pleasanter spot you never spied;
But, when begins my ditty,
Almost five hundred years ago,
To see the townsfolk suffer so

From vermin, was a pity.

*"The Pied Piper of Hamelin" by Robert
Browning*

My impatience rose, but I quelled it. This was a serious monkey-butt moment. Gidon had read "The Pied Piper of Hamelin" by Robert Browning so. Many. Times. What if I were just to calm my ever-busy brain and listen? I let the words in Gidon's soft cadence and slight but distinctive accent wash over me as he read, tenderly, as if for the first time:

Rats!
They fought the dogs and killed the cats,
And bit the babies in the cradles,
And eat the cheeses out of the vats,
And licked the soup from the cooks' own
ladles,
Split open the kegs of salted sprats,
Made nests inside men's Sunday hats,
And even spoiled the women's chats
By drowning their speaking
With shrieking and squeaking
In fifty different sharps and flats.

"So what's the poem all about?" Gidon asked me rhetorically at the poem's end, as was his habit.
"That—"
"That you should keep your promises," Gidon said confidently.

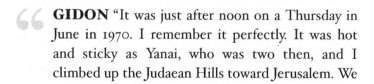 **GIDON** "It was just after noon on a Thursday in June in 1970. I remember it perfectly. It was hot and sticky as Yanai, who was two then, and I climbed up the Judaean Hills toward Jerusalem. We

could feel the cooler air as we got closer to Jerusalem. Yanai's red, curly hair blew in the wind as he sat in his booster seat in the back of our kibbutz-owned car. We were headed to a visit with my sweet, five-year-old daughter Maya and her mom, Naomi, who had been living in Jerusalem for most of the year, with her old boyfriend who had arrived from America."

The marriage between Gidon and Naomi fell apart incrementally but dramatically. The couple had split up and hammered out their own unusual, extralegal custody agreement. Gidon would keep Yanai and stay on Kibbutz Zikim while Naomi kept Maya and lived in Jerusalem with an American boyfriend with whom she had reignited romantic ties, and by whom she had become pregnant. It was a fragile peace and a precarious situation doomed to fail spectacularly.

 GIDON "As I was driving, Yanai had a constant flow of questions. 'Dad, why are those cows just sitting there?' 'What is that big green machine doing?' 'Where are those goats going?' and so on. I tried as best as I could to give him some explanations and not to discourage his inquisitiveness. I thought it was healthy and good to ask questions, not having done so myself when I was a child.

Traveling by way of the back road to Jerusalem is a shortcut and a great deal more interesting. We passed by a number of small Jewish settlements that were within the 'Green Line' (in pre-1967 Israel), one of them being Tzur Hadassah, where Naomi's identical, twin red-headed sister, Paula, resided with her husband. Sometimes on our way to Jerusalem, we stopped by for a short visit, a cookie, a cup of tea, and a short chat; we were good friends. Today, however, it was a bit later than usual, and I was anxious to see and spend time with Maya, and I am sure Naomi was looking forward to spending time with little Yanai.

Since Naomi and I had parted ways, we made an arrangement that once a month, I came to Jerusalem with Yanai, and spent about three hours with Maya while Naomi did the same with Yanai, of course. We would go for a walk to the nearest park, talk about past good times we had together and how much I missed her. Maya would tell me about her preschool day care center, what she did there, her friends, and other activities, but we did not talk about what was going on between her mother and me. Foolishly, in retrospect, I did not ask her about her family life in Jerusalem.

I loved this child of mine, with her long, blondish hair, petite body, lovely blue-green eyes, and quick intelligence; she was so lovely that it broke my heart that her mother and I had created this ridiculous situation.

Our three hours together were up, and, slowly, hand-in-hand, Maya and I walked back to Naomi's apartment. This time, by previous arrangement, I was, for the first time ever, leaving Yanai at Naomi's for the weekend, a payback arrangement for when Naomi, three weeks earlier, had left Maya with me at the kibbutz for the weekend, which was, of course, wonderful for all of us. I have lovely photos, to this day, of how we spent time playing in the sand dunes at Zikim.

Returning with Maya to Naomi's apartment, I picked up on some nebulous, heightened tension there but put it up to the hubbub of all of us being

in such a small apartment and Naomi's being eight
months pregnant. While eating a bowl of soup that
Naomi kindly provided me with, I remember being
struck by the sudden appearance of a buyer for
their VW bug and was told that because of their
growing family, Naomi and her boyfriend were
selling their car to buy something larger. It made
sense to me. Nothing more was said about it, I
hugged Maya and Yanai goodbye, and told them
that I would be back, of course, on Sunday to pick
up Yanai and take him back to Zikim. With
somewhat of a heavy heart, I returned to Kibbutz
Zikim, where another kibbutz member was
anxiously waiting for the car. I had mixed feelings
about my weekend off. On the one hand, it was
nice to be free for the first time in a year, but on
the other hand, I felt a bit lonely and forlorn
without either of my kids."

Gidon returned to Kibbutz Zikim and set to making
weekend plans for himself. On his list was a visit with an
intelligent, outgoing American brunette named Susan with
whom he had been friends for some time. To Gidon's great
disappointment, Susan begged off. Instead, Gidon went to
Kibbutz Ha'Zorea, where he met with old friends, made new
ones, enjoyed the food in the dining hall, and went on a hike in
the forest. But he was lonely. He couldn't wait for the weekend
to be over.

 GIDON "I remember that drive back to Naomi's
house. I had an uneasy feeling, and I didn't know
why. Even after I parked the car and entered the
building, my foreboding grew. It seemed quieter
than usual. Was everyone at work and the kids
already in school? Why didn't I hear Yanai? I came

to Naomi's apartment and noticed a note on the door, in an envelope, addressed to me. With shaking hands and a feeling of dread, I opened it and read the short note: 'We have gone to America.' My children were gone. I was in shock. There was no phone number and no address, nothing. My hands shaking, I noticed something rattling in the envelope: the key to the apartment. I opened the door. The place that I had visited only a day before was totally empty. Not a soul. No furniture, no pictures, nothing. The apartment was totally bare, down to the walls.

I slumped down on the floor and remembered how devastated I had been, so many years ago, when, after praying day after day, for weeks on end, to Dear God, to PLEASE bring my dad back, and it did not happen. My mother had been unable to comfort me or hug me or do anything to help me overcome my anguish. And now, here again, I found myself lost, abandoned, all on my own. It was so painful, that even today, forty-nine years later, I can hardly describe how I felt at that terrible moment.

How could Naomi have done such a thing? This must have been planned meticulously, I thought, as I stared around the empty apartment. How could I not have seen this coming?

I cried, I banged my head against the wall, and I slumped down and tears ran down my cheeks. At that moment, I had no idea what to do or how to go on living."

What happened that day in Jerusalem in 1970 couldn't have happened to a person less emotionally equipped to deal with it. Any parent would be devastated by the chain of events that

Gidon experienced, and in his pain and panic, he found himself triggered, in the parlance of today, once more feeling the bottomless insecurity, loss, and abandonment that he had experienced throughout his childhood. It made perfect, terrible sense that the most painful story in Gidon's life was a blow that stripped him of his agency, worth, and purpose. I could only imagine the deep sense of betrayal that Gidon must have felt, the anger, disbelief, and humiliation. On top of that, the wrenching feeling of being so starkly alone in Israel after having built a family. But the family Gidon and Naomi had built a bit hastily was vulnerable to such things given the shaky emotional foundations of the marriage. And the fact that, while Israel was Gidon's long-dreamed home—a place that would be unthinkable to leave—for Naomi, it had been but a chapter in her life. The relationship had ended, and Naomi felt trapped in Israel. She wanted to go back home to California.

 GIDON "As the reality set in, I realized that this must have been her plan, a long time in the making, orchestrated meticulously without Maya's knowledge. Now anger, disbelief, and anguish, and a terrible loneliness gripped me. Since the time I had lost my father, I had not felt like this.

What could I do? Slowly, I got my brain to work again and knocked on some neighbor's doors. I was told that, yes, Naomi and her boyfriend had moved out yesterday afternoon and, as far as they knew, were heading for the airport with a half a dozen or so suitcases."

Gidon returned to Kibbutz Zikim and told the stunned kibbutz members what had happened. There were a lot of questions. He found out that Naomi, her boyfriend, and the kids had, indeed, boarded an American Airlines flight the previous Saturday evening using his forged signature on the document allowing Yanai to be added to his mother's passport. Gidon recalled that a few weeks prior he could not find his ID card, but then it mysteriously showed up again, in an unmarked envelope. Had Naomi stolen it to forge his signature? His sense of betrayal deepened as Gidon thought back over his interactions with Naomi in the previous weeks and months. What happened had been meticulously planned; it wasn't a heat-of-the-moment kind of thing.

What happened here? Why did Naomi do such a thing? I went over it in my mind. I tried to put myself in her shoes. Why didn't this couple go to a social worker or hire a mediator if things were so bad between them regarding the custody of the children? Wasn't there something that could have been done differently? Of course there was. There always is. But that's not really how life goes, is it? I had my own regrets, my own bad decisions—so many things that I should or could have done differently.

 GIDON "I asked myself, 'What shall I do? Where to start? What can be done? How will I find them?' I called Interpol, but they told me that because Naomi was the kid's mother, there was nothing they could do. I had a meeting with the Kibbutz Secretariat, and the Kibbutz fully supported me and gave me money for the flight to the United States, with their blessing and a great deal of hope that I would find Maya and Yanai and manage to bring them back to Kibbutz Zikim."

It was forty-eight years later on a warm, dusky Israeli evening, the kind that made me love living here. All around were the sights and sounds of celebration. Children playing, jugglers performing. Fragrant food being served and festive music playing. And the stars were just beginning to appear, one by one, in the mauve sky. Egyptian fruit bats swooped overhead. There was a family wedding on Kibbutz Mishmar Ha'Emek. Noi, Gidon and Naomi's grandson, was getting married. Naomi was seventy-three years old by that time; she still had the red hair, now tinged with gray, and the petite frame that she had almost fifty years ago. We were seated at the same table. This wasn't the first time Gidon and Naomi had seen each other since those terrible days—far from it. They treated each other with a slightly forced cordiality but not much more than that. I harbored a crazy hope that maybe this book would heal the two, just a little tiny bit.

Naomi was polite but understandably wary of me; she didn't know me from Adam, and she knew I had been writing a book about Gidon's life. Two strikes. I didn't know what to say to her. I just wanted to understand. I wanted to tell Naomi, to reassure her, that Gidon's book would be no worshipful hagiography, nor an indictment of her. But it was not the time for a conversation like that.

I would never understand the landscape of her relationship with Gidon. That was something between them. Naomi didn't know it, but I understood her on a certain level. I, too, had made choices and mistakes that caused a lot of hurt. I understood following your heart, and I sure as hell understood regret. I know there are two sides to every story.

But this is the story that I am telling now.

CHAPTER 20
PAVED OVER PARADISE

Gidon and I were stuck in a traffic jam in an Arab-Israeli village called Tira. It was crowded; the *shuk* (outdoor market) is very large and had become a well-known place to visit and shop for fresh fruit, vegetables, spices, halvah, and an assortment of clothes and cheap electronics. The streets of the village are not designed for such crowds, and Gidon and I crawled forward at a snail's pace. We were just trying to go home. We were in the eastern part of central Israel, near the Samarian hills, on the Israeli side of the Green Line, but just barely.

The so-called Green Line in Israel is not actually green and is not visible to the naked eye. It's the 1949 Armistice Line (originally drawn in green on the map, thus the name) that serves to demarcate the border between Israel and Palestine. Tira lies within the Triangle, a concentrated area of Arab-Israeli villages that includes larger villages such as Qalqilya and Tayibe. During the Crusades, Tira was owned by the Order of St. John, which claimed a connection to the Knights Hospitaller, a chivalric order founded in the twelfth century by the Blessed Gerard in medieval Jerusalem. I wondered about this Blessed Gerard and many other blessed Crusaders and what went through their minds as they marched through this strange country and snatched it up, looking for treasure and salvation.

"But Gidon, what about the kids?" I asked.

Our small car was redolent with the scents of the fresh tangerines, strawberries, and cardamom we bought at the shuk. Perhaps it was good that we were stuck in traffic, unable to look at each other directly; we were discussing a very sensitive subject. I was floored that Gidon was encouraged by every authority and professional he spoke with to simply get the kids back, plain and simple. I hadn't been able to make it work in my head—this total lack of concern for the welfare of the children, much less a protocol for lawyers, detectives, consulate employees, and police both in Israel and in the United States.

"It was a different time," Gidon said.

I couldn't wait to get home to research this, but I was already pretty sure that the rights of parents and, importantly, of children were nearly nonexistent almost fifty years ago. In 1980, the Hague Abduction Convention adopted a multilateral treaty for such cases. Israel did not sign the treaty until 1991. I found the country profile for Israel on the Hague website and skimmed through forty-six pages of the PDF showing contact information and steps to take before I reminded myself that I was obsessing. These forms and steps simply didn't exist at the time.

Times were different, and Gidon was different then, too. In 1970, at age thirty-five, he was carrying a very heavy load of unexamined Holocaust trauma. He was so deeply distressed by the sudden disappearance of his children that he wasn't able to stop himself from his own worst, most triggered impulses: to make this right, immediately, no matter what.

I asked Gidon whether he went to the U.S. embassy to report what had happened. He hadn't. I couldn't imagine that the U.S. embassy would have done much, anyway. Naomi was a U.S. citizen, but a family dispute would surely be pretty low on the embassy's priority list. The trouble with international child abduction is that it's extremely difficult to pursue in a meaningful or timely way. For fathers, this task can be even more difficult. Once children are taken over a border—that's the tricky part—they can simply vanish, leaving the other parent more or less helpless. Authorities, in other words, were not particularly equipped—then or now—for the terrible situation Gidon had found himself in. "Possession," John Lennon once said, "isn't nine-tenths of the law, it's nine-tenths of the problem."

Five days after the kids had disappeared, Gidon landed in New York and went to the home of his second cousin, John. Using an address book that Naomi had inadvertently left in the home she and Gidon formerly shared on Kibbutz Zikim, John called Naomi's parents and said he'd heard from Gidon in Israel; he wanted to know where his children were. What John didn't say was that Gidon was beside him as they made the call and that he was listening in. It became clear from the call that Naomi was either already at or headed toward her parents' home in northern California, even as they spoke.

Gidon went to the Israeli consulate in New York and was told that if he could find his children, they would issue all the relevant documents and help him get home again. So he caught a flight to California and met with friends who had worked as volunteers on Kibbutz Zikim. With a place to stay and plenty of support and encouragement, Gidon was introduced to a family law attorney. Judging from the spacious office with a panoramic view of San Francisco, this lawyer was no slouch. The attorney reiterated the same advice: Get the children. Fast. But first, the attorney counseled, Gidon would need to hire a private detective.

In my mind's eye, I pictured some kind of Quentin Tarantino movie character, a guy with sideburns and a polyester suit. Gidon's description of the encounter did nothing to dispel my imaginings.

GIDON "The agency was located in a small, three-story building, on the ground floor, with a sign advertising a private detective agency. I entered, and a young woman received me on the main floor of the building, with hundreds of files everywhere. People came in and went out nonstop. After a while, a tall, stocky man invited me into his office, which was actually not a real office but a furnished basement lined on all sides with electronics. I told him what happened, and he asked me a very important question: Was I sure that I knew where the kids were? I needed to be sure before we could put a plan into action. The fee for this plan was $1,500."

The plan was this: Go to where Naomi and the kids were, with two cars, one for each child. Get the kids. Drive to the nearest private airport, where Gidon would be waiting, get in a private plane, and fly over the state line into Nevada.

"From there," Gidon told me, "I was on my own." One thousand five hundred dollars didn't strike me as a ton of money for such an elaborate plan, although it is almost $10,000 in today's dollars. But that wasn't the part that got to me.

"What does 'get the kids' mean, Gidon?" I demanded. "Who was going to 'get' them, and how?"

"Well, I don't know. The detectives, I guess."

"Just knock on the front door and take the children?" I was absolutely floored. I loved Gidon to pieces, and I knew this topic was very hard for him to discuss, but I was definitely judging. What would I have done? Not this, I thought. There was a line. But how could I possibly judge Gidon or Naomi, all these many years later?

All Gidon knew was that he needed $1,500—and fast. Until then, he had not told his mother, Doris, who was living in Toronto, Canada, what was going on. How was he going to tell his mother that he was in America because his children, her grandchildren, had been kidnapped and that, moreover, he needed a lot of money to get them back? With a heavy heart, though, Gidon made the call. Doris agreed to send the funds as soon as possible, but it was a bank holiday in the United States and in Canada, so Gidon had to wait for several days. He found himself in an unusual situation.

 GIDON "My dear friends realized how stressed out I was and, it being a holiday, suggested that the next day we all take ourselves off to the beach for some relaxation. We parked the car at the top of a ravine and climbed down steep steps that led to a totally hidden but lovely beach, where young and old, skinny and fat people were sitting, swimming, playing, and just talking, all without a stitch of cloth on them, all very calm, very friendly, and very free. For me, this being the first time ever, it was a bit of an unusual situation, but I quickly realized that I would be the odd man out if I kept my clothing on. I'm used to the warm Mediterranean, so the Pacific was very cold. I ran in for a minute up to my knees, and quickly decided this water was not for me. So, my friends and I talked and enjoyed the sun warming our bodies. Half an hour later, someone approached from a distance and called 'Gidon! Is that you? What are you doing here in California? What are you doing on this beach?' And it turns out it was none other than Dave, another volunteer friend from Zikim. What a coincidence to meet him here. It was totally unbelievable. I told him what was going on and then came a surprise. 'Gidon, do you have transportation?'"

Gidon's nude-bathing, kibbutz volunteer friend, it turned out, was headed to Spain for a month, and he offered Gidon his car while he was gone. "I started feeling," Gidon wrote, "that maybe I did really have a chance in getting the kids back. Things were going my way. I started to cheer up a little."

Another volunteer from Zikim who Gidon had gotten ahold of when he arrived in California agreed to drive up to the small, rural town where Naomi was staying with her parents, the kids, and her boyfriend, to stake things out. Gidon and Stuart drove up the Sacramento Valley for several hours, past fields of rice and corn, and came up with a plan. Stuart would knock on Naomi's door, unannounced, while Gidon waited about 50 yards away, hidden by trees and bushes. Stuart would pretend to have stopped by casually and then, seeing the kids, ask what was up and what their plans were.

The plan worked. After a friendly two-hour visit, Stuart bid his goodbyes and returned to Gidon. The couple seemed relaxed, said Stuart. They said that Gidon was back in Israel and that all was just fine. They were planning to head back to southern California after a brief stop in the Bay Area.

Gidon returned to San Francisco, excited. He had the information he needed. But there was still a snag: The money had not yet arrived. The detective made a proposition.

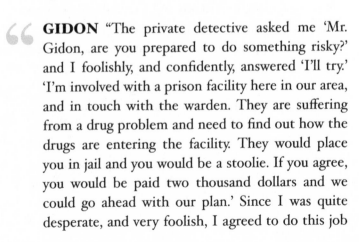

GIDON "The private detective asked me 'Mr. Gidon, are you prepared to do something risky?' and I foolishly, and confidently, answered 'I'll try.' 'I'm involved with a prison facility here in our area, and in touch with the warden. They are suffering from a drug problem and need to find out how the drugs are entering the facility. They would place you in jail and you would be a stoolie. If you agree, you would be paid two thousand dollars and we could go ahead with our plan.' Since I was quite desperate, and very foolish, I agreed to do this job but, luckily, beforehand, I had to be interviewed by two very experienced jailers to see if I fit the bill. After an hour's interrogation by these two gentlemen, it very quickly became clear that I did not in any way meet the requirements: I was neither hardened nor experienced with drugs—I couldn't even tell the difference between hashish, grass, and marijuana. I knew nothing about hard drugs, I was much too naïve and trusting, and the chance that I would come out alive was close to zero. I also lacked the criminal mind, so they told me. I simply was not the stoolie type. On the one hand, I was relieved, and, on the other hand, of course, I was desperate to find out how and when I could get the money I needed."

Having (thankfully) been rejected as a would-be jailhouse snitch, Gidon had to keep waiting for the money to arrive. But time was marching on—it had been days—and he knew that with every passing day, the likelihood that Naomi and the kids would head out rose. Plus, he'd come down with a bad case of poison oak from hiding in the bushes on his last escapade with Stuart.

Gidon was invited to a swanky pool party in Sausalito with some kibbutz volunteer friends. Although he enjoyed good food and wine, he found himself having to explain his story to another pool party guest—a doctor, who, having spotted Gidon's flaming red legs, offered to get him some medication, which obliged Gidon to spill the beans to the no doubt stunned doctor.

Finally, the money arrived, but now a new plan had to be made. The family was in the Bay Area. Gidon and an employee of the private detective drove to the address to stake out the situation. Dave stressed to Gidon that he should stay in the car at all costs. They were just doing a quick confirmation that the family was there, and they couldn't afford to blow their cover.

You can guess what happened next.

GIDON "After a while, I got out and, against Dave's protests, climbed the small fence surrounding their property, this time paying attention for poison oak or poison ivy, and slowly made my way closer to the house while hidden in the bushes. I was crouching behind a huge tree when all of a sudden the back door of the house opened and out came Maya, Yanai, Naomi, Naomi's sister Laura, and an elderly woman whom I supposed was her boyfriend's mother. I was about a hundred yards from them and could both hear and see them. Though I stayed hidden, I was terribly excited and not very much in control of my feelings. Though I stayed hidden, my brain and my heart just wanted to jump up and hug and kiss the kids. Seeing them and hearing them was just too much for me. I did stay out of sight, relying on all my self-control not to do what seemed to me to be so natural. At this point, it occurred to me that what I ought to do is retreat and get back to the car—mission accomplished. But just at that very moment, a large German Shepherd dog came out of the house and, without hesitation, immediately started barking and coming toward me. I hightailed as fast as I could, and as I jumped over the fence, I heard them yell 'Call the police! Call the police! He's trespassing!' I hid a couple of hundred yards away behind another hedge. As I crouched and hid myself, two police cars came up the road, sirens blaring, and entered the driveway. I, of course, stayed hidden, shaking and totally distressed. About an hour later, when the police cars had finally left, I carefully made my way to the car and joined Dave, who had, of course, heard and seen what was happening and quickly surmised that things did not go well. He was actually glad to see me, because he feared the police had caught me and I would be jailed, knowing that the trespassing laws in California are very strictly enforced. He, of course, was also angry with me that I exposed myself and that we lost the one big advantage of surprise we had till this moment. It quickly became clear that, having lost the element of surprise, Mr. Greenberg was no longer prepared to continue working with me, and that I would be on my own."

What a wild goose chase. Now Gidon had blown it. He was indeed on his own from that point on, but he had a car and he had an address book of names and phone numbers. He hit the road for southern California and drove for hours along the seaside, which calmed him. He had the money his mother had sent, and he knew where the family was headed. He was in too deep now; he had nothing left to lose.

He looked up a cousin on his father's side and showed up on her doorstep, hoping to find a haven in the seaside community where he hoped Naomi and the children were, if all accounts had been correct. But the cousin had changed dramatically since Gidon had known her.

 GIDON "I couldn't even sleep on the couch because, as she explained, this was the Lord's resting place, so I slept on a mattress on the floor, and realized very quickly that this was not going to be my home while I was there. I had my breakfast of tea and biscuits and said goodbye and decided that I would look someone else up."

That someone else was a lovely woman named Lee. Lee had

been married to Naomi's boyfriend before she had been abruptly dumped in favor of Naomi. She was more than happy to help Gidon. What's more, she had been living in the community for a few years and knew of her ex's routines, friends, and hangouts. She and Gidon, with their respective hurts, hit it off and became very close.

 GIDON "Lee worked as a social worker in Santa Barbara. She had a car, and in the morning would drive to work, leaving me the key to the house and giving me directions to where I could possibly try and track them down. After a few days, I started taking Lee to work and picking her up afterward, and then, together, we would cruise the streets of the town. This became our regular routine, covering various parts of this sprawling and growing city. We enjoyed each other's company, and the only part that was not good was, of course, that we found no trace of either Naomi or the children. This, of course, was very disillusioning and frustrating. As the days went by, it also meant that the time would shortly arrive when I had to return the car to its owner in San Francisco."

Back up the California coast Gidon went, and he returned the car to his friend. Unthwarted, he boarded a bus and headed right back to his search—and to Lee. On the bus ride, he befriended a German American woman traveling on her own with three small boys. She was headed to the same place Gidon was to join her husband, who was attending a conference there. The woman, Verena, was struggling with her boys, and Gidon offered to help her out. After the boys finally went to sleep, Gidon told Verena his story. By the time the two parted ways at their destination, Verena, too, was on board to help. They made plans to join her husband for dinner later that week.

Then Lee had a brainstorm. It occurred to her that if Naomi was in town, she would need to get a checkup at a medical clinic, being that she was expecting her third child at any time. Lee located several clinics in the area, went in, and asked about "a client of hers" that she was worried about. They found a clinic where Naomi had an appointment. Verena, the woman from the bus (who, with her husband, Jan, had treated Gidon to a lovely steak dinner earlier that week) jumped in to help. They'd sit in their family car near the clinic and wait to see if Naomi came in. Then they would confront her. Naomi didn't show up. Gidon was crushed. He was running out of time, money, and hope. Verena, Jan, and their three boys had to return to King City, where they lived, but they gave Gidon their address and contact information, urging him to be in touch with them should the situation change.

Lee and Gidon decided to divide the city into areas and cruise around, searching a different neighborhood every day. Days went by, with nothing. At the end of another day, just as the two were about to throw in the towel, Lee mentioned that she knew of a big supermarket that her ex frequented. The two drove to the parking lot and waited. Gidon went inside: nothing.

 GIDON "Returning to the car disillusioned and pretty much down, I got back in the car with Lee. As she was about to slowly back out of the parking space, I naturally looked around also, and let out a shout: 'Lee, there they are! Look!' Lee stomped on the brakes, pulled back into our parking spot, and, looking around, both of us saw—twenty yards away behind us—a station wagon pulling up and Naomi's boyfriend with his bright red bandana, getting out, walking past, and entering the supermarket about 150 feet away. Lee and I ducked down. I was, of course, beside myself with excitement and reacting on nerves only. Once he entered the supermarket, I got out of the car, my heart pounding hard and walked the twenty steps over to their station wagon. I slowly opened the back door and saw Maya and Yanai sitting next to Naomi's younger sister, Laura. Naomi was sitting in the front seat. She turned white as a ghost when she saw me."

CHAPTER 21

THE WAR OF ATTRITION

"There are two tragedies in life," George Bernard Shaw said. "One is to lose your heart's desire. The other is to gain it."

If the taking of his two children, several weeks earlier in Jerusalem, had seared itself into Gidon's soul, what happened next only magnified that pain. With the passing of so much time, Gidon's telling of this story no doubt differed from the memories of Naomi or the children. Memory is a famously mysterious phenomenon; the more we tell our stories, the more details we add, edit, or exclude. We direct a movie in our minds of the events that shaped us. To me, the accuracy of Gidon's memory was less important than the emotion it evoked in him today.

It was read-aloud time, only, Gidon was reading to me instead of the other way around. His voice was choked with emotion.

GIDON "I spoke to the kids in Hebrew and told them 'Shalom. I've missed you and haven't seen you in a long time.' Then I took Yanai gently into my arms and walked with him to Lee's car. Naomi sent her sister Laura running to the supermarket to get her boyfriend. Maya also got out of the car, and I called to her, but Naomi shouted at her 'Get back into the car!' I was in a terrible turmoil: What should I do? After a minute or so of hesitation I told Lee 'Let's get out of here,' and this while holding onto Yanai and leaving my dear Maya behind."

Mothers, children, separation, helplessness, anger, and trauma must have played a cacophonous orchestra in Gidon's mind in that awful moment. Gidon openly wept while relating this story. He took a moment to compose himself, and we hugged. Enveloped in Gidon's arms, I harbored a guilty thought: What had Gidon imagined a confrontation would look like? Had he thought about the long-term implications? What consequences did Naomi imagine when she took the children in the first place? What about the children?

I couldn't seem to stop myself from having Big Fat Judgments about this, something that made me feel ashamed of myself. How the hell would I have known what to do at the time? Chastened, I shifted into Good Partner mode and comforted Gidon. The entire situation was terrible, and—in a single moment in time, knowing that he had maybe five seconds until all hell broke loose—he did the best he could. Gidon did not consciously choose between his two children; pressure and desperation made him just plain panic as he ran out of time.

 GIDON "I asked myself then and I ask myself today why I didn't also take Maya. Could I have? Yes, I could, and I should have! Perhaps, had Lee offered to hold onto Yani while I went to get Maya, I may have done so. But she did not become active in this drama, and surely had some ambiguous feelings at this point. One other aspect of this momentous event was that had I decided to physically take Maya into our car, it probably would have necessitated a physical confrontation with Naomi, and that is part of the reason I didn't do it.

I told myself that, after all was said and done, Naomi and I did have an agreement that each one of us would raise one of the children, and though she drastically broke this understanding, I still felt that, perhaps, something could be salvaged. Both of us would in all likeliness suffer, but we would also be able to raise at least one of the children. None of this called into question at all how Maya felt and, over the years, it turned out that it had deep and damaging ramifications. Maya must have thought 'How was it that Dad took only Yani and not me? Why not? Didn't Dad love me? Didn't he care?' Only many years later did I realize how deeply this lack of sensitivity on my part toward Maya really affected her, and I'm sorry to this very day. I can hardly forgive myself."

Perhaps belatedly, it dawned on me why Gidon was so insistent and persistent about me writing this book. He had a lot to get off his chest, much of which was unexamined and disconnected. He needed a companion along the way, a sounding board—someone to listen, to understand, and to hug him when the pain was just too much.

In *A Primer For Forgetting*, Lewis Hyde writes:

"The French psychologist Pierre Janet once suggested that we think of memory not as a thing fixed in the mind but as an action, 'the action of telling a story,' and when it is successful, that action leads to 'the stage of liquidation.' Forgetting appears when the story has been so fully told as to wear itself out. Then time begins to flow again; then the future can unfold."

So maybe this was it: the last telling of a terrible event, as Gidon remembered it, that echoed with hurt and anger for decades.

Gidon and Lee took Yanai to the home of some friends and tried to calm down and plan their next steps. The following day, Gidon visited with a family lawyer who had just won another complicated custody case. The attorney told Gidon in no uncertain terms that it would take thousands of dollars and up to three years for him to legally sort out this situation and that, even then, there were no guarantees. Gidon would have to stay in California during this time. Therefore, the lawyer said, the best option was to simply return to Israel with Yanai and put it behind him.

With little Yanai in tow and his heart heavy about Maya, Gidon headed up to Jan and Verena's home in King City. While Gidon waited for the Israeli embassy to send him a passport for Yanai, the couple comforted, encouraged, housed, fed, and even employed Gidon for three weeks. Jan asked Gidon if he could drive a tractor. Soon enough, Gidon was an Israeli kibbutznik driving a John Deere tractor in the Salinas Valley, which reminded him of the Jezreel Valley in Israel. He was happy to be out, working in the enormous garlic fields, but his heart and soul were bruised by the whole experience, and he ached to go home. The passport arrived, and after thanking Jan and Verena for their generosity and kindness, Gidon and Yanai returned to Israel.

 GIDON "Arriving back in Israel, with Yanai, it was exciting to see the Tel Aviv seashore. The familiar landscape was heart-warming, although I was very sad that Maya was not sitting next to me as Yanai was. We were met at the airport by my neighbors and friends from the kibbutz, and, of course, their first question was 'Where is Maya?' I told them briefly and painfully what had happened and, as usual, couldn't control my emotions. We got back to Zikim, and Yanai went back to his little group of children as if he had never left, and I returned to my work in the cow barn. Just being back home, a feeling of wellbeing and security enveloped me, with many of the kibbutz members not only asking me about what had taken place in America, but also expressing a lot of empathy and support. I concentrated on being a good father to Yanai and felt secure and a sense of belonging on the kibbutz. One day, I was holding Yanai in my arms, walking down a sandy path on the kibbutz. I remember that there were Jacaranda trees everywhere, with their brilliant orange flowers. Suddenly, I had such a strong feeling of commitment and devotion that I stopped on my way and I vowed that I would protect and take care of Yanai with all of my strength for the rest of his life. I remember it to this day, that intense feeling. But I was also worried. What did the future have in store for me and Yanai? Would I see Maya again and, if so, when, where, and how? Must I stay on kibbutz, particularly Zikim? Would I find a new partner? Would I somehow rebuild my life?"

The Israel that Gidon returned to after a six-week absence was one in which tensions and conflict with its neighbors were still active. The Six-Day War had been over for about three years, but the Arab League Summit in 1967, which was attended by the heads of the state of Algeria, Egypt, Iraq, Jordan, Kuwait, Lebanon, Sudan, and Syria, had issued the Khartoum Resolution, which famously included the "Three No's" policy: no peace, no recognition, and no negotiations with Israel. Thus, the War of Attrition (or, *Ḥarb al-Istinzāf* in Arabic) came about, which was a series of attacks, counterattacks, cross-border mortars, border skirmishes, and hostilities—sometimes sustained, sometimes sporadic—that lasted for almost three years, from 1967 to 1970, primarily in Sinai. *Attrition warfare* is a strategy that is suggested by its name; it consists of simply wearing down the other side until their numbers and materiel are so depleted that they eventually give up.

 GIDON "As a single father, I was excused most of the time from reserve duty. But one time I did have to go and serve on the Golan, and that was very, very hard on me. I was more worried about Yanai's safety in Zikim than my own well-being on the Syrian border, with Katyusha rockets coming down on us at any time, night or day. We survived unscathed, though there was damage at some of the border kibbutzim. Of course, we retaliated relentlessly, but we never knew when or where the next salvo of rockets or heavy artillery or mortar fire would come down on us. It was very unnerving, to say the least. It was usually massive but short so that our forces, especially the air force, couldn't spot them."

The War of Attrition ground on. Remember those fifteen shipping vessels that were stranded in 1967 when Nasser closed the Suez Canal? Three years later, they were still there, trapped where they had been temporarily moored in the Great Bitter

Lake in Egypt. The Great Bitter Lake, as the name might imply, has a salinity double that of the sea under normal circumstances. But closed off, with fifteen vessels parked in it, along with the usual sand and dust storms of the Sahara, the slow deterioration and discoloration of the ships were inevitable. This group of stranded ships became known as the Yellow Fleet. The ships could not be abandoned where they were, but the canal was closed for the foreseeable future, acting for some time as the ad hoc border between Israel and Egypt. Their hands tied, the shipping companies thinned the crews considerably, lashed the ships in groups of three, and rotated crew members every few months. They had to keep watch over the ships. A mini-society sprouted up, with the Yellow Fleet creating their own postage stamps—which were recognized by Egypt—hosting pool parties on different ships, and even having their own mini-Olympics in 1968. The ships were stuck for eight years in a surreal no-man's-land, out of time and place as the world madly spun without them from war to war. The Suez Canal was not reopened until 1975, and when it was, only two of the fifteen ships could make it out under their own power.

Gidon stayed in touch with Maya by sending letters containing drawings from Yanai addressed to Naomi's parents in California. Eventually, Naomi replied by way of unaddressed envelopes. But these were few and far between, and the trust between the two had been broken beyond repair. Gidon hired a lawyer, applied for full custody of Maya and Yanai in Israel, and won before an Israeli Supreme Court judge. Although she contested it, unless Naomi came to Israel with Maya, this legal custody decision was utterly unenforceable. It was an empty victory.

It would be four years before Gidon saw Maya again and Naomi saw Yanai. Another four years after that, Naomi and Gidon came to a kind of détente. But it was and remained for decades a cold war of wills. Slowly, that terrible chapter became something new, something that looked a little like healing.

Since Gidon and I have lived together, there has been a slow, friendly war of attrition. Under my influence, Gidon has eaten and not complained overly dramatically about taco salad and pad thai and under his influence, I have come to appreciate a Czech dumpling called knedlícky, over which large quantities of gravy must be poured. (Gidon insists that any sauce is called gravy, and I have given up on that battle.) Gidon has not yet given up his argument that my cats should just eat whatever is left over instead of "that expensive pet food you buy."

Gidon has taught me to slow down and express myself more carefully rather than my usual stone-skipping-over-the-lake manner of communicating. I have taught Gidon how to make his own playlists on Spotify. Gidon likes to blast music when he cooks you see, and he rotates between Simon & "Garfinkle" (as he calls them) and Abba. For such a big age difference, Gidon and I have a surprisingly large musical taste crossover. My parents are close to Gidon's age, so I grew up listening to the music that they loved, which spanned the 1950s, '60s, and '70s.

"What's your favorite Simon & Garfunkel song?" I asked Gidon one day. I knew what he was going to say: "Bridge over Troubled Water." Or, no—maybe "The Boxer." That had to be it: the plaintive coming-of-age story of a young man lost and alone in the world.

"'Fifty Ways to Leave Your Lover.'"

"Gidon, that's not—" Okay. I decided just to slip out the back, Jack. Didn't need to discuss much.

Simon & Garfunkel has a special place in Gidon's heart for a reason. Susan Kashman, the expressive, intelligent friend he'd made on Kibbutz Ha'Zorea in 1961—and with whom there had been a simmering, low-level flirtation—had sent Gidon a Simon & Garfunkel album, an album of Brahms, a coffee percolator, and a Tonka toy truck for Yanai, all brought to him by her parents, Monte and Margie, who moved to Israel in 1970. Gidon and Susan had stayed in touch through correspondence and holiday cards for many years by that time, and Gidon was happy when Susan moved to Israel to join her parents.

Living on Kibbutz Zikim with Yanai was a nurturing and caring environment for Gidon, but he was again quite lonely. At the suggestion of the kibbutz psychiatrist, Gidon started attending group therapy sessions each week in Tel Aviv to try to work through the terrible events he had just experienced. Before his therapy sessions began, Gidon beelined to a pay phone to call Susan, who was then living in the heart of Tel Aviv. He had to use the famed *asimon* tokens that Israel used for pay phones up to 1987, which are now collector's items. Susan was everything that Gidon was not: expressive, educated, and creative. She was exactly what Gidon needed and missed in his life. But she was in a different relationship.

One day when Gidon called, Susan sounded stressed. She wanted him to come over. Gidon said he was on his way to group therapy, but Susan was insistent. "We'll have therapy together today," she said.

Mystified, Gidon went to her small apartment on Allenby Street in Tel Aviv.

GIDON "I arrived to find a distraught young woman, tears running down her cheeks, in utter dismay. We hugged, and she thanked me for coming. How could I not? I knew that Susan had been in a serious relationship with a musician named Victor, and that she loved him, and he loved her, but he was not prepared to marry her."

Susan was pregnant. She knew for sure that she wanted to have this child, but also that her relationship with the biological father was over. She definitely knew that single-parenthood was not for her. Gidon also was a single parent, and the two had been warm friends for many years. Susan had a feeling that if she and Gidon cast their fortunes together, crazy as it sounded, it might just work. She asked Gidon to marry her.

 GIDON "So many things to think about, so many questions to answer, and yet a glimmer of hope possessed me. Is this my second chance to rebuild my life? Will it be good for Yani to have a new mom? Will I be able to be a true and loving father to this child? Will Susan be able to live with me on Zikim? What will she work at on the kibbutz? Can she learn proper Hebrew? Will there be enough passion in our relationship? We come from such different backgrounds; how will we bridge those gaps? How will we manage?

The questions, doubts, and fears were all real, and yet I tended, as I do even today, to be hopeful, believing in the future, adventurous and ready to jump into the sea and start swimming. The truth is, I was also a bit taken aback that Susan would choose me out of a number of other male friends she had to become her partner, lover, friend—not to mention father to this unborn baby. This meant a great deal to me and about how she felt about me, trusted me, and was prepared to throw herself into this unknown territory; she, too, was being adventurous. She knew about my disastrous marriage to Naomi, and yet she was ready to go for it, as the saying goes. I wondered how hard it would be for her to be a loving and a giving mom to Yanai, having had no such experience before— with any children and especially not in this kind of a situation. Would she be able to cope? Would she be able to love both Yanai and me? And, yes, I would be there, and I would try to help and be patient, understanding and loving, but would it be enough?"

Forty-eight hours later, Gidon said yes. It was, as he said, "a leap into the clear blue sea." And what a leap.

CHAPTER 22

HADAS

Outside, there was a hill. And the hill was only one of many hills. And the hills were laced with dusty green, ancient olive groves and stone walls spilling over with purple morning glory and vibrant bougainvillea and pomegranate trees heavy with fruit. Inside the house on the hill, children and grandchildren played, sang, and prepared food. Voices layered on voices; generations layered upon generations. These were the children and grandchildren of Gidon and Susan Kashman Lev.

Somebody built a bonfire in the growing dusk under a grape arbor. Lebanon was only about twenty kilometers away, sharing the same scrubby Mediterranean landscape. Jerusalem was two hours southeast; Damascus, three hours northeast. Susan's eldest, Gidon's second daughter, had organized a beautiful family gathering for the weekend in the northern part of Israel. Gidon lounged on a bed, resting for a few minutes. He was staring at the beamed ceiling overhead, wistfully, longingly.

"What are you thinking about?" I asked. I supposed that whatever was on Gidon's mind, it would be sentimental, or even sad.

"How great the construction of this house is," he said. "Look at those beams!"

That's Gidon for you; a man who defies expectations.

The family weekend was in Klil, an agro-ecological model settlement in northwestern Israel. Nonorganic agriculture is forbidden, sustainable orchards are a must, developing the native plants of the region is key, and the homes have solar panels and generators, which hum at night, partially obscuring the yipping of jackals as they prowl for food. Klil is within the Mateh Asher Regional Council, so named after the Tribe of Asher, said to have been allotted this land in antiquity, according to the Book of Joshua. Klil is verdant in a scrubby, Mediterranean way, but not particularly forested.

Trees and forests are important in Israel. In fact, since it was founded in 1901, the Jewish National Fund has planted more than 185 million trees in 280 forests. "In most countries, people are born to forests, and forests are given to them by nature," said Moshe Rivlin, the former world chairman of the JNF. "But here in this country, if you see a tree, it was planted by somebody."

The Ottomans cleared much of what is today Israel of its pine and oak trees to build railways for their empire. Israel was "afforested." In the world for forestry, to *reforest* means to plant a forest where one had been before, whereas to *afforest* means to put a forest where there was nothing before. Big difference. The JNF afforestation, much loved both inside and outside Israel as a symbol of rebirth and renewal, was, naturally, controversial. The JNF was criticized for planting non-native trees, planting trees to obscure the remains of Arab villages, and restricting Bedouin herding and for "overreliance on highly flammable pine trees."

"A lot of that is probably true," Gidon said. "Or at least part of it."

He fanned smoke away from his face. It was a chilly day, and he was wearing a sweater and an ill-fitting baseball cap that he found somewhere. Back from our family weekend in the north, and inspired by the firepit in Klil, Gidon was "making a cookout" in a spot that is not entirely legal. What he built this fire with, I did not know. I hoped it wasn't highly flammable pine tree detritus. We'd gotten into trouble over Gidon's cookouts before. Building a fire is not legal in most urban areas of Israel. I stood beside him, dutifully holding a plate, nervously looking around for whoever might bust us this time.

We live next to a beautiful park, Gan Avraham. Cut into the hills of Ramat Gan, it has winding paths, a community garden, and a dilapidated amphitheater. For a while, the municipality had an outdoor ping pong table there, but by the time Gidon and I bought paddles, it was gone.

It's a bit of a breathless walk to the top of the park, but once you reach it, there are sweeping views of Tel Aviv. A school is perched nearby, and the snippet of a jazz tune drifts in the air. Israel's schools don't use bells to indicate recess or lunchtime. Instead, they play tunes: nursery tunes for the little kid schools, Yiddish or Israeli folk music for others, and a range of unidentifiable but pleasant tunes like this one. It seems that everything in Israel has layers; this school was also once the secret headquarters of the Haganah, the Israeli proto-army, from which David Ben-Gurion commanded his forces before 1948.

Ramat Gan had been beautifying the municipality and adding historical markers at various sites that denoted historical events or remarkable people from the past. A few blocks away, installed long before this current historical marker/beautification plan— by the look of it—is a replica of a pioneer cabin. Through the large glass window, what looks like leftover department store mannequins are poised, reading a book or stirring porridge.

I grew up in the Cascade Mountains of northern California, among evergreen trees—conifers, tall and swooshy in the wind.

The trees in Israel don't seem as tall, lonely, or blue-green as the ones I was used to: Douglas fir, ponderosa and sugar pine, and incense cedar. The trees in Israel are different: wild, branching, climbing, hugging the soil for dear life. They have names that echo the region from antiquity: Aleppo pine, terebinth, Mt. Tabor oak, cedar of Lebanon, tamarisk, cypress, olive, sycamore, fig, pomegranate, eucalyptus, acacia, almond, and date palm trees. Israel is indeed the land of milk, honey, and very many trees and parks.

The myrtle tree (or *hadas* in Hebrew) has special meaning in Israel; prized in antiquity for its fragrant leaves, it was used in weddings and special ceremonies. It symbolizes peace, justice, and righteousness. So much so that Queen Esther, of the Purim story's Hebrew name, was Hadassah. The Purim story, which is thought to date back to something like the fourth century BCE, is from the *Megilla* (book of) Esther and tells of how the brave and righteous Queen Esther foils the evil vizier Haman from his plan to massacre the Jews in ancient Persia under the rule of her husband, King Ahasuerus. Scholars believe that the Ahasuerus from this story might, in fact, be the historical Xerxes. Which of these two names is more fun to say three times fast is up for debate.

Deciding to take a leap of faith and marry a woman whom he was very fond of but didn't know all that well was a completely Gidon thing to do. It was a very Susan thing to do as well, it seemed. It's the small things that remind Gidon so powerfully of Susan that he weeps from time to time. A book she loved. A picture in which she smiled radiantly, her hair pulled back with her oversized 1970s glasses on. A card she made. A funny story of something that she did. Her journals. Her poetry.

Born in Florida and raised in Brooklyn, Susan hailed from a liberal, progressive family. Her father was an engineer and a part-time, quite gifted artist; her mother was a politically active homemaker. An emotionally complex and inquisitive woman, Susan was a lover of literature and had a bachelor's degree in American and English literature and a master's in English literature and American history. She had a rebellious streak. An anti-intellectual intellectual, Susan was a seeker who interrogated life, love, and meaning through her writing and conversation. She didn't do things in half measures.

Although on paper they were so different, Susan and Gidon seemed *b'shert*: fated. They had three things in common: both were headstrong, both wanted a committed life partner, and both were game enough to take seriously the crazy idea of hitching up. For Gidon, a woman better suited for him would have been hard to find. Susan wrote:

> It's true that my heart
> Is sometimes a forest
> So dense, it's fearful.
>
> Like the rain forest,
> An ecosystem so complex,
> So ferocious.
>
> There are meadows, though,
> And glades where friends
> Come to play and rest.
>
> You need to be persistent
> And brave and want
> To believe love is here.

Upon the news of the engagement, Susan's parents, Monte and Margie, drove their Mini-Minor car to Kibbutz Zikim for a family get-together. While sitting in the shade of an ancient olive tree, they quizzed Gidon about whether he really knew what he was getting into. They had met Gidon before, yes, but Monte and Margie were doing their due diligence. Susan was twenty-seven years old, and they were eager for her to find happiness and a measure of security. Was Gidon really up to the task? Yes, Gidon was an enthusiastic bundle of energy, but he had some baggage—and so did Susan. Was Gidon the right person to be a good husband to their only daughter and a good father for their first grandchild? I could only imagine how Gidon reassured them with his cheerful optimism, bright blue eyes, and authentic sincerity. Gidon didn't do things in half measures either.

 GIDON "The next day after my meeting with Monte and Margie, Susan and I decided to go to the sea, a fifteen-minute walk through the sand dunes. I carried Yani most of the way on my shoulders. The sea and the seashore were empty and just beautiful. I used one of our blankets to make us a bit of shade, we stripped, and into the blue sea we plunged. It was all so calm, warm, as the Mediterranean usually is in the summer, and quiet, a *mechaya*, as the saying goes. Susan, who was a good swimmer and loved the waves, (not like me) swam right out there, while Yani and I stayed close to the seashore. Since there were hardly any waves, I started to teach him how to swim. It was just so wonderful and hopeful. Yanai built sandcastles while Sue and I talked and rested, both body and soul. The building of our relationship had begun in earnest."

Susan and Gidon were married on Kibbutz Zikim on April 21, 1972, in a civil ceremony on a green lawn overlooking the Mediterranean. The whole kibbutz was in attendance, and two of Susan's beloved aunts came from America. Susan wore a white wedding dress embroidered in the Yemenite style. There were singing and dancing and, as with all good celebrations, an abundance of food.

Margie and Monte encouraged the couple to make their marriage official, and ten months later, the couple was married again, this time by the chief rabbi of Ashkelon. Jewish religious ceremonies require a *minyan* (i.e., ten adult men present), so Gidon, Susan, and her parents and friends had to go out into the street to find a few more people. It is not uncommon in Israel for random Israelis to join a minyan when asked; it's another aspect of this country that I find endearing.

In Susan's journal she wrote:

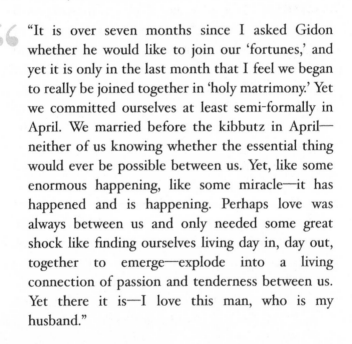

"It is over seven months since I asked Gidon whether he would like to join our 'fortunes,' and yet it is only in the last month that I feel we began to really be joined together in 'holy matrimony.' Yet we committed ourselves at least semi-formally in April. We married before the kibbutz in April—neither of us knowing whether the essential thing would ever be possible between us. Yet, like some enormous happening, like some miracle—it has happened and is happening. Perhaps love was always between us and only needed some great shock like finding ourselves living day in, day out, together to emerge—explode into a living connection of passion and tenderness between us. Yet there it is—I love this man, who is my husband."

In August 1972, while Gidon's cousin John and his wife, Lilly, were visiting, Susan and Gidon stayed in the kibbutz guesthouse and lent their guests their home, as was the kibbutz tradition. Susan's inevitable birth pains started (as they often so conveniently do) at 3 a.m. Borrowing his cousin's rental car, Gidon rushed Susan to Barzilai Hospital in Ashkelon. Fifteen hours later, he would find himself in the branches of a broad sycamore tree.

 GIDON "The hospital was a single-floor hospital, in the center of which there was a lovely courtyard with a wonderful tree. In the waiting room, friends from the kibbutz told me that, if Susan gave birth after dark, I might be able to see it happening if I climbed up the tree. This I did do. As I left Margie and Monte, Susan's mother asked where I was going. 'I can't tell you. Not far. Don't worry.' I climbed up on one of the branches of the tree in that wonderful courtyard and watched our baby being born. It was stupendous to say the least. I could see Susan, the midwife, nurse, and doctor, all helping, and only wished I could be there, too. As soon as I saw that the baby had arrived, I climbed down, ran to Monte and Margie, and told them we have a baby. 'Is it a boy or girl?' they asked. 'I don't know yet,' I said. Twenty minutes later, they showed us, through a glass window, a wonderful, beautiful baby girl. And everyone present called out '*Mazel Tov!*' A little while later, we were allowed to see Susan, who was smiling, exhausted but extremely happy. A new life, another beginning for all of us had just begun!

I told Yanai that he had a new sister, and, in the morning, we made it to the hospital, with Yanai asking a lot of questions: 'How big is she?' 'What does she look like?' 'What color hair does she have?' 'Is she nice?' And I just kept on telling him, 'You will see her shortly, and know all the answers.' 'Will I be able to hold her?' 'Yes, of course. Just be gentle and careful,' I replied. We entered the room where Susan was staying, together with three other women who had just given birth, and there in a little sort of basket, right next to Sue, was this most beautiful little baby, all neat and smooth, and just lovely. We all loved her from the moment she appeared, and Sue was overcome with joy and emotion. We kissed, we hugged, and Yanai, too, was really affectionate. 'So Yani,' Susan said, 'you see, she is so very small, but she will grow, and you will be able to play with her. Her name is Hadasa.'"

It was August 13, 1972, when Hadasa Lee Lev was new to the world. She would grow up to become a tall, willowy architect with sea-green eyes and the most melodious laugh I have ever heard.

Gidon. (1960)

Gidon in the Israeli Army (IDF) on the Israel/Lebanon border. (Approx. 1961)

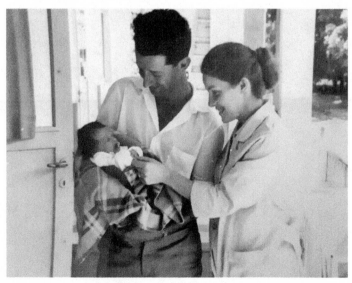

Gidon and Naomi with baby Maya. (1965)

Susan Kashman Lev at Antioch College.
(Approx. 1966)

Gidon and Susan at the Red Sea. (1977)

Left: Monte and Margie Kashman, Susan's parents. (Date unknown).

Below: Gidon and Hadasa in Wales. (1973)

Above: L-R: Elisha, Shaya, Asher, Hadasa, Yanai. (1984)

Left: L-R: Hadasa, Yanai, Shaya. (Approx. 1975)

L-R: Gidon, Yanai, Elisha, Susan, Hadasa, Shaya and Asher. (1998)

Gidon and Maya. (Approx. 2003)

Gidon and Susan. (2008)

CHAPTER 23
A LIFE LESS ORDINARY

I wish it were possible to sum up the next forty-one years in Gidon's family life, of birthday parties, summer camp, karate and dance lessons, soccer practice, holidays, births, deaths, jobs, failures, successes, house moves, and other ordinary yet extraordinary things that make up most of our lives. Gidon wrote thousands and thousands of words detailing these four decades of his life. Naturally, what made perfect sense to Susan and Gidon at the time, sounded hectic and confusing to me so many years later. There were six moves and three kids born during an eleven-year period. There were jobs, opportunities, dirty diapers, camping trips, flat tires, laughter, and shouting. I tried to strike a balance with Gidon and describe the big picture with less granular detail. But, to Gidon, all the details were necessary. All of them. But isn't that the challenge for all of us? To make sense of our narratives as they play out in the moment and then to put them into context for someone else? I turned to what I imagined must be relatively accurate data:

The True Adventures of Gidon and Susan Lev by the numbers:

- married forty-one years
- raised five children
- resided in three countries
- 14,965 breakfasts, lunches, and dinners
- 42 boxes of photos
- 14 buckets of tears
- 5,526 hours of laughter
- undisclosed number of bandages, splinters, and blisters

Gleefully, Gidon added some additional "data," cracking himself up as he did:

- thousands of moving boxes!
- one monthlong camping trip with me and five kids across America! (Asher was only two!)
- one family trip across Europe!
- many empty bottles of the red wine Sue so loved!

After their marriage in 1972, and the birth of Hadasa, Susan and Gidon took advantage of a job offer that Gidon had received from an English dairy equipment manufacturing company and moved to Wales in early 1973. With little Hadasa and Yanai in tow, Susan and Gidon were now expecting a third child, their first together.

Over time, Susan and Gidon added three sons to their family —Shaya, Elisha, and Asher—all born between 1974 and 1981. Each son was born in a different country: Wales, Israel, and Canada. Gidon and Susan were chasing jobs, experimenting with living closer to Gidon's increasingly lonely mother in Toronto, looking for opportunities, and trying to make ends meet.

Gidon grumbled at this summary. It left out the details of Shaya's birth:

"Shaya popped out of Susan in a breech birth that the doctors thought would be so difficult. I didn't even make it to the end of the hallway before they cried out, 'Mr. Lev, you have a son!'"

Gidon told me that, in 1974, Naomi came to England with Maya to visit; Gidon got to see his daughter, and Naomi got to see Yanai. It was emotional but strained. The separated children and parents would not see each other in person again for another four years.

After an eleven-month job contract in Wales was up, Susan and Gidon decided to move to New York and then Canada to be closer to Gidon's mother. By then, Gidon's stepfather, Jus, was very ill, having had a stroke.

Just one of the jobs Gidon and Susan took during their one-year sojourn in Toronto in 1974 was as superintendents of a twenty-five-story apartment building. Most of the tenants were students at the University of Toronto. The family got free rent, water, and electricity, but to Susan's amusement, she found herself washing the windows in the lobby yet with an advanced degree in American literature. Once, when confronting a tenant about the fact that the swimming pool was closed, Susan was shoved into the water herself. She came back home dripping wet and furious. The tenant was given a thirty-day notice to move out.

In 1975, the couple and their children returned to Israel. Rather than returning to Kibbutz Zikim, Gidon and Susan decided to take advantage of generous government subsidies offered to young families willing to make their homes in the further reaches of Israel. But the hilly, rocky landscape—so different from the humid coastal, central Israel—gave the couple doubts. This area was known, Gidon told me, as "the peripheria."

Today, this "peripheria," which includes the large city of Nazareth, is an exemplar of coexistence in Israel. With a majority Arab-Israeli population, Nazareth and its half a dozen surrounding villages are considered the Arab capital of Israel.

Gidon and Susan soon became a part of one of the most diverse, integrated Arab and Jewish regions in the country. The family moved to Nazareth Illit, a Jewish enclave established in 1957 perched on the hills just above Nazareth, meant to offer young families affordable housing, good schools, and modern municipal services.

Susan and Gidon lived and loved in Nazareth Illit for the next six years.

"No," Gidon said. "Forty years."

"Well, I'm counting from 1975 to 1981 before you went back to Canada for three years."

"Well, I'm counting from 1975 to 2016," Gidon said.

"But you were gone for a few years," I pointed out.

"That doesn't count."

In Israel during the 1970s and '80s, things were anything but peaceful. The region was—as it perpetually seems to be—on the brink of war. It makes sense that living outside a Middle East on fire might be a good idea. Gidon and Susan had been abroad during both the 1973 Yom Kippur War and the First Lebanon War.

 GIDON "During most of the time, when the first Lebanese war was being fought, we were living in Canada, and one of the reasons we were in Canada was to put a bit of distance between us and the troubles, at times painful and bloody. We needed a respite from all that. The fact is, for a while we were even thinking of giving it all up—sell our house in Israel and staying in Canada. Then, in 1981—while we were living in Toronto, Canada—

Susan had given birth to our fifth child, a feisty little boy, Asher, and a new war broke out called the First Lebanon War or Peace for Galilee. For months, there had been shootings and incursions by the PLO (Palestinian Liberation Organization) across the border, and it became quite clear that the PLO had made Lebanon and Beirut its main base, with the help of Syria and others, stockpiling large amounts of arms and ammunitions not far from our very vulnerable border, so the reasons to do away with this very real threat were there. How it was carried out, how far to go, I don't think was very clear to anyone, not even to Begin, and he was the prime minister! In the end, Arafat and his man were totally surrounded—with Henry Kissinger brokering an agreement that helped create Hezbollah and allowed Arafat and his remaining fighters to leave Lebanon for Tripoli-Tunisia. The Israeli Army retreated to our border and helped create the South Lebanese Army right along our northern border, which more or less guaranteed quiet in the north for the next few years."

Despite the unrest in Israel, the family returned to Israel for good in 1984. For a time, Susan taught English in a local high school, but her creative, innovative approach proved too exotic for the unruly students who did not share Susan's love of the English language. Bruised and disheartened from the experience, Susan devoted herself to full-time homemaking. Gidon tried his hand at so many things throughout his life that he printed his own booklet, called *My Working Life*. On its cover, Gidon wears a cap and is taking a test sample of milk from a large glass container of milk in a dairy barn. Gidon wrote tellingly of his relationship with work and its role in his life.

GIDON "Work. In Russian *rabota*, in Hebrew *avodah*, in Czech *prace*, and, finally, in German *arbeit*. During the war, the Germans wrote that on almost every concentration camp gate, very cynically: *Arbeit macht frei*, which it did not. In many cases, it brought the prisoners closer to death, from sheer hard work, undernourishment, and horrendous work conditions. In a way, it did make the people *frei*, if death can be thought of as being set free, and, perhaps, in a way, it was since the suffering was so great so that many a prisoner, male or female, preferred to die rather than go on.

In a different time and place, and in another context, there is a deeper and more significant meaning to that famous—or, should I say, infamous —quote that the Germans used. For me and for millions of others around the globe, work does and did give a person a certain amount of freedom and independence because it enables us to stay alive and choose how we want to live, where, and even with whom. Yes, it is dependent on a thousand and one factors, but the base is there, and it does give each one of us a certain amount of power and control over our life. For me, personally, it always gave me a base from which I was able to organize my life and a feeling of controlling my destiny. That dear work ethic was a strong force in formulating my daily, weekly, and monthly existence, at times to the detriment of my social, cultural, and even personal life. As far back as my incarceration in Térézin, as a boy of eight, I worked cleaning the stalls of the German officers' horses. I enjoyed brushing and keeping the horses clean. It was frightening at times. Many of us boys were, from time to time, kicked or slapped if the officer was not satisfied with the work done, but I managed it and survived."

Here is a short list of jobs Gidon has held:

- gas station attendant
- building superintendent
- Filter Queen vacuum cleaner sales (total sales: one—to Gidon's mother, Doris)
- takeout food management
- import/export administration at a gold jewelry factory
- plastic pipe factory, day and night shifts ("Which was awful," Gidon noted)
- banking assistant
- community center cultural director and folk dance instructor
- dairy barn supervisor
- milk tester
- taxi driver
- flower delivery ("Even at age eighty-five!" Gidon added)

"Life!" Gidon exclaimed during manuscript read-aloud time. "Sometimes even I don't know how I did it!"

"What should other people take away from this, Gidon?" I asked.

He sipped his tea thoughtfully. "Well, you have to believe in yourself."

"And did you always believe in yourself?"

Gidon laughed. "Mostly. But not always."

Dammit. I wanted a takeaway from this, something I could use in my own life. As I looked back at Gidon's life, I grew exhausted just thinking about what he had been through, over, around, and beyond. I couldn't seem to get to the bottom of what made this man tick.

"Even I don't know!" Gidon laughed.

I wanted to know his secret, to apply it to my own life, which seemed so full of tall mountains and deep, dark valleys. How had Gidon been able to face so many challenges, setbacks, and difficult times and yet maintain such an optimistic disposition?

Then I remembered: *hineni*. Hineni is from the Hebrew Bible, and it was what Abraham said to God when he asked him to sacrifice his only son, Isaac. It was what Moses said to God at the burning bush. Hineni also appears (famously so) in the chorus of Leonard Cohen's song "You Want It Darker." Hineni means "Here I am," and to me, a kind of proud showing up: I'm ready. I'm here. Count me in.

For me, it is clear that Susan and Gidon lived hard, loved hard, and worked hard. They uprooted themselves several times and lived the whole adventure, good and bad, at full throttle. Susan had been an only child and so had Gidon. Raising a family with Susan was and remains the single most satisfying, fulfilling, memorable part of Gidon's life. In Susan, Gidon had found a true life partner; she was beside him through it all. When Gidon was with Susan, he was home, and that's where he always wanted to be.

CHAPTER 24
SHE LIFTED UP HER WINGS

In a slim, bound manuscript titled *Letters From Tanganika*, Susan wrote:

"I think I should tell you a little about how we do in Tanganika. First of all—when you love someone, you let them know. It's considered a great blessing to feel great feelings. A privilege. Those who cannot or do not—are poor in spirit. Not that people are not afraid of being hurt, but even to be hurt is not so terrible because people are open-hearted, filled with the sense of joint adventuring on the planet. And curiosity is a good thing: since it is simply a way of knowing how someone else does it—gets along, manages.

And there is great passion for all kinds of things: Mozart, colors, birds, babies, rainy days and sunny days. Happiness is to be engaged with up and down, in and out, man's time and cosmic time, before and after. And it's all pulled together by each person balancing his inner and outer reality.

Yet there is always the under-toad—an inner

eye alert to disaster: it could be me, it might have been me, perhaps it will be me caught in some tragedy. As if one barely escapes with each good day lived.

In Tanganika, the spirit illuminates time and experience. But this doesn't mean we are SOLEMN. No . . . we are ridiculous, silly yet serious.

Oh, people get angry, too. And like to shout and curse and scream but that has never broken any hearts. Because it doesn't shut out, close down, obliterate.

If you ask someone in T, 'Can't you be serious?' He says, 'No, because I'm already too serious.'

It is easy with contradictions because the sense of wholeness is so strong.

Finally, life and people are so interesting, surprising, changing. No one is bored or boring.

I didn't say it's an easy place to live."

I never got to meet Susan, but what I knew for sure was that she was the love of Gidon's life and that the family she and Gidon created together is an incredibly creative and expressive one. All six of Gidon's grown children write, teach, paint, dance, sing, cook, and perform. The grandchildren are all following suit in their own ways. At Passover, family members put on a short play or performance, and every place card at the Seder table, mostly from Susan's time, is handmade and unique. Creating and expressing have been a part of the Lev family tradition, always. Susan encouraged her children—and Gidon—to communicate and to express themselves fully. It was a passion of hers, and her legacy is apparent everywhere in the family, which is a very bonded tribe. The love and connection shared between them are obvious.

Gidon still has many of Susan's books. He arranged them

carefully: fiction, nonfiction, poetry, and history. I can tell by the number of titles of particular authors that Susan liked V.S. Naipaul, Peter Matthiessen, Franz Kafka, and Laurens van der Post. She read William Somerset Maugham, A. B. Yehoshua, Amos Oz, Thomas Mann, and Alice Walker. She read Fyodor Dostoyevsky, James Joyce, Oscar Wilde, and D. H. Lawrence. She wrote her thesis on Lawrence and became thoroughly disenchanted with him afterward. There are coffee table books of the art of Henri Matisse and Paul Klee and the sculptures of Henry Moore. There is a family medical guide and a copy of *Our Bodies, Ourselves*. In photos, Susan looks like the mother anyone would want to have, with a toothy, confident smile and strong, suntanned arms with which she affectionately holds her children and Gidon.

On our refrigerator, there is a handmade sign that Susan made. It says: "Let's Make Things Better." Susan, Gidon recalls, would not let anybody go to bed until they had made up for and smoothed over misunderstandings and hurt. This sometimes resulted in marathon discussions late into the night. I think of this quite a lot: *Let's make things better.*

I cannot imagine planning, shopping, and cooking day after day for five kids. But Susan was the queen of her kitchen and an excellent cook. Her spaghetti Bolognese is legendary. Gidon still has many of her dishes, pots, pans, graters, sieves, and other accoutrements of a skilled cook. When I met Gidon, he still had dozens of small jars of spices that Susan had labeled carefully. They had grown dusty and lost their scent, but he was attached to them; each had been at one time potent additions to meals made with love.

"She also had an unbroken rule," Gidon added. "At the end of each and every day, she would go over our large living room floor with a mop before settling down to some telly program or going to bed. This was sacrosanct!"

In a letter to one of her children, Susan wrote about marriage:

> Perhaps marriage, like all the great events and mysteries in life, is a mass of contradictions that fleetingly achieve a harmony from time to time. Like freedom and the absence of freedom. Like profound good feeling in the midst of unbearable surface tensions. Like different and sometimes opposite characteristics complementing each other and making each person feel more whole than they would alone. Like feeling bound to your commitment and yet free to re-choose and reaffirm it every day of your life. Or not. Being patient but also vigilant.
>
> As with life in general, there's no magical formula for making marriage work well all the time. Maybe it's enough to try to make it work each day. A little. And especially in the hardest times, to try to find something each day which is redeeming. Sometimes, this involves willfully remembering what it is you love (or remember loving) in the other person. This is not easy. We'd like to think that love and happiness are spontaneous and free flowing. But sometimes it's not. And there's no certain way of knowing when a commitment or a decision has come to the end of its natural life. But in a broader, philosophical way, that's what makes a life exciting: there's so much to think about, so much to feel about.

Gidon knew that Susan loved to write and wrote often, but he hadn't realized how prolific she had been or how gifted she was. Susan had left behind boxes and boxes of poems, letters, and other journals. One of the first things he shared with me when I met him was a book of Susan's poems that Asher, Shaya, and his wife, Tamar, lovingly put together after her death. I didn't know what to expect when I read it. Now my copy is filled with Post-its and paper clips and dogears to mark pages and poems that I particularly love, like this one:

Raising Our Children

Once love was an ocean
We splashed in all year long.
It was the sun that lavished
Praise on our bodies and
Grew wild flowers in our hearts.

This is what it felt like
Raising our children.

Once love was a riddle
Creating riddles. Once
It was a question asking
Questions. Once love was adventure
Sending us off and bringing us home.

And this is what it felt like
raising our children.

Now love is a resource
Like the sun and the wind;
It's the heat of summer
And the chill of winter.
When we harvest the stars
And gather the sands, when we
Love with all our hearts and souls,

This is what it feels like
Raising our children.

In one of Gidon's many photo albums, there is a series of pictures of Susan's adult children, each individually positioned under the purple Jacaranda tree in the front yard of the home in Nazareth Illit that Hadasa had designed. Elisha, the photographer of the family, took the photos. In the last picture, there is Susan, weak, in a wheelchair. Susan's death in June 2012, after a yearlong battle with lung cancer, marked the end of an era. She died at home, with Gidon and her children by her side.

 GIDON "We buried Susan in the cemetery of Kibbutz Mishmar Ha'Emek, among trees and flowers everywhere. It was a very solemn and moving ceremony, mostly nonreligious. We played some of Susan's beloved songs, we read some of her poetry, we tried, as best as we could, to connect to her soul, and, of course, we cried. Then we went over to Yanai and Dafna's home, had some tea and coffee, and just talked. Though we are not religious, we did decide to have the traditional *shiva* in our house in Nazareth Illit, which we so loved. During the seven-day period of mourning, so many people came: all of our friends and our boys' friends, even past and present neighbors. It was really a heart-warming and nurturing time of reflection and expression of love and care, for Susan and for all of us, and I came to appreciate this old Jewish tradition of sitting shiva.

I must admit, I felt very lost and lonely. I had always thought, being the cancer man, that I would go first, and, now, here I was, all by myself. Afterward, when everyone had gone home and the days passed, I tried, ever so slowly, to get back to some sort of daily routine. I prepared meals for myself, I took my showers, I returned to driving a taxi four to five days a week, and slowly started to deal with all the paperwork that one must cope with as a result of a death in the family. I arranged for a cleaning lady, went for my checkups, and kept in touch with all my offspring, wherever they were. In this way, four to five months went by. I functioned, but I was sad and struggling."

"I want to add something else," Gidon said.

I set up a Google Doc for Gidon, and he settled down to write. I was pretty sure I was going to get another page of details and dates and facts. But I didn't. Gidon allowed himself to write freely and with emotion. And it was beautiful.

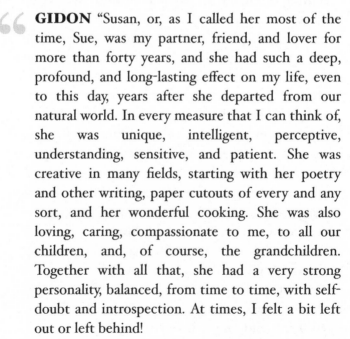 **GIDON** "Susan, or, as I called her most of the time, Sue, was my partner, friend, and lover for more than forty years, and she had such a deep, profound, and long-lasting effect on my life, even to this day, years after she departed from our natural world. In every measure that I can think of, she was unique, intelligent, perceptive, understanding, sensitive, and patient. She was creative in many fields, starting with her poetry and other writing, paper cutouts of every and any sort, and her wonderful cooking. She was also loving, caring, compassionate to me, to all our children, and, of course, the grandchildren. Together with all that, she had a very strong personality, balanced, from time to time, with self-doubt and introspection. At times, I felt a bit left out or left behind!

She was also, in many ways, adventurous and

definitely fun-loving, while at the same time very sensitive and easily hurt. Sometimes just the wrong tone of voice from me or one of our children could bring her to tears and cause her much pain for hours. In those situations, it was I who managed to bring her out of that depressed state, and I think she was very grateful and appreciated my being there for her.

I learned a tremendous lot from Susan, and grew and changed, becoming more self-confident and at peace with myself and who I was. Interestingly though, this self-awareness and introspection became more evident and part of my daily existence after Sue's departure! Our children, I think, saw us often at odds with each other, but what they were not so aware of, especially in our later years, was the deep love and commitment we had for each other. Looking back, I know we had endless hassles over minor and, at times, even silly issues, that today I can hardly remember or comprehend. It seems so silly now.

Two days before Susan died, while she was sitting in her wheelchair (too weak to stand on her own two feet) under the Jacaranda tree that we had planted together thirteen years before, she demanded a can of Coke. Sue never touched soft drinks, but I ran to the nearest super to get it for her, with her firmly reprimanding me, 'Don't you know I like a Coke? Can't you have it for me in the fridge?' This was Susan, not having lost her strong character to the very end. I miss her dearly and loved her and love her to this day, but the Coke she never touched!"

I have often wondered why the story of the untouched Coke

had stayed with Gidon so. Maybe it's because Susan lapsed into unconsciousness only a day or two later, and that was the last time she was able to ask Gidon to do something for her, even if it was a small, illogical, even unnecessary thing. Surely she had felt terrible at that time, very near death. Perhaps Gidon remembered the Coke that Susan didn't really need or want as a final affirmation of his devotion to her and the life they made together.

CHAPTER 25
A JOURNEY OF 10,000 STEPS

Gidon was sitting on his usual spot on the sofa, his hands folded over his lumpy belly, which had two grapefruit-sized bulges that strained his shirt and pants buttons. One was what remained of two hernia operations, and the other was where Gidon's urostomy was. I called it his porthole. Gidon lost his bladder and much of his urinary tract in 2011 when he had stage-four bladder cancer. Now he had, as he put it, "new plumbing." I frequently tell him he's the Six Million Dollar Man.

With some trepidation, I handed him the latest chapter of the book. I knew that the previous chapter had been hard on him. He misses Sue so. But he had been such a trooper, reading chapters once, twice, three times and adding his notes and thoughts, sometimes writing entirely new sections when he wasn't pleased with something he'd written earlier. He'd been getting better at feedback, finally learning to say something nice first and then point out what he didn't like. I had to wait to see what he would say about today's pages.

"Thanks," he said. "You look funny by the way."

I knew I looked funny. I was wearing my goofy sun hat, complete with a chin strap and a pedometer. I had reached the age of not caring how I looked, especially when I was trying to get ten thousand steps of fresh air and my body moving after hours of sitting. Reaching the age of not caring how funny you look is a wonderful thing. I headed out into the warm sunshine.

Outside our building were old suitcases, dust, plaster, and piles of lumber that used to be cabinets. This was what remained of Maria, our upstairs neighbor. The workmen were mostly Palestinian and typically took the bus here from Ramallah. They were cheerful and hardworking. A few times a day, I heard the call of the muezzin; one of the workmen had an app on his phone so he could be reminded of when to stop working and pray. This, too, as Gidon would say, was Israel.

Maria spoke Yiddish, Hebrew, and Polish but very little English. She was a cheerful fixture of the building for the past thirty years, with a habit of sitting outside in her wheelchair with her Ukrainian caregiver, Natalie, enjoying the fresh air and saying hello to all who passed. One night, we heard a scream. Gidon and I ran to the front door and flung it open. From up the stairwell, the scream continued to echo. We ran up the two flights. Maria was on the floor, unconscious. Natalie was panicked. Gidon got down on his knees and gave Maria CPR. I had no idea he knew how to do this. I tried to calm Natalie (not possible), and I found a neighbor to help call an ambulance. Later, I tried to remember the exact moment that Maria died, but I couldn't quite tell. I just knew we were there when it happened, and it seemed like a privilege.

I had no way of knowing if Maria heard our voices or felt me stroking her forehead. I didn't know if she knew it was Gidon, with whom she had long enjoyed chatting, who was pumping her chest to get her heart going again. Within minutes, the paramedics arrived and surrounded Maria with their beeping machines. But it was clear that it was too late. Gidon and I stood and watched helplessly.

That was a few months ago. Maria's death left a pall over both of us for some time.

Gidon handed me a piece of paper on which he wrote further thoughts on Maria. "Gidon felt," he added, "while he was giving Maria CPR, that once she had closed her eyes, this was it. She was tired, she had a long life, and no amount of pressing would bring her back. She had had enough. She had said her goodbyes. She was at peace."

A few minutes later, Gidon returned to my office. "When I moved into the building, Maria was still driving, you know. She had a terrible time parking." He chuckled at the memory. "She would get so frustrated. So I would help her." Gidon looked down at his feet. "That was only four years ago."

Oof. I wondered what it must feel like to be at Gidon's age, when the death of even an acquaintance felt like—was—a premonition. Sometimes when Gidon sleeps, he goes completely still, and I touch him to make sure he is breathing. I know that one day, he won't be. I tell myself that this would be much better than long days suffering in a hospital, or languishing in a nursing home with dementia. Then I tell myself not to be so morbid and just to be in this relationship, in this moment, and stop thinking about the end all the time.

We talked about this when we first decided to be together, Gidon and I. The fact that he would have to leave me at some unknown point in time, that the length of our relationship already had an expiration date, a fact that we could not change. Gidon is unafraid of death, but what about me, I sometimes said with tears flowing down my cheeks. It's easy for Gidon to be in this relationship; when he gets ill and passes away, he will have been loved right up to the last minute, but I will have decades ahead without him.

"Oh, you'll find someone else," he said.

"And now that you have been with me," Gidon added later, "you know better what you want!"

Perhaps Gidon is not frightened by the prospect of death because he has cheated it so many times. He survived a concentration camp and the diseases there. He survived the Six-Day War, the War of Attrition, and cancer—twice.

In his paper clipped, early writings, there was a chapter called "The SCOURGE of Cancer."

GIDON "First it was Monte, Susan's dad, who died of pancreatic cancer in 1977, only seven years after coming to live in Israel. He did battle with this disease for an entire year, even returning to work and his beloved occupation: painting. But he finally succumbed, right there on Yehoshua Bin Nun Street, fourth floor, with all of us there to say goodbye. Then Margie, Susan's mom, came down with breast cancer—refusing any kind of operation or other therapies. 'Just give me painkillers,' she said to her doctor. She died in the fall of 1988. She waited for the holiday of Sukkot to be over. It was in our house in Nazareth Illit, surrounded by her loving family, which by then had grown to seven souls!

Next my mother got colon cancer in 1992. She called a day before her surgery. We didn't know she was sick! I flew to her immediately to be there for the operation. Later, she moved to Israel. She died in 2003, having managed her stoma for ten years. It took me many years to realize how difficult that is to do! Just a short while after my mother had her operation in 1992, I was found to have stage-four colon cancer and went through an entire year of intravenous chemotherapy every two weeks, in the Rambam Hospital in Haifa.

For the first three to four days after the chemo, I would rest. I felt weak and suffered from nausea. I felt like doing nothing, even television I didn't want to watch. Slowly, I would regain my strength and appetite. Then I would start my work for the next ten or so days, doing the milk test program in the surrounding *moshavim* (agricultural villages), with the help of my kids, who worked with me and were a wonderful help. Just as I was feeling good and energetic again, back to the hospital for another treatment. The cycle started all over again. It was clear, as the treatments continued, and are cumulative, that the side effects were more and more pronounced. Halfway through, I became disillusioned, to put it mildly, and considered the idea of stopping treatment altogether! To me, a year seemed a long time to bear this, and I was getting tired of it all. Susan, my sweet, dear wife, spent many an hour talking to me and helping me to get out of this depressed state, and so I gradually did. I continued the treatment for the rest of the year, even when I had to go to Canada for a month, to help my mother sell her house, pack up, and move to Israel. I simply took the medication with me and had my old family doctor arrange to have it done—not by him, mind you, doctors are really not that great at giving these kind of injections—but by a very experienced nurse at the Mt. Sinai hospital in Toronto. One interesting aspect, though, evolved over the years, that this protocol that I was following for an entire year could have been done for just half a year, with, according to statistics and later research, the same results.

Of course, there is no question that Sue's help

and firm encouragement—and the warmth of my children, too—helped me to overcome my depressed state. I continued the full protocol, and, in the end, I was pronounced clean of cancer. Then, a month or two after my mother died, in 2003, I was diagnosed with cancer again. I had what is called TCC—transitional cell carcinoma, which my doctor, Basel Fahoum from Nazareth, kept in check for seven years by performing a cystoscopy every three months. I had to stay in the hospital for two to three days for that. Sometimes it was painful, getting a spinal injection, and sometimes it was even funny, as I would lie there naked on the table. I remember once when an English nurse held my hand when I got the spinal injection. The nurses and staff got to know me. I became a fixture. You have to remember, I was there every three months for seven years!"

I could not imagine what this medical minefield would have cost Gidon in another country, or if it would have been possible for him to receive this care at all. In Israel, every citizen is entitled to health care services under the National Health Insurance Law, and it is illegal to deny this right based on preexisting conditions or risks.

So there's a silver lining in Gidon's painful medical odyssey: it was affordable and of some of the highest standards. But, even so, the physical and psychological pain was, at times, almost unbearable.

 GIDON "Finally, in 2010, the cancer finally penetrated into the wall of my bladder, blocking one of my kidneys. A few months later, I had a seven-and-a-half-hour surgery to remove my bladder. So here I was, 'the cancer man,' and, yet,

> Susan, half way through 2011, came down with lung
> cancer and died within a year."

I returned from my walk, which took me in a circuitous route
through Ramat Gan, past the little shops and cafés, zigzagging
through a park or two. It took me about 90 minutes and 7
kilometers, a little over 4 miles, to get to 10,000 steps. Often, I
tried to game this: Should I walk faster? Uphill? What is the best
path to maximize my exercise but also get back home and get
back to working on this book? I felt more and more urgency to
finish; Gidon would be eighty-five soon. I wanted, more than
anything I had ever wanted, for Gidon to hold this book in his
hands.

I opened the door, and Gidon looked up. "I don't like this,"
he said testily. This was not like Gidon, this tone. "There's not
enough information here."

I made us both a cup of tea, and we sat at our small kitchen
table. "Tell me," I said.

When Gidon launches into a conversation that he is
passionate about, he really launches. It's very difficult to stop the
train. He started by giving me the names of specific doctors, the
dates of various treatments, the way the room was big or small.
It became clear that Gidon had a lot of pent-up emotion about
this terrible period in his life. He shifted to the details of his
treatment for bladder cancer, stressing his points carefully. I told
Gidon that this long list of details might be too tedious for a
reader to connect with. He was not satisfied. It seemed clear
that Gidon was projecting onto me his frustration of being
unable to convey the depth of his suffering with not just his own
struggles with cancer but with the way it affected his family.
There was something more going on here, something in between
the lines. Some enormous, unresolved grief. I wanted to get to
the bottom of it.

I told Gidon about the very first time in my life that I
experienced utter fear and panic. I had lived in Israel only for a

few months when there was a military operation called Operation Pillar of Smoke. I had never before heard air raid sirens, nor had I been forced to run to the bomb shelter. I couldn't even understand what the news reports were saying, so bad was my Hebrew. It was utterly foreign and it ~~scared me deeply~~ scared the shit out of me (Gidon amended on my behalf).

I had visited Los Angeles only a couple of weeks after it was over, eager to talk to my friends about it. While my friends showed genuine concern and interest, they just couldn't relate. It was as if I were speaking another language. The topic petered out. That was when it struck me that the experience I just had was one that made my world smaller. Anybody could relate to stories about relationships or jobs with bad bosses or a fun vacation. But when you experience something very specific, such as war or the suicide of a loved one or cancer, you occupy a different space. A lonelier one.

Gidon agreed in principle. He saw what I was getting at.

Sensing an opening, I asked him to tell me more about Susan's struggle with cancer. When did she find out? What was the first diagnosis? Gidon's demeanor changed: no longer testy or demanding, he was just sad. He told me everything about that terrible year while Susan suffered. How, at first, the doctor thought Susan had pneumonia. The antibiotics didn't work because the diagnosis was incorrect, but nobody knew that yet. Tearfully, Gidon told me about how he and his sons helped Susan go to see her absolute favorite musician, Paul Simon, in his first live concert in Israel. She was so weak she needed help walking.

Gidon told me about how every test, every doctor visit was marked by bad news, then promising news, then bad news again. He told me how Susan and he managed to go on a cruise in the Mediterranean to help a childhood friend suffering from multiple sclerosis enjoy one of her last wishes. It was the last vacation Gidon and Susan spent together before cancer completely took over their lives. The experimental treatment Sue tried was ineffective, and the usual treatments didn't work either. She grew weak. The cancer had spread from her lungs to her brain. She stopped cooking and reading.

"She even stopped watching her favorite show, *The Dog Whisperer*," Gidon added.

Susan was disappearing before the family's eyes. Gidon told me how his youngest, Asher, who had returned to Israel from abroad, spent hours at his mother's side, talking with her about everything under the sun, helping her cope. It was Asher who, together with Susan, chose the poems that would go in her book of poetry that the family so cherishes today.

When Gidon twice struggled with his own cancer, even though he came close to wanting just to quit the fight, he was able to define his struggle, to contain it. He worked, he showed up for his treatments, he carried on. But when Susan got cancer, it was different. All the hard work in the world—planning and being a good, supportive partner—did not stop the inexorable progress of cancer within Susan's body. There was no way to simply carry on, and that became clear only a few months after the initial diagnosis. I asked Gidon how Susan felt when the doctor told her and Gidon that nothing more could be done.

"She was quiet," he said. "She only wanted no hospitalization and no pain."

That made sense. I became quiet, too. I could tell this conversation had worn Gidon out, emotionally and physically. As cheerful as he usually is, he also has a deep well of grief.

"Gidon misses his partner of forty years. Her photos, poems, and journals and of course her spirit are the only things he has left," Gidon added. "And the children."

And . . . my heart just broke.

CHAPTER 26

THE LIKE OF THIS

"Has the like of this happened in your days or the days of your fathers? Tell your children about it, and let their children tell theirs and their children the next generation!"

1 Joel, 2-3

Gidon and I were prepared for our visit to Yad Vashem. At least, we thought we were. We had collected and stapled Doris's records and looked through family photographs that Gidon kept in a cracked leather pouch. The photos smelled of age and dust. The writing on the back was in German and in Czech. Pictures of aunts, uncles, cousins, brothers and sisters, grandparents and great-grandparents, some in daguerreotypes from before the turn of the last century. Gidon's great-grandfather, who was perhaps three years old at the time, was posed holding a Czech sword of some kind. There was one photo of Gidon, in 1946, laughing in the snow, wearing his American cousin's U.S. Army cap, his cousin looking for all the world like Elvis Presley, standing nearby. Gidon had been liberated from the concentration camp for only about a year when this photo was taken.

The name Yad Vashem literally translates to "hand and name" but is more commonly understood as "monument of names" and is taken from Isaiah 56:5: "To them I will give within my temple and its walls a memorial and a name better than sons and daughters; I will give them an everlasting name that will endure forever."

The sprawling museum, research, and education center is located on Mt. Herzl—named after the early Zionist leader Theodor Herzl—and overlooks the hilly Ein Kerem neighborhood of Jerusalem in the southwest of the city. Yad Vashem first opened its doors in 1957 and, in 2005—about forty-eight years later—debuted a footprint four times larger than the original, designed by famed Israeli Canadian architect Moshe Safdie. During his long career, Safdie, a Syrian Jew from Haifa and a gifted and prolific architect, also designed, among many others, the Hebrew University, the main branch of the Salt Lake City Library, the Skirball Cultural Center in Los Angeles, and the National Gallery of Canada in Ottawa. In no small part due to Safdie's design, Yad Vashem is more than a museum; it is the experience of entering a darkening maze before gradually returning to the light.

The day Gidon and I went, it was 101 degrees Fahrenheit in Jerusalem. The heat wave that descended had brought with it a fine dust from North Africa, and it hung over Israel like a yellow shroud. In Israel, this is called a *chamsin* (kham-seen), an Arabic word that means "fifty"; it is said that these dust storms strike the region about fifty times a year. They seem to come more often now, probably as another sign of climate change. This weather phenomenon is also called a *sharav* in Hebrew.

I drove to the museum, which gave Gidon the rare opportunity to enjoy the golden fields of his country from the comfort of the air-conditioned car, rather than wrangling with traffic as he usually and expertly does. "Even now, at his age!" Gidon added.

Lumbering tourist buses filled one of the several parking lots near the museum, which receives hundreds of thousands of visitors yearly. A long list of world leaders and presidents have visited, not to mention notables like the Dalai Lama, Pope John Paul II, Prince William, Duke of Cambridge, and film star Marlene Dietrich. In the Garden of the Righteous Among Nations, more than twenty-six thousand non-Jews who risked their safety, freedom, and lives to help Jews during World War II are commemorated.

Not an especially large space, the reading room at Yad Vashem is filled with encyclopedias, ledgers, maps, and records of names. This is but a fraction of the information to be found in the museum's database, which is available to search on the ten or twelve computers located at the desks clustered in the center of the room.

Outside, there was a sweeping view of Jerusalem, shimmering in the heat. Inside, Gidon and I happily enjoyed the air-conditioning. About eight or ten other people were there. Some seemed to be American tourists, taking advantage of being in Israel to look up information about relatives. At another desk, a whole family sat around a computer, listening to the filmed testimonial of an elderly man, who, I presumed, was their grandfather. The testimonial was in a language that I did not recognize, but the family seemed to understand just fine, exchanging smiles and sad looks with each other as they watched their relative speak. The American couple stood to leave, and the librarian told them in English that she was so sorry they didn't find what they were looking for. The couple shrugged apologetically and left. The librarian sat down with an older, religious couple, the man wearing prayer fringes under his heavy overcoat; his wife, wearing modest long sleeves, also had her head covered.

As Gidon and I waited our turn, we leafed through books about villages in Ukraine and browsed the names of Jews who lived in Łódź. With effort, I picked up a coffee table-size book that had to have been four inches thick. It was a list of villages destroyed during the Holocaust. Villages under the letter *A* alone took up forty pages. A whole world. Gone. Disappeared. The librarian, Mickey, was a young and graceful Orthodox Jew. Her head was covered modestly as she flitted efficiently from one person to another in the quiet space. Occasionally, a young girl of about six or seven, with a head full of unruly, curly red hair, sidled up alongside her and spoke urgently to her in hushed Hebrew. Finally, it was our turn.

"What country?" Mickey asked.

"Czechoslovakia," I said and pointed to Gidon. "Theresienstadt." Mickey's demeanor changed instantly. She peered at Gidon then said something sweet and sincere about how Gidon appeared much younger than he was. It's true.

Mickey invited us to sit at a desk. The keyboard clattered away under her touch. The database at Yad Vashem is incredibly complete but not very user-friendly, which was half the battle. In only a minute or two, Mickey had located the records of Arnošt Löw (Ernst in German), Gidon's father. She clicked through several pages of documents and information, written in both Czech and German, then she stopped and looked at Gidon.

"Who did your father piss off?" she asked. Ernst had been transported from Térézin to Auschwitz on a "family transport"—without his family. "Something happened here," Mickey murmured as she flicked through documents.

Whether Ernst was punished by being sent alone in a family transport or whether he managed to keep Doris and Gidon off the same transport, we would never know.

"Ah. Look at this," Mickey said. "From Auschwitz he was sent to Buchenwald."

"No," Gidon stammered. He explained that his father was sent to Auschwitz and then died on a death march right before the end of the war, in spring 1945, as far as he knew.

Mickey tapped a fingernail against the computer screen where the records of Ernst—who had by then been tattooed as number B12156—blinked gloomily. "He was quarantined for a time"—she peered more closely—"probably with typhus. Then he was sent on a transport to Buchenwald." Mickey clicked away. "This is odd. There is no record of his arrival at Buchenwald. Only of his transport out of Auschwitz."

Gidon sat between Mickey and me. He was uncharacteristically quiet.

One of the many things that make the Holocaust unique among atrocities is the care with which the perpetrators documented their own crimes; so sure were they that they would be hailed as heroes of efficiency in the annals of history, Mickey explained. At Buchenwald, prisoners and transports were tracked meticulously. She showed us documentation of ration cards, health cards, and ledgers of the names of those arriving on this week or that.

Mickey clicked back to Ernst's record. He had no card upon his arrival.

"I don't understand. What happened?" I asked.

Mickey looked at me as though I had asked whether the moon was made of cheese. "He must have arrived dead."

The air was sucked out of the room with a wrenching yank. Gidon knew his father had died in the camps; he'd known this since 1946. But this—this detail. It was too much. Gidon closed his blue eyes. His shoulders shook. I put my arm around him, asking, "You okay?"

"Yes, yes," he said, wiping his eyes. "Sort of."

I took Mickey aside. I had a question that I didn't want to ask in front of Gidon. I told her that in her Yad Vashem paperwork, Gidon's mother had written that she believed that her own mother had been "electrocuded" [sic] in Belzec. Perhaps as a way to cope, Gidon thought this ridiculous. But I had looked at this entry over and over again: E-L-E-C-T-R-O-C-U-D-E-D.

A stupid rumor, Gidon had said. She didn't know what she was saying. She had no way of knowing. This was true; Doris could not have known what happened to her mother. But,

Mickey told me, Belzec did indeed experiment with putting people on platforms and electrocuting them, and that fact—even though Gidon's grandmother Alice actually went to Treblinka—will never leave my brain.

"How do you do this?" I asked Mickey a few minutes later.

"Oh, I'll cry after you leave," she said. "I don't usually cry in front of people."

Suddenly, the cute redheaded curly-haired little girl was back. She threw her arms around her mother's waist. "I'm hungry!"

"The natives are getting restless," Mickey said with an apologetic smile.

"I don't know how to behave around someone who has received this kind of knowledge," I told Gidon as we made our way back to the car and readied for the hour-long drive back home. The truth was, I didn't know how to react to my own knowledge of these horrors, made so personal through Gidon.

"Just be yourself," Gidon reassured me as he buckled up. I wanted to put on some cheerful music or to unroll the windows and scream into the dusty yellow heat. I didn't know what to do or say.

I turned to Gidon. "Have you ever heard that saying that 'if wishes were fishes, the sea would be full'?" I had no idea why that came out of my mouth.

"But the seas are full of fishes!" said Gidon.

A day later, a picture of Gidon's father, Ernst, came crashing out of the past and into our possession when a friend on social media managed to find it in an online database. The photo was taken in 1941 in or near Prague. It showed Ernst trying to apply for a visa.

I stared at the photo, hoping that maybe it was a mistake. The resignation and fatigue on Ernst's face were heartbreaking, and the resemblance to Gidon was uncanny. How would Gidon handle seeing this photograph after the news of the previous day? Gidon had not seen a photo of the father he barely remembered in years, and never at this age and stage of his life. I asked him to sit down and handed him a copy of the photo and the paperwork it came with. Gidon stared at the photo at length.

"Yup," he said.

In three years, Ernst would no longer resemble this picture. He would be in Térézin and then Auschwitz, emaciated and skeletal.

∼

There truly has never been anything like the Holocaust. But there have been very many acts of genocide and mass brutality akin to Nazi atrocities. Between 1914 and 1923, 1.5 million Armenians were systematically murdered by the Ottoman Empire. To this day, diplomatic battles rage about whether to term these horrible events as genocide. In Cambodia, between 1975 and 1979, roughly 1.5–2 million Cambodians were murdered by the Khmer Rouge in the infamous killing fields. Between 1992 and 1995, thousands of Bosnians and Serbs were murdered in a horrific orgy of ethnic cleansing. During just a few months in 1994, 800,000 Tutsis were massacred by Hutu tribesmen.

In *A Primer For Forgetting*, Lewis Hyde reminded me of an old Jewish legend.

 ". . . the Angel of the Night, Lailah, places the fertilized soul of a child in the womb, and kindling a light so the soul can see the world from end to end, teaches it about the just and the wicked, those who follow the Torah and God's commandments and those who do not. When it comes time to be born, the angel lightly strokes the child's upper lip, leaving a small indentation. Immediately, the

242

newborn forgets all it has seen and learned and comes into the world crying."

In autumn 2018, CNN conducted a poll that revealed that one-third of Europeans reported knowing little or nothing at all about the Holocaust and that one in twenty Europeans in the countries surveyed had never even heard of the Holocaust.[1] Americans didn't fare any better. A different survey found that 10 percent of American adults were not sure they'd ever heard of the Holocaust, rising to 20 percent of millennials. Half of all millennials could not name a single concentration camp, and 45 percent of all American adults failed to do so.

There's more. In 2018, there was a 74 percent rise of anti-Semitic attacks in France, a 60 percent increase in Germany, and in the United States, according to the Anti-Defamation League, "the number of acts targeting Jews and Jewish institutions rose 34 percent in 2016 and jumped 86 percent in the first quarter of 2017".[2]

I am shocked and dismayed by these figures. Hasn't the Holocaust been represented time and again in major books and films such as *Schindler's List*, *Sophie's Choice*, *The Pianist*, and *Life is Beautiful*? Aren't there dozens of documentaries on Netflix about Hitler and his henchmen? What about the stacks of historical fiction about World War II available in libraries and bookstores?

What is happening?

Maybe in this post-everything world, the Holocaust just doesn't matter anymore. Or it might be worse: Is it possible that the past doesn't matter anymore? What are we doing wrong?

The usual suspects come to mind: underfunded education systems; smartphones and, with them, the dazzling number of ways to distract ourselves; social media and its endless feedback loop of self-centeredness; movies, those seductive machines of myth-making and happy endings reassuring us that the good guys, who usually wear capes, always win and that we need not look back unless it's the prequel origin story of the hero. Is the Joker more well-known than Hitler these days?

Okay, boomer, a voice says in my head. End rant. Calm down.

I do not believe it's useful to assume from these surveys that 10 percent of Americans, half of all American millennials, and one-third of Europeans between the ages of eighteen and thirty-four are stupid, ignorant, lazy, or anti-Semitic. We have to be particularly careful not to further alienate millennials by accusing them of ignorance or stupidity: not being able to name a Nazi concentration camp does not signify an endorsement of the Holocaust. Correlation versus causality is important here. Maybe we're just not asking the right questions in these surveys.

I suspect that the usual collective amnesia plus a sense of despair and detachment in these sped-up times are more to blame than anything else. What percentage of Europeans or Americans know about the Uyghurs in China, or the reasons for and the details of the wars in Syria or Afghanistan? Is that not also shameful? Doesn't this willful ignorance shine a light on our all-too-human tendency to filter out that which we think does not affect us, that seems far away, long ago, or otherwise not affecting us personally?

"Excuses," as Thucydides did not exactly say, "are an expensive commodity. It's better to be prepared."

When Gidon and I visited the oddly named Ghetto Fighters Museum in northern coastal Israel not far from Acre, we had an unsettling but instructive experience. There was a large room on a subterranean level devoted to the Auschwitz concentration camp. As Gidon and I made our way through the exhibits in the room, a flood of animated Russian teenagers poured down the stairs like a wave of pure energy. The kids were a bit boisterous for such a solemn place, but they were on a field trip. The teacher explained to me that they were students from an international boarding school in Israel.

The far end of the large room featured an imposing black map of Europe. Red, blue, and yellow circles and triangles of various sizes marked the sites of concentration camps, extermination camps, and transport centers. Big blue boxes marked the places of mass killings. The teens swarmed the map. Excitedly, they pointed out Odessa and Kiev, places they were familiar with. A group of teenage boys clambered over themselves, arranging themselves on the floor just below the map. They posed themselves at length, making sure each face would be seen. A compatriot focused his smartphone camera on the group. They counted to three and stuck out their tongues.

I wanted to be angry at them, or offended, but I couldn't. How were twenty-first-century teenagers supposed to feel in this room, with these awful images, with this overwhelming, devastating information presented in blinking lights and behind glass? How did we expect kids to react?

There were troubling connections between the form and function of Térézin, of World War II, and of the rise of intolerance and right-wing politics today. Térézin, you might say, was among the original bits of fake news: Hitler wanted the world to believe that he had built a city for the Jews—a model camp, a Zionist experiment, a resettlement program. Such nice words used to mask such horrors.

The vocabulary we use when we preserve our narratives and how and if they might be understood in the future is critical. Fake news locates the events of Térézin within the fabric of our current battle with disinformation, lies, and social media bots. Some have suggested that Térézin wasn't a real concentration camp because it lacked gas chambers. Some even have suggested the Holocaust didn't happen at all. Such lunacy is not worth entertaining.

The writer in me is well aware of the semantics: concentration camp. Those two words bring to mind awful images that we've all seen in black-and-white. Stacks of corpses. Emaciated survivors staring at the camera lens vacantly. In German, *lager* means camp. The German word *vernichtung* means obliteration, annihilation, destruction, and extermination. Three million Jews were exterminated in these camps. It's no mistake that the word *extermination* was used. It's what we do to pests. The Nazis were meticulous about everything, including semantics.

In the United States, the use of the words *concentration camp* to describe the detained immigrants on the U.S.-Mexico border has been hotly disputed as inaccurate, misleading, and even offensive. Two points of view are ostensibly in agreement with one another and yet meet in the queasy middle; supporters of cruel, inhumane conditions on the border are offended by any allusion to the evils of Nazi Germany, so loathe are they to be compared to the ultimate evil. Another point of view is that the Holocaust occupies a singular sphere of horror and, therefore, there is absolutely no equivalence between a Nazi concentration camp and any other type of concentration camp. We argue about semantics while the building burns down around us.

The Auschwitz-Birkenau Memorial and Museum in Poland weighed in with this statement:

> "When we look at Auschwitz we see the end of the process . . . It's important to remember that the Holocaust actually did not start from gas chambers; this hatred gradually developed from words, stereotypes & prejudice through legal exclusion, dehumanization & escalating violence".[3]

To paraphrase, the Holocaust didn't begin with Auschwitz and gas chambers. They're how it ended.

There is hope. Rachael Cerrotti's *We Share the Same Sky* is a moving podcast series about Rachael's journey as she walks in the same footsteps of her grandmother, who lived in hiding in the Netherlands during World War II. Rachael is young, and her voice is melodic. The podcast is multilayered and gripping. In my correspondence with Rachael, she said:

"I think we are in a strange (and, of course, unprecedented) space right now with Holocaust history, anti-Semitism, Jewish identity, etc. It seems that a lot of people are talking about it, but there is less understanding of what it actually was. I had a friend (not Jewish) write me as I was releasing the [*We Share the Same Sky*] series, and she commented that she always thought she knew what the Holocaust was because she had heard the word so many times, but in listening to my story, she realized that she actually didn't know anything about it. I found this to be profoundly honest and see it as being a truth for many people, Jews included. But, this is why we do what we do. The way I told the story is resonating with people of all ages. The podcast, aside from being for the general public, is now being placed in classrooms around the country as a way to teach Holocaust history."

Rachael isn't the only one doing her best to educate everyone about the realities of the Holocaust. In 2019, Israel tech executive Mati Kochavi and his daughter, Maya, created Eva's Instagram account, which was based on the 1944 diary of a Hungarian teenager named Eva Heyman. A normal, relatable teenager with the requisite hopes and dreams, Eva also happened to document her days in a journal—and, now, in the Instagram series with a smartphone—as her ordinary prewar life grew darker before it faded to black. Eva died in the Auschwitz concentration camp in October 1944. The series generated controversy: how dare the Holocaust be discussed with the use of emojis!

I disagree. How shall we tell these stories when the eyewitnesses are gone? Any way that we can.

CHAPTER 27

MOTHER

  GIDON "My poor relationship with my mother, who didn't care, interest herself, or speak to me about anything of real importance, was painful for me. For most of us males, the most crucial and important relationship we have is with our mothers, and that influences our future relationships, not only with the female gender, but relationships with people in general. My mother oppressed, depressed, and suppressed me. She knew nothing about my emotional or intellectual being, nor was she concerned about it. She never told me she loved me."

It had become evident to me that, in his long life, four events were most painful for Gidon: the Holocaust, the end of his first marriage and the consequences of that, the death of Susan, and his relationship with his mother. He wrote pages and pages about his mother, but he had written the same thing, over and over, just changing words or sentence order now and again.

GIDON "My mother insisted I sleep after lunch, and most of the time I was not able to do so. So I developed a very instinctive system of faking that I was asleep, just out of fear of being punished. I also remember her absolute demand that I finish the food on my plate, including spinach, which I hated. I remember at least once when, after being forced to eat it, I vomited it up and mother made me eat it again, standing over me! Sometimes, she made me kneel in the corner, on dried peas."

Mothers forcing kids to take naps and kids pretending to do so is as old as time. Kneeling on dried peas is horrible, but punishments like these were probably not uncommon a few decades ago. But forcing a child to eat his own vomit? Can that be true? My God.

I asked some of Gidon's grown children how they remembered Doris. "Hard." "Sharp." "Difficult." These were the words that came up. She did, though, make a particular kind of pastry, Shaya noted kindly, that was delicious.

Susan wrote a few poems about Doris. In them, she searched for compassion and understanding, but they are painful, even angry poems. One is called "My Mother-in-Law, the Scorpion." Another is "My Mother-in-Law, Angry."

One day, Gidon took an old, broken wooden spoon out of a drawer in the kitchen. This, he explained, was the same wooden spoon that Doris used to beat him with. I very much doubted this was the actual spoon but it didn't matter—to Gidon, it was.

GIDON "I actually remember the time, as if it was today, when, for the first time, I physically stopped my mother from hitting me. We were standing in the hall of our house on Cranbrook Avenue in Toronto. She was prepared to hit me, for some reason or other, this time with a *kochlefl* (wooden spoon), and I, by this time bigger and stronger than her, pinned her hands to her side and said, 'No more, Mother! You can punish me, you can yell at me, but no more hitting!' She truly was taken aback that her little 'Peterl' would dare do this to her."

Doris had experienced a terrible childhood trauma herself. In a painful and mysterious family dispute, when Doris was about eight years old, her parents divorced. It was ugly. There were allegations that Doris's mother, Alice, had been unfaithful to Doris's father while he had been away during WWI. Mother and daughter were separated. Alice was "banished," as Gidon put it, to Vienna, some hours away from Karlovy Vary. Doris found herself without a mother for reasons she did not understand, living with a father she barely knew. There was no evidence of a custody arrangement or visitations. Thereafter, Doris saw her mother only two or three times in her lifetime.

It wasn't long before Fritz, Doris's father, remarried. Together with his new wife, Elsa, he had another child, a son named Heinz. Later in life, Doris told Gidon that she loved her younger brother, Heinz, but that her stepmother, Elsa, was unloving. Eventually, Doris was sent to a boarding school in Prague. Doris had not been mothered lovingly after the age of eight.

Fritz, Elsa, and Heinz all died in the Warsaw Ghetto.

Gidon had long known about his mother's separation from her mother and ascribed this terrible episode as the source of Doris's "oppression, depression, and suppression." What he didn't add to this calculus was the trauma, deprivation, and terror of Doris's own concentration camp experience.

Her bad behavior both preceded and continued after the Holocaust, he was quick to point out.

None of my attempts to emphasize that, no doubt, Doris's experience in Terézin must have had an enormous impact on her shifted Gidon's pain on the subject. He seemed unwilling or unable to notice the patterns of abandonment and broken families in his lifetime. I so badly wanted for Gidon to inch toward a modicum of, if not forgiveness, at least understanding of his mother. But there are some conclusions that we just have to come to ourselves, if ever we do.

Inspired by the book project, Gidon had shifted into high gear, joining a Jewish genealogy website and adding many friends on Facebook. He reconnected with cousins in Canada. One day, Gidon got a package in the mail. Inside the envelope were letters that Doris had sent to a cousin. In them, Doris wrote with pride of her Peter and extolled the merits of his wonderful wife, Susan, and their children. In another letter, Doris mentioned that she suffered anxiety attacks and that the past was very painful for her. This peek into Doris's thoughts surprised Gidon. He softened, just a little.

"I do remember times," Gidon mused, "when my mother was happy, joyful—even in Prague—when she was working at home making hats. Sometimes she would sing—she had a beautiful voice—and loved to dance. She also had a great love for opera, and this love she did instill in me. I want to admit here," Gidon added, "that I was not the most sensitive and kind son I could and should have been, especially in my adulthood. Had I been more forgiving, I probably would have known and understood a great deal more about my mother's and my family's life. I realize this only now, a bit too late."

I told Gidon that it was natural that he felt anger toward his mother but that he shouldn't turn that anger into guilt. I thought he might have been making some small movement in the direction of forgiving his mother and himself. For such a garrulous person, Gidon very often did not wish to speak on this particular subject, so I was always cautious when broaching the topic.

"Maybe she wasn't cut out to be a mother," I offered lamely.

Gidon pulled out a binder called *My Mother*, stuffed with photographs, notes, forms, and birthday cards from grandchildren. There were cards to Gidon and eulogies for Doris upon her death. One is from Susan:

> "Don Juan the Shaman says to Carlos Castaneda 'find yourself a worthy tyrant, if you want to improve your spiritual abilities and moral strength.' In many ways Safta Doris was a worthy tyrant, and I respected her for that! . . . Doris was a survivor. She went through life as if always on the lookout, always seeking a safe landing from a stormy sea. Always making sure there was a piece of wood strong enough to support her and her son through the gale."

There was something else in the binder: twelve yellowed, crinkled handwritten pages titled "Koncentrationcamp Years 1941–1945, as written by Doris." Gidon said that he had never seen this document, yet he was a keeper of records. He had boxes and files of photographs, clippings, and papers. Had he truly never seen this? Or was his memory playing selective tricks on his mind?

The twelve-page letter was written in English, so I had to guess that Doris wrote it some years after the war. I had never heard anything from Doris's point of view about this chapter in Gidon's life. It was like opening a time capsule. I must admit I was surprised by Gidon's reaction.

"This isn't true," he said, pointing to a paragraph. "That isn't true, either."

"Gidon—"

"She just made that up."

I was at a loss for words. She *made it up*? Wasn't Doris the grown-up in the situation? Wouldn't her memories—if anything —be *more* accurate than Gidon's?

But Gidon was on a roll now. He spotted something else, shot up and went to his files. He was keen to prove his mother wrong about one specific point: that his grandfather was with Gidon and Doris when they were transported to Térézin.

"If my grandfather was *with* us, he would have helped me carry my bag!" Gidon sputtered, his face reddening with emotion. "He would *not* have let me carry it so far in the snow!" Gingerly, I showed him the transport paperwork again – his, his mother's and his grandfather Alfred's. They were all on Transport M, on December 14th, 1941.

"Gidon," I said, as gently as possible, "your grandfather was prisoner number 339. You were prisoner number 885 and your mother was number 884. The Nazis probably separated the men from the women and children. He was there. He just wasn't with you."

Gidon was experiencing a terrible emotional flashback and I felt responsible for it. Angrily, he picked up a pen. I intervened: no writing on this document. I made a copy for him so that he could correct away if that was what he was moved to do. The end of the following passage set him off yet again:

> "Thru all this we saw Ernst for a few minutes every day and even some times a little longer and he made plans for the future—that kept us going. Ernst loved his little boy so much and truly tried his best to stay alive. Ernst's father, Alfred Löw, came down with a twisted [illegible] and died an awful death in Theresienstadt—nobody operated on him! He had a heart of gold and loved us all so much.
>
> [illegible] that is the woman I lived with in the dorm was [illegible] when I read them from my cookbook which somehow I had in my suitcase—

recipes about rich cakes and good rich foods with lots of butter, eggs, etc. That was our dream.

There was something in the coffee the Germans gave us—which prevented the women to have their periods. Actually it was a good thing—as we had only cold water to wash us, the children, and our laundry. Of course, we all had lice and tried the best we could to keep clean.

Also I came down with T.B. by then there were sickrooms established and Jewish doctors from the transports helping us. I was lucky—there were two doctors from Karlovy Vary—one was our family doctor, Dr. Feldman Fisher, the other Dr. Löwenstein. They got me into a sickroom and helped me as best they could. There was one small cup of milk and a little supper every day—but no medicine. But I had a cot at an open window so there was fresh air. My Peter, who slept with me before, miraculous[ly] did not get the disease (T.B.) as we later found out. Those two doctors saved Peter's and mine life. All the sick people had to be reported and they were shipped to Auschwitz. Those two doctors kept my name and number from the list twice or three times. All the Jewish doctors who worked for us were later shipped out and perished! I was nearly a year in the sickroom and Ernst as best he could looked after Peter."

"Absolutely not true," Gidon said with angry finality. "I saw my father twice."

"But she writes, right here—"

"She's wrong."

Gidon was more than affronted, he was triggered. Doris's accounts contradicted his own memories. I was left only to surmise that, for Gidon, the thought that his grandfather couldn't help him when he first arrived at the camp and that he saw his father from time to time but had no memory of those visits was just not bearable.

One warm autumn afternoon in Tel Aviv, Gidon and I stood knee-deep in the Mediterranean. We were throwing breadcrumbs into the water as part of the Jewish new year tradition of throwing away regrets and wrongdoings of the past year and leaving an opening for doing better in the next. Gidon had never done it, but he was game. Moments later, as we walked back over the sand, avoiding crunching over seashells, I asked Gidon what he was thinking about when he threw his bread into the water.

"My mother," he said stiffly.

"What about your mother?" I asked a little disingenuously. Gidon knew I wanted so badly for him to forgive Doris.

"I want to think about her more kindly. I guess."

We clambered back up and over the concrete wall meant to keep us out of the estuary from whence we'd made our way to the sea.

"Don't tell anybody," Gidon said as he held out a hand to help me up and over the rocks.

"Is it okay if I include this, Gidon?" I asked months later.

"Yup," he said without skipping a beat.

CHAPTER 28

HINENI

"Have you read the article?"

I had just finished reading a long, depressing article about climate change. I was taking it too seriously, Gidon said. I was being too pessimistic. Angrily, defensively, eager for Gidon to share my view that life was terrible, I printed the twenty-plus-page article and handed it to him to read. Everything seemed futile.

From the other room, I heard pages turning quietly. Gidon had set himself to reading the article. Half an hour passed. I laced up and got ready for my daily walk. Then I heard Gidon's shuffling steps approaching.

"But they're going to find solutions," Gidon said, handing the article back to me. He shuffled away stubbornly. There is no changing this man.

It seemed like a million years ago that I met Gidon Lev. Early in our acquaintance, he was bent not just on publishing a book about his life but also on having that book read by very many people. Thousands of them. As many as possible. Maybe, he said, it would even be a movie. Gidon, the improbable warrior, was not afraid to dream big. But he also wanted validation, and maybe some admiration, too. Don't we all? It's like that funeral fantasy that we all have, whether we admit it or not. The touching things people will say about us and how we affected their lives. What an inspiration we were! How it all added up to a cohesive, inspiring, uplifting story that makes sense. How fondly we will be remembered! What music should be played at said funeral? What really captures who we were?

Each of us has memories that we file, rearrange, embellish, and sculpt so that we can learn from them—if we can bear to think about them at all. Maybe as an octogenarian, Gidon was able to be so honest about his life because he felt he had nothing to lose, having not just survived but also flourished and embraced that most essential part of himself—his complicated, contradictory humanness—and made peace with it. We are all inventions of ourselves, in the end, and curators of our narratives.

Being so enmeshed in Gidon's life was not always easy for me. I had sometimes felt a loss of my own identity. Eventually, I was able to recognize that among the lessons for me in this experience was that the infinitely complex process of being alive and finding meaning in our stories was generous and inclusive.

Gidon had not studied spirituality or feel-good books or philosophies the way I had, so tirelessly, in my search for comfort, meaning, and maybe even a helpful aha! moment or shortcut. He didn't have any books by Jack Kornfeld or Tibetan Buddhist nun Pema Chödrön on his bookshelves. He hadn't read Eckhart Tolle or listened to the inspiring Ted Talks by Brené Brown. Gidon, it seemed, didn't overthink. He just lived. He considered life a great gift without ascribing to any belief of pop theories, cosmic sensibilities, or wishful thinking. He is just happy to wake up every morning. It's that simple.

Gidon is a mischievous person, a man drawn to risks, to jerry-rigging things, to making things work in the moment. He likes to get away with things, to beat the system and the odds. Having experienced his childhood in a concentration camp, Gidon had to behave accordingly to survive. He had to fall in, to make do, to adapt. He was inculcated with both a sense of order and discipline and violent outcomes but also with a kind of survival-thinking: get what you can and run. This sometimes made him a bit reckless.

He rarely, if ever, experienced life according to his individual needs. He adapted to each situation and, in some ways, became a bit of a Zelig figure, morphing into whatever was necessary at the moment. I am quite sure this impish quality of Gidon's is much more endearing when he isn't your dad. He told me that, when he was a young father, he had a temper and did not countenance laziness or disorderliness. *Dor v dor*, (from generation to generation), our history follows us; our wounds are handed down.

In winter 2018, Gidon gave me a four-sided silver ring. One side was a heart. On another was Gidon's name. On another, the date. On the last side, the word *Hineni*: Here I am.

Because of Gidon, I am constantly reminded that life is fleeting and that real love is rare and that every moment spent living fully —the ups and the downs—is a moment well spent. I will benefit for the rest of my life, with lessons learned, patience taught, and memories made, with Gidon Lev. He has taught me to slow down and to be kinder, more patient, and more deliberate in what I say and do. He's taught me to be both shrewder and more trusting.

Gidon gets scared sometimes, it's true. It frightens him when he doesn't feel good, which isn't that often, thus the fear. I imagine that when I am eighty-five years old, I likely won't give a damn about anything at all, having already lived so much. Maybe giving a damn or not giving a damn in just the right moments and in just the right measure is another takeaway.

No matter what life threw at Gidon, he was willing to show up for whatever came next. *Setback, schmetback.* Carrying on is as natural as breathing to Gidon. That, I realized, was what I wanted to learn from him, that willingness to keep creating and living, no matter what had happened before or could happen again.

Gidon's story is not just that of a Holocaust survivor. His is the story of a man who lived and the people lucky enough to have known him. I count myself inexpressibly lucky to have been one of those people.

Gidon's eldest daughter, Maya, grew up in California with her mother, Naomi, and her other siblings. Yanai grew up in Israel with his father, Gidon, and his other siblings. Susan raised Yanai as her own son, and the bond between them was a deep one. Gidon, Susan and Naomi made sure that Maya and Yanai got to see each other from time to time and to know their half-siblings living on the other side of the world. It wasn't always easy, but there is a loving and enduring bond among all of Gidon's offspring today. Gidon and Naomi don't see or speak to each other very often, but they seem to have made some effort to heal and move beyond the past. If the lives of the children they had together are any indication, that is exactly what has happened and more.

Gidon's relationship with Maya is a loving and tender one, and he enjoys loving relationships with all of his kids. Four of the six Lev offspring live in Israel, and Gidon regularly sees them. Gidon has fourteen grandchildren ranging in age from thirty-five years to eighteen months old, and another one on the way. He also has one great-granddaughter—so far.

We never did get to the bottom of the dated pendant with

the emblem of Térézin on it that Gidon's father gave to his mother before he was sent to Auschwitz. We don't know what the date on the pendant signified or how Ernst was able to come by it. Through Doris's testimony, we confirmed that Gidon's childhood family doctor, Dr. Feldman Fisher, was, indeed, imprisoned in Térézin. Some question remains about whether Gidon's grandfather Alfred was transported to Térézin on the same date as Gidon and Doris were; his transport papers show that he was but the records at Beit Theresienstadt differ.

A black marble memorial plaque memorializing Gidon's father, grandparents, and other relatives who died in the Holocaust can now be found on the wall of the New Jewish Cemetery in Žižkov, Prague. It includes a special name: Theresie Löw, Gidon's grandmother.

Gidon's mother, Doris, is buried on a hillside overlooking Nazareth Illit. Gidon has not visited her grave in some time, but together, we shall. The wooden spoon that Gidon said Doris beat him with has mysteriously disappeared.

On March 3, 2020, on Gidon's eighty-fifth birthday, just before the global pandemic that would make such things impossible, we went zip lining in the Judaean Hills outside of Jerusalem. Gidon went first, and his delighted laughter echoed off the canyon walls as he flew over the rocks and between the trees. I buckled up and followed him.

Gidon and Julie in New York. (2019)

*Gidon and Julie camping on the
Jordan River. (2018)*

Gidon protesting in Tel Aviv. (2019)

The last page of Doris' Holocaust testimonial.

The pendant Ernst gave to Doris before he was sent to Auschwitz.

The family memorial plaque at the New Jewish Cemetery in Žižkov, Prague.

Gidon in Karlovy Vary. (2019)

Above: The stairs that Gidon and Doris went down for the last time before being transported to Theresiendstadt

Below: Gidon's Star of David and transport paperwork.

Gidon enjoying a spa in Karlovy Vary. (2019)

Gidon and Julie in Karlovy Vary. (2019)

Gidon mid-shave, with the book's whiteboard behind him. (2018)

GIDON'S AFTERWORD

Julie and I worked on this book for more than two and a half years. We spent hours talking and discussing and writing and rewriting, all in an atmosphere of loving and caring. In the last chapter of my life, Julie has been my best friend and my partner and my love.

It has been for me a revealing, interesting, and exciting journey working on this book. Of course, it has not always been easy and surely not simple. We old-timers know that nothing is ever simple, especially when writing about eighty-some years of living in a very turbulent and constantly changing world. I have learned a lot about myself, about the suffering of others, and about memory itself—and how fickle it is at times. I have, in this process, changed—hopefully for the better. I always say that change is the one rule of nature that is universal and enduring!

I hope that you, the reader, are inspired by the stories of my life and that my adventures can give you the courage to have your own. I am alive and kicking and hope to be for some time!

I want to thank, of course, first and foremost, my love, my partner, and my friend, Julie, without whose endless drive, support, help, love, and care I could not have accomplished this project and made my dream come true. I also wish to thank all of those friends and relatives, all over the world, who encouraged, supported, and cheered me on in my life and in the writing of this book.

INTERVIEWS WITH GIDON LEV

Julie: What is your idea of perfect happiness?
Gidon: Perfect happiness? First of all, I don't believe in anything perfect. For me, there is no perfect, no 100 percent in anything. I only know of one 100 percent, and that is death itself. That, I accept. Everything else is relative and changes with the circumstances and a thousand and one factors that we are not nearly in control of. But I can truthfully say today that I am happy, as, indeed, I am—where I am, and with who I am. I am healthy in mind, soul, and body, which at my age is almost impossible, but it's true!

Julie: What is your greatest fear?
Gidon: I think my greatest fear is to succumb to an illness such as Alzheimer's, where I cease to be me, physically, mentally, or a combination of both. I think I would rather die than go on living not being who I am. I also fear an illness where I am in constant pain. Almost everything else I think I can deal with—even if, at times, it is hard.

Julie: Which living person do you most admire?

Gidon: This is a difficult one to answer since, at close range, I really don't know enough people well enough to be that sure of them. Let me say that one of my sons, Asher, I admire and respect most, for his intelligence, creativity, talent, tenacity, and adventurism. He is truly out there, putting himself on the line and willing, not always happily, to suffer the consequences.

Julie: What figure from history would you most like to spend an hour with?

Gidon: One of the following: Tomáš Garrigue Masaryk, David Ben-Gurion, or Yitzhak Rabin.

Julie: When and where were you happiest?

Gidon: I think I was the happiest at a number of times, and it is hard to tell which of those times I was the happiest. I was very happy in 1959 when I got on the boat, the *S.S. Zion*, to come to Israel, the fulfillment of a dream I had looked forward to for many years. I was also very happy at two other special occasions. The first was when my daughter Maya was born in the Afula hospital on April 18, 1965. It was like a dream come true. I was especially happy when, in 1981 in Canada, Susan gave birth to our youngest son, Asher, and I was right there with her as she was giving birth. It was fantastic!

Julie: Who are your heroes in real life?

Gidon: I am not sure I have heroes in everyday life. I think I look up to people that have overcome hardships in their lives and made a good life for themselves, both on a personal level and on a more social, general societal level.

Julie: What is your earliest memory?

Gidon: My first memory that I truly cherish is my grandfather Alfred taking me to a playground in Prague before the War and the camp.

Julie: What gives you the most satisfaction?
Gidon: I get a lot of satisfaction to this very day in working; it is something that gives me satisfaction and fulfillment, as a sort of foundation of being a human being.

Julie: Who are your favorite writers or poets?
Gidon: Howard Fast, Jack London, Shakespeare.

Julie: Who is your favorite musician?
Gidon: My favorite musician is Paul Simon, for two reasons: the incredible lyrics and wonderful music to go with it. I also love Pete Seeger and The Beatles.

Julie: Who is your favorite Israeli politician or leader?
Gidon: There were two that I could see as leaders with a vision, daring, and character. They were from opposite political streams but were able to change and rise above their narrow political dogmas. They are Menachem Begin and Yitzhak Rabin. The present prime minister, Benjamin Netanyahu, is the one I most dislike and have no faith in. To say I despise him is a bit extreme, but I hold him responsible for the lack of any advancement toward the most important task before our country: to bring a measure of peace, hope, and real security to this area and our country. He does not lack education or intelligence; he lacks the vision that it can and must come about, and only we can do it, since we have the control and power to carry it out. As the saying goes, "You make peace with your enemies, not your friends."

Julie: What is your one wish for Israel?
Gidon: My one wish for Israel is to get out of the West Bank as soon as possible, with some compromises as to territory, and allow us and the Palestinians to have separate, independent democratic countries, living in peace, side by side!

Julie: How much (or little) did your experience at Térézin form your personality?

Gidon: No doubt my Térézin experience had a profound influence on shaping my personality, but it was not the only factor. My mother, the lack of a real father, our flight to America and Canada, and, last but not least, my commitment to Israel and Socialist Zionism all had a great deal to do with shaping my personality as it is today.

Julie: Are you surprised by the political direction Israel has taken since 1959?

Gidon: No, I am not surprised by Israel's present political direction. Rather, disappointed and, at times, horrified. I was hoping—perhaps dreaming—of a more egalitarian and just society. Perhaps that was a utopian dream and, for a while, it seemed to work. To do your best, work the hardest that you could, and to receive, in return, all the things you need to live a good and satisfying life, without having constantly and consistently to compete for your livelihood. That was my dream.

Julie: What do you wish your father knew about your life, had he lived?

Gidon: I wish my father would know that, in spite of him not being there for me, I did learn to work hard and raise a family, of whom he would be very proud!

Julie: Would you rather be a river or an ocean?

Gidon: I would rather be a river because it flows and constantly seeks new paths.

Julie: Would you rather be a mountain or a meadow?

Gidon: I would rather be a mountain. I love the adventure of height and climbing and discovering new vistas.

Julie: What is your favorite word or words?

Gidon: Love, dance, and life.

GIDON ON GERMANS: TRANSCRIPT

Julie: You told me that, until about ten years after the War, you felt very angry at the Germans.

Gidon: I really didn't want to have anything to do with the Germans or with the history of the Holocaust, or recognize or deal with my loss. It took me, perhaps, another five to ten years more until I finally came to a point where I said, "Okay, you know, I have to start dealing with this somehow." And, at that point, I even agreed to do a stopover in Germany on my way to Canada to visit my mother, and just to allow myself to feel whatever I would feel being there. And I remember, to begin with, when I arrived and I was taken to a hotel for the night, I didn't speak German. I spoke English and just listened to the German. But slowly, I relaxed and said, "Okay, I can be angry and I can be unhappy, but most of these Germans here and alive now weren't truly part of what took place many years ago."

Julie: Did you find yourself at any moment looking at older Germans who might have been and wondering how they could have done such a thing?

Gidon: No. Not really. Not, not in any depth. I—I guess I just decided that most of my dealings are with Germans who, twenty years ago, either were not alive or were just little kids, were youngsters. And, over a period of time, I simply made peace with it without feeling deep hate, even though I think that . . . I do find the German nation, the German people as a whole, guilty for what took place. Because it was such a vast system, set up so that only a few people would know what was really going on. Still, I do feel that those who didn't take an active part in the killing and torture and humiliation of the Jews—and not only of the Jews—they knew things were not right, that things were being done that were just horrendous. In a way, all the Germans [who were adults during the war] are guilty, because they knew that, just over the hill, they were burning Jewish bodies in a crematorium. You can see the smoke and hear the shots, but you don't do anything about it. It's just impossible that they didn't know—even if not exactly what was going on. There should have been enough Germans that rose up against it. Had that been so, Hitler would never have been able to do what he did.

Julie: Why do you think that so many Germans didn't do anything?
Gidon: I think partially—probably—it was the fear, an atmosphere of terror. And it reminds me of the [George Orwell] book *1984*, where you never know whether if you say something or don't say something, do something or other, somebody will report you and you, too, will end up in a camp, or be shot or tortured.

Julie: Is there anywhere in the world right now where you see that kind of environment forming again? Could this happen again?
Gidon: Well, I hope not. But I'm sure that there are many places in the world today where fear rules over the population. The scene in South America, certainly in a place like Chile, during the rule of, uh, I don't remember who it was . . . people were afraid.

Julie: Pinochet?
Gidon: Pinochet. And I imagine, though I certainly don't know firsthand, that is also true in places like Iraq or Iran, and places in Africa. Hitler was an authoritarian.

Julie: Which led to this control and this fear. Let me ask you specifically about politics in the United States and the new president there if there's anything you see there that alarms you.
Gidon: Yes, I think America today is struggling with the ideas of fear vs. democracy, the power of the rich, the power of controlling the media, controlling the army. There are a lot of things going on in the United States that need to be taken

seriously and need to be changed and guarded against. And I hope that this will happen. Perhaps [Donald] Trump is what will actually motivate people to change things. Somebody—an Israeli —who a little while ago spent half a year traveling across the United States and visiting a lot of little towns and villages, not the main cities, came back feeling that things are really in very bad shape. He felt that before things get much better, things will have to get a lot worse.

Julie: So what do you say to people who might look at America today and say, "Oh, no, it's going to be like Germany and Hitler." And what about those who laugh at that and say, "That's ridiculous. It could never happen again." What do you say to that?

Gidon: Well, I think that anything can happen and things can happen again, not only in America. They can also happen again in Austria, in Germany, in Poland, Hungary, Romania, and even the Czech Republic, because we are going through a period of a great deal of extremism. And all the sides, including Nazism and Neo-fascism and Muslim extremism pose a great danger. I would even go as far as to say that here, too, in Israel, we also have our extremists, who are a danger to the State of Israel.

Julie: Do you ever feel, as a Holocaust survivor, that that label follows you, that you have a special responsibility or urgency to chime in on this topic?

Gidon: I think I have a responsibility to be who I am and express my feelings and my thoughts, as openly and as strongly as I can, in whatever situation I find myself. I don't feel, certainly not at this late age and stage (maybe mostly age), that I want to go out of my way and climb the barricades. But I do feel that whenever I have an opportunity to express my feelings—for example, when I'm giving a talk to high school students in public schools during the week of Holocaust Memorial Day—I should do it. I can do it, and I have done it, and it's been very rewarding to see the response of the students.

Julie: What kind of responses have you gotten from the students?
Gidon: Very engaging and very positive. I actually have it on a video from the last time, and you can see from the questions that they were very much involved and connected. I managed to connect to them on a very personal level.

Julie: What were their questions primarily about? What about your story most engaged them, do you think?
Gidon: I think they were a little bit surprised that I have come out of the Holocaust and, not only survived, but have gone a step or two beyond that and created a new life, and that I still have a positive attitude toward life itself. And, actually, there was at least one or two questions such as, "Well, how do you explain your positive attitude?" I could hardly answer it because I really don't know, but that's been my way of surviving.

Julie: So your positive attitude toward life exists still and has existed throughout your life, even though your childhood was really taken from you?
Gidon: Yes, that is definitely true. It's hard to say that I had a childhood. I certainly didn't have a family.

GIDON ON REPARATIONS

It comes to my mind today: Can the loss of dignity, humanity, the loss of family members close and distant, the loss of normal family life, let alone property, small and large, suffering in ways that are almost unimaginable, be repaid in monetary ways? I emphatically claim, even today, it cannot!

So, the idea that I would accept German reparations, when they became available sixty-five years ago, was totally unacceptable. Yes, I was young then, full of passion, proud to be a Jew, and proud of finally having my own country—Israel— where I was energetically preparing to immigrate. The truth is, the war years—the Holocaust—was all too painful for me to think about, let alone talk about. It was all too raw! The four years of hunger and suffering in Térézin, the loss of my father and all the rest of my family, the deprivation and humiliation, was just too much. I refused to apply. But my mother did apply and received a lifelong pension and a $5,000 (have I got the right currency?) one-time grant for me. I took the money and gave it to HaShomer Ha'tzair to be used for scholarships for kids that couldn't afford the entire fee for our summer camp, known as *Moshava*. Perhaps, had I had a mother who would talk to me and explain things in a supportive way, I would have listened. But she did not do so; she only berated me and called me an emotional idiot! And maybe I was?

I was young. I didn't think of the future in terms of having kids and a family. I could only think of going to my Israel and my kibbutz, and of working the land. There were, and there probably still are (if they are alive today?) quite a number of survivors who did not accept reparations, refused to drive German cars or buy German products, and, last but not least, to speak the German tongue.

It took me over twenty-five years to deal with and make peace with these deep, deep feelings of disdain and outright hate of anything German! But I did.

GIDON ON EXTREMISM AND MEIR KAHANE

Thinking about my life of about forty years of living in Nazareth Illit (Upper Nazareth, an exclusively Jewish section of the large town of Nazareth, inhabited by Palestinians, roughly 70 percent Muslim and 30 percent Christian), I recall the visit by Meir Kahane, the orthodox extreme-rightwing rabbi. He actually advocated the transfer of our Arab citizens to Jordan, Syria, or any Arab country that would be prepared to receive them (not that any of them would!), without any consideration for what they wanted and disregarding the fact that they have been in this land longer than most of us. At the time of his visit, there was already good amount of tension between us and our Arab neighbors from Nazareth and some of the Arab villages that abound in the region. We were trying to deal with it and build bridges—find common ground to coexist together as respectful neighbors. I was very upset about his impending visit, as I had read about him and heard about him, and he reminded me of Germany and Hitler himself. I saw the same kind of delivery: rabble-rousing, half-truths, hate-mongering, that brought Hitler to power. To me it was terribly painful that we, too, could produce such a monster. The Hebrew word for this is *mifletzet*. I knew I must protest in some way!

The same method, the same message: hate, hate, and hate again, against anyone that was not Jewish! Hitler had done the same some thirty-five years earlier (and we and others paid the price!), preaching against anyone that was not an Aryan German. Kahane, to our credit, did not have a great following in our town. Nevertheless, they organized a wooden platform for him in one of our commercial centers, and I decided, with some anxiety and a bit of fear, to stand beside his 150 or so supporters and express as much as possible my abhorrence to this man and his political agenda. Of course Susan, my wife, was not happy. She, too, could not stand this man; however, she feared for my safety.

If you can, imagine this rabble-rousing man standing on a platform made of wooden fruit crates, surrounded by his fiercely aggressive supporters shouting their support for him every time he expressed his racist views, castigated Arab citizens, and actually called for their expulsion from Israel, here and now. And, now, imagine me, in the middle of this crowd, shouting out my abhorrence at this man and his message of hate. As loudly as I could, I shouted out, denouncing him, heckling, interrupting him as much as I could! It didn't take too long before I found myself surrounded by a bunch of thugs, threatening me and warning me that if I didn't stop and get out of there, they'll take care of me!

Then, all of a sudden, four policemen surrounded me and

whisked me out of there. They put me in my car and told me to go home, "For your own sake!" I did go home, feeling that I managed in a small way (I was all alone opposing this hateful person) to express my deepest feelings and disgust.

True, I was upset, and it took me a while to calm down, but the fact that we Jews, who for centuries had suffered at the hands of others from this same kind of racism, were allowing one of ours to expound the same hatred, I found terribly disturbing! The very idea that there were people among us (not too many, mind you, but even one is too many!) who hadn't learned from our own painful history was unforgivable. Though I do not often put much weight into old sayings, there is that one that does make sense: Do not do unto others what you do not want others to do unto you. Let us hope that the larger majority will remember this!

GIDON ON DOGMATISM AND REGRET

Looking back on my time in HaShomer Ha'tzair, I have few regrets, though today I do feel that I could have done things a bit differently and still made it to the Promised Land. HaShomer Ha'tzair had too dogmatic an approach, and that cost us dearly. It was too narrow, and, in this doctrinal approach based on strict principles, we suffered from the damaging dogma that we must become tillers of the soil and hewers of wood, not doctors, lawyers, or teachers. This approach did not allow for other paths to the same goal, and as a result, many, many good people did not make it to Israel and on the kibbutz. At that time, the kibbutz was not such an easy and simple community to live in. Were it not for this dogmatic frame of mind, a good number of the people who left would be here, in Israel, today.

Too often, when individuals for one reason or another could not adjust to the new and very different lifestyle on the kibbutz, instead of trying out a *moshav* (communal agricultural settlement with private property and much more personal autonomy) or *chas vechalilah* (God forbid) even a city, they gave up on everything and went right back to the United States. They simply couldn't cope, adjust, or compromise. They didn't have the tools, because we, in the movement, hadn't provided them with such. They and I, too, were so completely locked into the dogma of kibbutz principles that nothing else would do. They were unable to see that there are many ways they could contribute to the growth, development, and existence of the State of Israel, that living on a kibbutz was only one of them. In a way, I am angry at us, at the movement, and at myself. I, too, was much too dogmatic! Israel lost many a good and wonderful person. I myself struggled, but I stayed the course.

My long-time best friend, Dan, and his wife, Ne'ima (Judy), didn't even make it to Israel. Dogma is dogma, whether political or religious: It is just that. It locks us up in a hermetically sealed box, doesn't allow for innovation and for questioning, and is set up as an absolute. It must be avoided.

I tell people today: there is only one absolute, and that is death itself. Once that occurs, there is no way back, at least not so far! The HaShomer movement was my home away from home, a savior for a long, long time, and I am thankful to the movement without reservation. I even had my first serious girlfriend in HaShomer, and that relationship lasted more than three years. Though no sex took place—that was taboo in the movement—we were quite intimate with each other and very good friends.

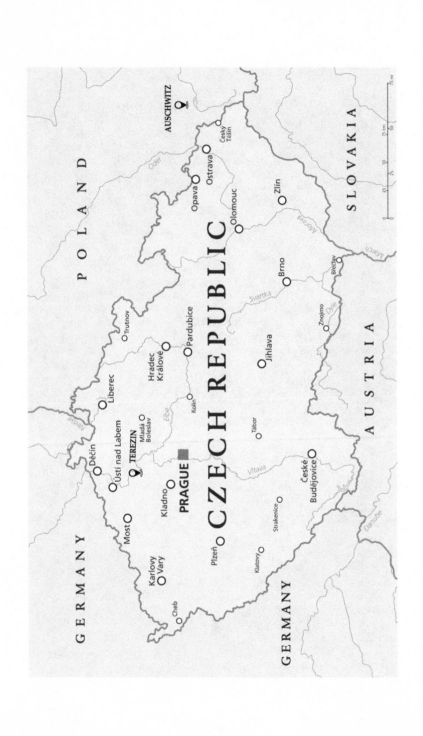

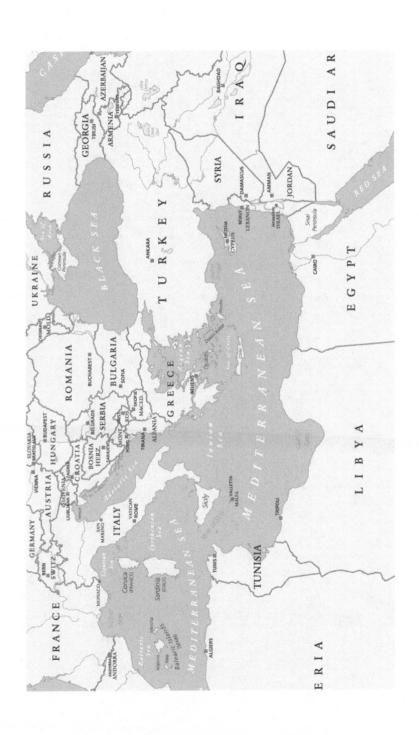

APPENDIX

JEWISH HISTORY, ANTI-SEMITISM, ZIONISM, AND THE JEWISH QUESTION

Zionism, as an idea, has been around for as long as there have been Jews. "Next year in Jerusalem" are the traditional words that conclude the Passover Seder in every Jewish home, when Jews remember the story of Moses and the flight from Egypt. What is the story of Exodus, if not a triumphant return?

The Jews, one of the original displaced people, have been exiled from and longing to return to what we today call Israel for millennia. In 587 BCE, the Babylonians (modern-day Iraqis), led by King Nebuchadnezzar, invaded what was then called Judaea. They destroyed the temple in Jerusalem and sent the Jews back to Babylonia as slaves. Some seventy years later, Cyrus the Great of Persia freed the Jews, and fifty thousand returned once again to Judaea, where they rebuilt the temple.

In 70 CE, Roman general Titus destroyed the second temple. This time, the Jews were stripped of property, sold into slavery, and driven out of the land—and were not able to return for more than two thousand years. That isn't to say that there were no Jews left in the region; miraculously, a small population of Jews remained and gradually rebuilt their numbers and became a part of the fabric of the Middle East and North Africa.

But the others, the exiled Jews, believed that they were being punished by God for all manner of sins and transgressions. They also believed that, when the time came, God would bring them back to their land.

As happens with all civilizations, resources by way of stones, buildings, temples, walls, and beams were used and reused over and over again (preservation of artifacts was apparently not much of a thing). Floods, sieges by invading armies, and other cataclysmic events made for an abundance of second-, third-, and fourth-hand building materials. A visit to Rome, for example, will provide ample evidence of this somewhat disillusioning fact. Just about any given ancient Roman ruin is generally comprised of several layers of other—earlier and later—civilizations.

The Temple Mount in Jerusalem, the historical site of the first and second Jewish temples, likewise has been the site of much destruction and rebuilding, depending on the desires, budget, and power of the latest landlord. For example, in the second century CE, the Romans used the Jewish temple remnants to build a new temple to honor Jupiter, the god of the sky and thunder; his wife (and sister), Juno, the queen of the goddesses; and his daughter Minerva, the goddess of wisdom.

After the Arab Conquest, in 638 CE, Caliph Omar ibn al-Khattab cleaned the place up; it had fallen into great disrepair over hundreds of years. Then he began construction of a place of worship to honor the site of the ascendance to heaven of Muhammad, who apparently used the same rock to ascend to heaven that the first Jew, Abraham, almost sacrificed his son Isaac on. This is also, conveniently, the same site where God gathered up the dust to make Adam (thus the nickname of the place as "the bellybutton of the world"). It's been a very busy spot, the Temple Mount.

For the Jews, the destruction of the temple and Temple Mount, once the center of Jewish administrative, religious, and economic activity, was a devastating moral and spiritual blow that has been handed down for generations. Both Judaism and Jewish thought were fundamentally changed after the destruction of the second temple. A dispersed people learned how to make their peoplehood and faith portable. Synagogues acted as substitutes for the temple, prayer replaced animal sacrifice, and religious study was ascendant over the now temple-less Jewish priests and judges.

Jews being Jews, a stiff-necked (read: argumentative) people, ideas about how to grapple with this exile and what it meant became baked right into the Jewish experience and is reflected in prayer, liturgy, philosophy, and, later, politics. Over time, Jews that had been sold into slavery or otherwise forced to emigrate wound up throughout central and western Europe, Russia, and beyond. The locals saw these slightly mysterious and most decidedly unsavory (to them) new immigrants arrive in waves over time. The Jews tended to live on the outskirts of villages, speaking strange languages and practicing a peculiar religion. Forbidden from owning land because they did not fit into the power structure of feudalism, which consisted of monarchs, nobles, the clergy, knights, and peasants or serfs, the Jews were (surprise!) outsiders. They upset the social order.

More than that, with the advent and growth of Christianity and its power and influence in Europe, Jews became threats. The stubborn Jewish insistence on hewing to their religion was a theological contradiction and a political problem. The Jews not only were mysterious outsiders, but they also threatened Christianity itself. Something had to be done.

Jews became an exceedingly useful tool for the power structure meant to spread and administrate Christianity in medieval Europe: the Church. Though it was the Romans who condemned and crucified Jesus because his rebellious teachings (which, to be historically accurate, were not well received in the Jewish world at the time, either) threatened Roman rule in the region. Blaming this on the Jews was, for some hundreds of years, the *modus operandi* for the Church. This was the seed—the lie—that stuck. It feeds anti-Semitism to this day.

If we fast-forward over a bumpy and uncertain thousand years, we will come upon the Edict of Expulsion, expelling all Jews out of England, which was ordered by King Edward in 1290 and stayed in effect until 1657. In 1643, fully one-third of the Jews in Poland were slaughtered. The Jews were expelled from Austria in 1421, from France in 1394, from Spain in 1492, from Lithuania in 1495, and from Naples in 1510.

The Jewish Question first arose in mid-eighteenth-century England in debates about the status and treatment of Jews within the context of rising political nationalism and new nation-states.

Nationalism is the idea that in a nation, which is a group of peoples, citizens should be united with a common culture, language, and heritage. A country is a geopolitical entity marked by borders; citizens need not have anything in common. A country is, by definition, more inclusive. So the Jewish Question—the Jews were a distinct people living in nation-states that, by definition, excluded them. Many solutions were put forth, including the Nazis' Final Solution, which was nothing less than wholesale murder. Anti-Semites later appropriated the Jewish Question to mean the Jewish Problem.

The Jewish desire for a return to their ancestral homeland in Israel coincided with the European question of just what to do with (or about) the Jews. Non-Jewish figures championing Zionism had intentions that ranged from ridding themselves of the problematic Jews to the Christian Restorationist (now known as Christian Zionist) belief that if the Jews all lived in the Holy Land, prophecy would be fulfilled and Christ would return. Some modern-day Christians still view "the in-gathering of the tribes" as an apocryphal (or end-of-times) goal; thus, many Jews are slightly suspicious of Christian support for Jews and its possible messianic ulterior motives. Jews wanted the right to choose, not be seen as a problem to be solved. They wanted self-determination and equal rights wherever they lived.

Mind you, when one says "the Jews," one is talking about a singular yet very diverse group. Then and now, not all Jews view Zionism in the same way (which reminds me of something Ben-Gurion once said: "two Jews, three opinions"). Judaism, many Jews argue, was different from the polytheistic religions that came before it precisely because it was an idea, not a place or a thing. Judaism is a portable religion. It is alive in the heart of every Jew, wherever he or she lives, and if one wanted to live in France and be a French Jewish citizen, or in Poland or Cuba, then a Jew should be able to do just that. Zionism could be seen as an idea, an ideal, and a choice.

A timeline of the history of Zionism from 1561 to 1896 is a mind-boggling list of more than sixty events, publications, pamphlets, speeches, leaders, rabbis, Christians, and even empires that weighed in, in one way or another. One such event that stands out as emblematic in many ways is when, in 1840, Lord Shaftesbury presented a paper to the British Foreign Minister calling for the "recall of the Jews to their ancient land." Shaftesbury was the president of the London Society for Promoting Christianity Among the Jews, which had been established in 1809 and did just what they said they would: try to convert Jews to Christianity.

Of course, many important Jewish figures played significant roles in the evolution of Zionism, and these figures represented different approaches within the movement. Theodore Herzl was a proponent of political Zionism, which is to say that he and his adherents felt that the best way to secure a homeland for the Jews as a nation was through political means, per international law, and through obtaining a legal charter from a powerful nation. Herzl knew that the Ottoman Empire was on the verge of financial failure and thought that perhaps the empire would grant land to the Jews in exchange for loans to the Turks. The sultan, it turns out, was game for the loans but not for the land exchange, and Jewish financiers didn't want to do business with the sultan.

Practical Zionism was another approach: Jews could immigrate to Palestine, settle, and begin to create some kind of foundational proto-state. What good would a charter do, practical Zionists argued, if there were not enough Jews living in Palestine to build the critical mass needed? Practical Zionism operated with flawed information and tunnel vision; the seeds for today's conflict were already sprouting.

Cultural Zionism argued that the land of Israel could not become a cultural and spiritual center for diaspora Jews until there was both a revival of Jewish cultural expression and a new, secular identity along with the strictly religious identity that Jewish young people were taught almost exclusively. These three different interpretations of Zionism would weave themselves together before, during, and after events in nineteenth-century Russia.

NINETEENTH-CENTURY ZIONISM

Nicholas and Alexandra by Robert K. Massie is an epic book that tells the story of Nicholas, the last Czar of Russia, and his wife, Empress Alexandra, and the tragic end he and his family met at the hands of Bolshevik Revolutionaries in 1918. It is a sweeping read: The hemophiliac son! That wily monster, Rasputin! The collapse of a dynasty!

What I didn't glean from the book was that the handsome, photogenic czar was more than regal or tragic; he was a weak ruler who supported anti-Jewish policies. Under his rule, pogroms (vicious, anti-Jewish riots) were frequent in the region administered by Imperial Russia called the Pale of Settlement. For more than 125 years, Jews were forbidden to travel or live outside of what we today call Belarus, Lithuania, Moldova, much of Ukraine, and eastern parts of Latvia and Poland. The

Bolsheviks who murdered the czar and his family didn't come from nowhere.

In March 1881, Nick's grandfather, Tsar Alexander II, emperor of Russia, who was also, conveniently enough for him, the king of Poland and duke of Finland, was killed in St. Petersburg when an assassin threw a bomb in his carriage. He was known as Alexander the Liberator because, in 1861, the same year the U.S. Civil War began, Alexander magnanimously freed the serfs in Russia. Fully 38 percent of the Russian population, or 23 million people—who had not had the luxury of education (largely farmers, servants, and peasants) and had lived for generations as indentured servants—were finally free to own property, to own a business, or to marry without having to gain consent. The liberation of the serfs in Russia was a social shift of seismic scale, impossible to overstate and crucial to consider in the trajectory of Russia to this day, from the communist state it became to the oligarchy that it is.

What did this mean for the Jews? Alexander II's death in 1881 set off a wave of anti-Semitic pogroms in Russia. The Jews, the apparent source of all inexplicable problems ever, must have been responsible—or so it was believed. In the Russia of 1881, things were horrendous for the Jews. The Southern-Russian Worker's Union mass distributed a leaflet that read:

"Brother workers. You are beating the Jews, but indiscriminately. One should not beat the Jew because he is a Jew and prays to God in his own way—indeed, God is one and the same to all—rather, one should beat him because he is robbing the people, he is sucking the blood of the working man."

In 1882, a sixty-year-old physician and activist named Judah Leib "Leon" Pinsker living in Odessa wrote a pamphlet called *Auto-Emancipation* in which he argued:

"Since the Jew is nowhere at home, nowhere regarded as a native, he remains an alien everywhere. That he himself and his ancestors as well are born in the country does not alter this fact in the least . . . to the living the Jew is a corpse, to the native a foreigner, to the homesteader a vagrant, to the proprietary a beggar, to the poor an exploiter and a millionaire, to the patriot a man without a country, for all a hated rival."

It was crystal clear that the Jews were not welcome, much less safe, in Russia. Zionism became an imperative. Pinsker established *Hovevei*, and later, *Hibbat Zion* (Lovers of Zion) to actively promote Jewish settlement in Palestine. In 1890, the Society for the Support of Jewish Farmers and Artisans in Syria and Eretz Israel was officially registered as a charitable organization in the Russian Empire. In only a few short years, its members numbered in the thousands. A trickle of Jews began to immigrate to the *Yishuv* (prestate Israel).

Of course, the establishment of Yishuv didn't stop the attacks on Jews, in Russia or elsewhere. The Dreyfus Affair, which took place in France, is probably the most well-known tipping point for the fight for Jewish self-determination. In 1894, Captain Alfred Dreyfus, an officer in the Third French Republic Army, was convicted of treason for allegedly giving away French military secrets to the German embassy in Paris. He was imprisoned for five years on Devil's Island in French Guiana. Although evidence was uncovered that pointed directly to a different perpetrator, Dreyfus was a Jew—and, as such, could not possibly be loyal to France, his rank, or the French army (or so the thinking went). Eventually, he was tried again, and the legal battle for Dreyfus's freedom and honor continued, ultimately culminating with his exoneration in 1906. He went on to fight for France as a major in the First World War.

The late nineteenth and early twentieth centuries marked a watershed moment for the Jews. Several Jewish organizations came into being, ushering the Jewish people into the modern, international age. At the inaugural Zionist Congress in 1897, in Basel, Switzerland, the World Zionist Organization was founded. The Jewish Agency was established in 1929 as the operative branch of WZO. The Jewish National Fund was founded in 1901 to purchase land in Ottoman Palestine from private Arab and Ottoman landowners. Hadassah was founded in 1912 by Henrietta Szold (who hailed from Maryland in the United States) to "promote the Zionist ideal through education, public health initiatives, and the training of nurses in Ottoman Palestine."

No more would the Jews be voiceless or totally reliant on the whims and politics of the local ruling power. New organizations ensured that they could be represented and supported politically, legally, or financially, wherever they were. The Jews had a collective voice for the first time in almost two thousand years. But they still needed a home. Just where that would be was up in the air.

JEWISH SECULARISM AND YOUTH GROUPS

By the mid-nineteenth century, the Jews of Europe were more or less divided geographically between western Europe and eastern Europe, with eastern European Jews typically living in more rural settings and adhering to more traditional religious practices and western European Jews living in France, England, Germany, or Czechoslovakia and so on, becoming more and more cosmopolitan, integrated, and secular.

These were tumultuous times for the Jews. What it meant to be Jewish was tested: Should Jews, the "people of the book" be scholars who spend their days in *yeshiva*, praying? Should Judaism be an intellectual pursuit to the exclusion of all else? How could the regular guy living in a shtetl, and who was not a scholar, express his Jewishness?

Jewish youth groups, which began to spring up as early as 1912, filled a void. There, Jewish youth could connect to their

Jewish heritage in secular, cultural ways and, at the same time, learn about the ideas of political and pragmatic Zionism.

WWI OUTCOMES: THE OTTOMAN EMPIRE AND THE BALFOUR AGREEMENT

In 1917, the Ottoman Empire, a former cultural and military powerhouse for hundreds of years, was in its death throes. At its height, the Ottoman Empire had ranged from the Balkans in the north (what we now call Bosnia, Serbia, and Croatia) up to Hungary, as well as west and south in the modern-day countries of Macedonia, Greece, Lebanon, Syria, Palestine, Egypt, and even Libya. It was a sprawling empire ruled by Sultans and populated with Muslims and Greek Orthodox Christians. European Christendom was terrified of the Ottoman Empire.

Like all good empires do, for both good and ill, the Ottoman Empire created a massive change in the ways of trade, politics, and culture in the region. And, just as all empires eventually do, it also collapsed.

The nail in the coffin of the Ottoman Empire was the First World War, which, incidentally, ended three other empires: the Russian Empire, the Austro-Hungarian Empire, and the German Empire. In 1920, after winning the war, the Allied Powers formalized the 1916 Sykes–Picot Agreement and drew the lines of the modern Middle East, which have been warred over ever since.

To really put the Ottoman Empire out of commission forever, what remained of the empire was divided into two spheres of influence.

France got Area A, consisting of southeastern Turkey, northern Iraq, Syria, and Lebanon. Area B was the British Mandate or Mandatory Palestine, which included what we today call Israel and Jordan. A whole lot of people got new landlords, as it were (outsiders yet again). Everything, it seemed, was up in the air.

It doesn't take a history major to intuit that this arbitrary line-drawing and divvying-up of a vast area comprised of dozens of languages, tribes, and cultures—all of which had just suffered the collapse of its ruling power of more than six hundred years— was not going to go smoothly.

As an interesting point of trivia that is not actually trivial, you may remember *Lawrence of Arabia*, the 1962 film directed by David Lean, which depicted just some of the adventures chronicled in the book *Seven Pillars of Wisdom* by T. E. Lawrence, the British officer who led the Arab armies in their revolt against the Ottomans.

The Balfour Declaration, so named after Arthur James Balfour, the British Foreign secretary, was announced on November 2, 1917, just five days before Bolsheviks stormed the Winter Palace and set off the Russian Revolution. The Balfour Declaration referred to what remained of a region of a particular longitude and latitude of the former Ottoman Empire:

"His Majesty's government view with favor the establishment in Palestine of a national home for the Jewish people, and will use their best endeavours to facilitate the achievement of this object, it being clearly understood that nothing shall be done which may prejudice the civil and religious rights of existing non-Jewish communities in Palestine, or the rights and political status enjoyed by Jews in any other country."

But there was a slight demographic spanner in the works. In 1850, there were roughly 350,000 inhabitants of Palestine: 85 percent Muslim, 11 percent Christian, and 4 percent Jewish. So that's something like 10,000 Jews. Census reports from 1900 show 600,000 inhabitants, 94 percent of which were Arabs, mostly Muslims. In 1914, the population was 657,000: 517,000 Muslim Arabs, 81,000 Christian Arabs, and about 59,000 Jews. These figures and those of other census reports from the

Ottoman Empire and, later, the British Mandate are hotly disputed.

What would become a catchphrase for Jewish and non-Jewish Zionist supporters—"A land without a people for a people without a land"—originated among Christian Restorationists in the United Kingdom, such as our friend, Lord Shaftesbury, and was incorrect, to be polite. But let's not mince words: it was also insufferably racist. A land without a people? I can think of several hundred thousand people who might have disagreed.

OTHER IMPACTS OF WWI: SOCIALISM

By the end of the First World War, and after the flu pandemic of 1918, the deaths of an estimated 5 percent of the world's population created widespread despair and disillusionment in Europe and a cascade of political consequences in the Middle East that continue to reverberate today. In Europe, the revolutionary ideas of Karl Marx and Friederich Engels ended empires and monarchies. Humankind, it was widely believed, had to learn how to live more rationally, more scientifically. Class systems, nationalism, capitalism, imperialism, and colonialism: Each had to be re-examined, and much had to be tossed out—at any cost. New ideas and ideals of governance, communalism, meritocracy, and equality were on the table.

JEWISH POSTWAR IMMIGRATION

For postwar Jews who wanted to immigrate to Palestine, there was virtually no legal or safe way to get there. The British were losing control of what was by now an explosive situation quickly devolving into a civil war, and they restricted immigration to Palestine. The Arab population was increasingly angry and felt betrayed; what was a trickle of Jews returning to Israel before became a stream in the 1930s and then a flood. The United States was willing to take only a small number of Jewish refugees and pressured the British government to allow them into Palestine. The British found themselves in an awkward position. The situation was getting out of control.

A resistance movement smuggled approximately 70,000 Jewish refugees from Europe to Palestine on 65 run-down ships. The British deployed a naval blockade to try to stop the refugees from arriving and set up camps in Cyprus for those passengers on those ships they caught. More than 50,000 refugees were detained. Holocaust survivors found themselves again in concentration camps, albeit in different circumstances in sunnier climes. You may remember the story of the Exodus, a ship carrying 4,500 Jewish refugees, which departed from France, headed to Palestine, and was boarded and turned back by the British in July 1947. The refugees aboard the ship were returned to camps near Hamburg, Germany. The debacle was a public embarrassment for Britain.

The United States wasn't particularly prepared—or willing—to accept a wave of immigrants and, at the time, did not even have an official refugee policy. In fact, the States had strict and controversial quotas dating to the Johnson–Reed or National Origins Act of 1924, which was meant to solve "the midnight races" problem (*controversial* might not be the word we want here: *racist* is more like it). The National Origins Act heavily favored emigrants from the United Kingdom or northern Europe and disfavored those from eastern and southern Europe —including the Jews.

Before 1945, U.S. immigration law had yet to evolve to deal with the humanitarian crisis of refugees and displaced persons across Europe. A poll taken in 1945 shows that fewer than 5 percent of Americans favored accepting more European emigrants than before the war began. The International Refugee Organization was created in 1946, as part of the newly formed United Nations, but wasn't fully funded until 1948. The IRO also operated the International Tracing Service, and it is likely through this organization that Gidon and Doris were found by a relative in the United States.

BUT WHERE SHOULD THE JEWS GO?

One day in the early 1900s, Joseph Chamberlain had an idea. A career politician and former mayor of Birmingham, Chamberlain, endearingly described as "ruthless, arrogant, and hated," was on a train in British East Africa (most of modern-day Kenya, up to the border of Uganda). He had a lot of time to think. He was traveling as the British Colonial Secretary, and he wondered what would happen if Britain gave thirteen thousand square acres of British East Africa to the Jews so they could sort things out. Chamberlain met with Theodore Herzl and proposed what is commonly yet oddly known as the Uganda Scheme. Herzl deliberated but ultimately rejected the idea, as did the British colonialists already living there. Oddly enough, no word from the Kenyans.

In 1928, cynically and tragicomically, the Russians conducted an experiment, land set aside for the Jews named the Jewish Autonomous Oblast (a village called Birobidzhan in far eastern Russia). It was the first territory in the modern age intended specifically for Jews.

In 1939, the Jewish population made up less than 20 percent of the population, reaching a peak of thirty thousand after WWII. Today, only about two thousand Jews (about 0.05 percent of the total population) still live in the region. There were Stalinist purges. There was mass emigration.

In 2016, journalist Masha Gessen published *Where the Jews Aren't: The Sad and Absurd Story of Birobidzhan, Russia's Jewish Autonomous Region* detailing the bizarre history of "the best worst idea" of Birobidzhan. Strange, misbegotten Birobidzhan still exists, in case you are wondering, and its sister city, among others, is Beaverton, Oregon. It is located fully seven time zones away from Moscow, in a large crook of land that borders China and nearby North Korea.

The Nazis had an idea, too, though it came much later. In 1940, Adolf Eichmann released a memo that laid out a plan to resettle one million Jews per year in Madagascar. The island would be a police state controlled by Germany's *Schutzstaffel* (i.e., the SS). There were other plans, too: British Guiana (modern Guyana) was another candidate that was seriously entertained, as was Italian East Africa. These territorial solutions were abandoned in favor of the Nazis' Final Solution, which called for the annihilation of the Jews.

Gidon's family, living peaceful, stable, and even prosperous lives far from the pogroms in Russia and eastern Europe, were not part of the Zionist movement and may have been only dimly aware of the First Aliyah (i.e., the first wave of immigration to Palestine), during which somewhere between twenty-five thousand and thirty-five thousand Jews immigrated to what then was called Ottoman Syria. They probably read about the Dreyfus Affair in the newspaper but likely took it in stride that yet another Jew was being thrown onto the bonfire. Gidon's family was assimilated into their local culture. Far-flung places like Uganda, British Guiana, or Birobidzhan were unlikely to have been on their radar at all. The Zionist Project was, in other words, an ardent but still peripheral movement on the radar for the majority of European Jews before the Holocaust.

SUGGESTED READING

If you would like to delve more deeply into the history of the Holocaust and Israel, check out the books on this reading list. The order of their presentation is alphabetical by last name and by no means indicates any priority or preference.

- *I Shall Not Hate: A Gaza Doctor's Journey on the Road to Peace and Human Dignity*, Izzeldin Abuelaish
- *After Auschwitz: The Unasked Question*, Dr. Anthony D. Bellen
- *Growing Up Below Sea Level: A Kibbutz Childhood*, Rachel Biale
- *Jews, God, and History*, Max Dimont
- *Man's Search for Meaning*, Victor Frankl
- *The Arab-Israeli Conflict: Its History in Maps*, Martin Gilbert
- *We Stand Divided*, Daniel Gordis
- *Letters to My Palestinian Neighbor*, Yossi Klein Halevi
- *Like Dreamers*, Yossi Klein Halevi
- *Lioness: Golda Meir and the Nation of Israel*, by Francine Klagsbrun
- *Survival in Auschwitz*, Primo Levi

- *The Drowned and the Saved*, Primo Levi
- *A Tale of Love and Darkness*, Amos Oz
- *In the Land of Israel*, Amos Oz
- *The Chosen*, Chaim Potok
- *The Book of Dirt*, Bram Presser
- *Contested Land, Contested Memory: Israel's Jews and Arabs and the Ghosts of Catastrophe*, Jo Roberts
- *Maus*, Volumes I and II, Art Spiegelman
- *The Lemon Tree: An Arab, a Jew, and the Heart of the Middle East*, Sandy Tolan

NOTES

2. PRAHA

1. Ebert, R. (1985, November 24). *RogerEbert.com/reviews/shoah-1985*. Retrieved from RogerEbert.com: https://www.rogerebert.com/reviews/shoah-1985#:~:text=%22Shoah%22%20is%20a%20tor-rent%20of,where%20the%20deaths%20took%20place.
2. Weiner, R. (n.d.). *https://www.jewishvirtuallibrary.org/prague#today*. Retrieved from The Jewish Virtual Library: https://www.jewishvirtuallibrary.org/prague#today

3. ITALSKA

1. Tait, R. (2020, May 5). *https://www.theguardian.com/world/2020/may/05/prague-revamp-reveals-jewish-gravestones-used-to-pave-streets*. Retrieved from The Guardian: https://www.theguardian.com/world/2020/may/05/prague-revamp-reveals-jewish-gravestones-used-to-pave-streets

5. THE FORTRESS

1. Lichtblau, E. (2013, March 1). *https://www.nytimes.com/2013/03/03/sunday-review/the-holocaust-just-got-more-shocking.html*. Retrieved from The New York Times: https://www.nytimes.com/2013/03/03/sunday-review/the-holocaust-just-got-more-shocking.html
2. *The Jewish Virtual Library*. (n.d.). Retrieved from The Jewish Virtual Library: https://www.jewishvirtuallibrary.org/history-and-overview-of-terezin

9. 1947

1. Shir Ha'Emek, Lyrics: Nathan Alterman, Music: Daniel Sambursky. Lyrics taken from: Nathan Alterman, *Pizmonim Veshirey Zemer part 2*, Hakibutz Hameuchad Publishing House 1979.

26. THE LIKE OF THIS

1. Green, R. A. (2018). *Edition.CNN.com*. Retrieved from CNN: https://edition.cnn.com/interactive/2018/11/europe/antisemitism-poll-2018-intl/

2. *ADL.org.il*. (2017, September 17). Retrieved from ADL: https://www.adl.org.il/en/research/u-s-anti-semitic-incidents-spike-86-percent-so-far-in-2017-after-surging-last-year-adl-finds/

3. Folley, A. (2018, November 27). *https://thehill.com/blogs/blog-briefing-room/news/418487-auschwitz-museum-says-its-important-to-remember-holocaust-did*. Retrieved from The Hill: https://thehill.com/blogs/blog-briefing-room/news/418487-auschwitz-museum-says-its-important-to-remember-holocaust-did

ACKNOWLEDGMENTS

It has been a very long road and quite an adventure. Gidon and I couldn't possibly have reached this moment without the support, encouragement and kind words of so many people. We'd like to thank:

Ruth Yudekovitz, traveler, writer, yogi and chef, for reading a chapter of one of the *earliest* drafts of the manuscript, and calling me immediately from the National Library of Israel in Jerusalem to say: "I think you have something here. Keep going." You were the key that opened the door and made this book possible.

Yossi Klein Halevi, who mentored me throughout the process of writing *The True Adventures*. Yossi was stern with me when it was necessary and also encouraging and generous—in equal measure. What an honor and privilege it is to call Yossi a friend.

Michele Chabin, for her contribution not only to the manuscript but to the project as a whole. Her belief was steadfast and her writing and research superlative.

Eva Hoffman and Lewis Hyde, two authors who I respect and admire, who allowed Gidon and me to reprint portions of their books to give readers more context and intellectual and emotional understanding of the themes in the book.

Rabbi Susan Silverman, for your humor, unconditional love, and unwavering support. You are a role model and my idea of the perfect rabbi.

Elisabeth Becker, without whose support, wise words, and memorable visit on a cold, rainy night in Jerusalem, Gidon and I might never have taken our first step toward realizing this book.

Judy Labensohn for introducing me to Gidon in the first place! What great things came from that.

Anne-Marie O'Connor, who was such a sport and put up with my endless emails and questions with grace and equanimity.

The staff at the Yad Vashem Central Reading Room and Archives and the Beit Theresienstadt Museum for a wealth of information and a great deal of loving patience and tissue paper for the tears.

Cayce Berryman, the dream incarnate of a copy editor who came to the project at the last minute and saved the day with her astute notes and corrections—not to mention her sense of humor and Texan wit. Also, she raises pygmy goats, so it was all done for the shouting when I found that out.

Kelli Christiansen, copy editor extraordinaire, who lavished the manuscript with her attention, astute professionalism, and good catches!

Andrew Zinnes, Cindy Jewkes, Rachel Peck, and Kate Healy for their no-holds-barred, honest feedback and fact-checking prowess, which saved me from myself.

Lynn Poritz, my Tel Aviv Salon friend who not only transcribed Gidon's words but also sang with him in our living room.

Dahlia Lithwick because you are my friend and that, in your view, this project was worthwhile is something that I will never forget or take for granted.

Nir Katz, for your Solomon-like wisdom, patience, faith, and excellent legal advice.

Paula Wagner, for shedding light where there was darkness

and shining your positive, healing light when it was needed and welcomed.

Nadene Ghouri, for your stalwart support and faith in this project as it continued to evolve and evolve yet again. And again. Julie and Jessie Miller for putting us up in Brooklyn during our momentous and emotional visit and being such gracious hosts. Debby Miller and Grape Minkoff, for hosting Gidon and me during the same visit and being willing to be such a loving and accepting part of our story together.

Pavel Rubin, for touring Gidon and me around Karlovy Vary, introducing and (re)introducing Gidon and me to the places and sights that make Karlsbad an utterly unforgettable place.

Ted Friedgut, for allowing Gidon and me visits to your lovely home perched on a hilltop in Jerusalem to talk about HaShomer Ha'tzair for hours and hours over tea and cake.

Yehuda Bacon, for the lovely afternoon we spent in your home in Jerusalem, talking about "glimmer" and survival. I will never forget your merry laughter and your creative spirit.

Ruth Chernia, Ken Skolnik and Lenny Shuval for your belief in Gidon and in this project over many years.

Batsheva and Avraham Golan because you are family and even more than that, you were always kind and encouraging about the project. You have meant so much to Gidon over the years.

Ofer Liraz Friedman, for being the very person to patiently type up and organize Gidon's writings in Nazareth Illit.

Jeff Camhi and Laura Nelson Levy for being dear friends and an example of love at any stage of life.

Marney Blom, for the stories you shared with Gidon and me about the experience of your grandparents in the Dutch East Indies during World War II and your genuine warmth and beautiful, generous Canadian spirit.

Rachel and David Biale, for hosting Gidon and me in your lovely Berkeley home and swapping stories about life on kibbutz.

You took Gidon and me seriously at a time when we were feeling doubtful. We carry that evening with us, always.

Zelia Sousa, for your beautiful writing and loving support for Gidon and me.

Zahra Zomorrodian and James DeMarco because you supported this project and Gidon and me every step of the way, through hail, sleet and snow. Also heatwaves.

Lynda Reiss for your general amazingness and friendship and for making the audiobook possible through your generous networking.

Sarah Williams because you are an amazing warrior and my north star on many levels.

Eetta Prince-Gibson, for your loving support, wisdom, and including Gidon and me in your family Rosh Hashana family tradition, year after year. It is a privilege.

Cindy Bayer, for hosting Gidon and me at your Place of Stories overlooking the deep blue of Lake Kineret. It was an unforgettable visit.

Dan Miller, the author of the wonderful Dry Bones Society for being there for me, time after time, with my oh-so-many questions.

Andrew Chapman, our incredible typesetter who went over and beyond — again and again.

The incredible editors, transcriptionists, and helpers who came to this project through social media: Surit Das, Samantha Perez, Mary Phillips, Carolyn Davis, Kariann Farrey, Emily Monaco (how fun it was to meet in Paris!), Pamela Smith, Diana Rosenthal Roberson, Katherine Swailes, Kathryn Barnsley, Daniela Yumiko Edwards, Karina Sinclair, and Heidi Sutherlin. Without you, this project would never have felt achievable. Thank you to the Binders for allowing a request for help to blossom into a tidal wave of loving support that eventuated in a book.

Vickie Sampson, Rabbi Janet Bieber, Elli Rahn, Liraz Avni Segal, Philip Hurd-Wood, and Nigel Groom for having the faith and vision in Gidon, me, and this project and giving hours of your life to the audiobook version of *The True Adventures of Gidon Lev*.

My family and Gidon's: Maya, Yanai, Hadasa, Shaya, Elisha, Asher, Truman, and Quincy, for putting up with Gidon and me both and believing that, eventually, we would be "done" with "the book."

Susan Kashman Lev: your spirit infuses Gidon's life on so many levels. I wish we could have met. One day, I will meet you in Tanganika and we'll talk for hours on end.

My mom and dad, Bruce and Sally Batchelder, for believing in me and in this project, 100 percent.

My brother, Peter—I miss you every single day.

ABOUT THE AUTHORS

Gidon Lev, eighty-five years old, delivers flowers part-time, is an avid reader, and volunteers at the Jaffa Institute, where he teaches English to elementary school students. Julie Gray's writing has appeared in the Huffington Post, Moment Magazine, the Times of Israel, and others. She has volunteered with The Afghan Women's Writing Project, Creativity for Peace, the Middle East Partnership Initiative, and Kids for Peace. Gidon and Julie met in 2017. They have been Loving Life Buddies ever since.

Made in the USA
Coppell, TX
25 May 2021